Embracing, Evaluating, and Examining African American Children's and Young Adult Literature

Edited by
Wanda M. Brooks
Jonda C. McNair

Foreword by
Rudine Sims Bishop

D0731497

THE SCARECROW PRESS, INC.
Lanham, Maryland • *Toronto* • *Plymouth, UK*
2008

SCARECROW PRESS, INC.

Published in the United States of America
by Scarecrow Press, Inc.
A wholly owned subsidary of
The Rowman & Littlefield Publishing Group, Inc.
4501 Forbes Boulevard, Suite 200, Lanham, Maryland 20706
www.scarecrowpress.com

Estover Road
Plymouth PL6 7PY
United Kingdom

British Library Cataloguing in Publication Information Available

Library of Congress Cataloging-in-Publication Data

Embracing, evaluating, and examining African American children's and young
adult literature / edited by Wanda M. Brooks, Jonda C. McNair.
    p. cm.
Includes bibliographical references and index.
ISBN-13: 978-0-8108-6027-8 (pbk. : alk. paper)
ISBN-10: 0-8108-6027-9 (pbk. : alk. paper)
1. American literature–African American authors–History and criticism.
2. Children's literature, American–History and criticism. 3. Young adult literature,
American–History and criticism. 4. African American children–Books and reading.
5. African American young adults–Books and reading. 6. African Americans in
literature. I. Brooks, Wanda M., 1969– II. McNair, Jonda C., 1970–
PS153.N5E45 2008
809'.89282'08996–dc22   2007025703

To my children, Nilah Jordan and Wesley Jordan—WMB

To my parents, Wanda B. McNair and the late John O. McNair—JCM

Acknowledgments

This book grew out of our friendship as colleagues who, upon our first encounter at the National Reading Conference, recognized in each other a profound and enduring appreciation for African American children's and young adult literature. Soon after meeting we realized that a significant portion of our academic training and career mentorship occurred synergistically among six interrelated literacy scholars to whom we owe our gratitude: Drs. Rudine Sims Bishop, Anne Haas Dyson, Vivian L. Gadsden, Violet J. Harris, Linda Leonard Lamme, and Lawrence R. Sipe. In its conception and development, *Embracing, Evaluating, and Examining African American Children's and Young Adult Literature* has truly been a collaborative effort between both editors.

We sincerely thank each of the authors who contributed to this edited collection. Each has written in thought-provoking ways about a body of literature that absolutely deserves more recognition in literary and scholarly arenas. We further acknowledge all of the writers of African American children's and young adult literature mentioned throughout this book, who within their narratives tell stories that others often pass over or disregard. Some of these enduring writers are Mildred Taylor, Walter Dean Myers, Patricia C. McKissack, Julius Lester, and Nikki Grimes. A special thanks is extended to Rudine Sims Bishop for her gracious and careful reading of this volume and the foreword that lays the foundation for each of the chapters.

Another note of appreciation goes to Allison Bechberger, who, as a Temple University research assistant, provided invaluable editorial support during the preparation of this publication. Her diligence, careful editing, and communication with each author allowed the editorial process on the publisher's end to proceed in an expedited fashion. We also appreciate the editorial guidance provided by Martin Dillon and the production staff at Scarecrow Press.

Finally, we are grateful to our families—Will Jordan, Nilah Jordan, Wesley Jordan, Wanda B. McNair, Jada McNair, and Jonah McNair—who continually support us and provide inspiration for the significance of this edited book and the eventual good it will do in the world.

Contents

Foreword

As someone who has been working in the vineyard of scholarship on African American children's literature for more than two decades, I was pleased to be invited to write the foreword for this book, in part because the co-editors and many of the contributors are representative of a group of younger scholars who are making African American children's and young adult literature the center of their research and scholarship. Serious scholarship on African American children's and young adult literature is a relatively recent phenomenon, having followed by several years the emergence, beginning in the late 1960s, of a substantial quantity of such literature. To date, only a handful of book-length volumes—aside from doctoral dissertations—have been devoted to the exploration of this body of literature and the historical works that are at its foundation. This volume, therefore, is a welcome addition and a gratifying sign that research and scholarship on this literary legacy will continue into the future.

In this book, Wanda M. Brooks and Jonda C. McNair offer a bouquet of diverse perspectives on African American children's and young adult literature, focusing attention on texts, on readers, and on pedagogical strategies that have the potential to bring the texts and the readers together. The scholars who contributed to this work view the literature through various theoretical and critical lenses, including literary theory, critical race theory, reader response theory, and feminist criticism. Literature scholars, literacy researchers, and teachers should all find relevance in these essays.

A reader unfamiliar with African American children's literature will come away from this book having made the acquaintance of some canonical African American writers such as Mildred Taylor and Walter Dean Myers. Mildred Taylor's historical fiction is particularly prominent in these essays, in part because it encapsulates and comments on some issues that continue to be critical in the lives of African Americans and in American society. Readers may indeed be struck by the extent to which these essays emphasize the complex social, cultural, and historical factors that influence the creation, criticism, comprehension, and classroom consideration of African American children's and young adult literature.

As a whole, this volume fosters an understanding of the ways that African American children's and young adult literature connects to larger contexts. The discussions of specific texts, for example, demonstrate that these books reflect some of the same literary traditions as African American literature aimed at an adult audience. The section on response shows how readers often find relevance and acquire insight by making connections between the literature and their own lives. The section on pedagogy makes clear the importance of a social context in which readers have the opportunity to construct meaning through dialogue with each other, with the texts, and with an insightful teacher-leader. This book invites readers to make their own connections with African American children's and young adult literature, to discover or rediscover its potential to engage readers, to educate, and to foster insight into some critically important social issues.

Rudine Sims Bishop
Professor Emerita
Ohio State University

Preface

The purpose of this edited volume is to stimulate continued discourse and serious thought in regard to the scholarship and criticism of African American children's and young adult literature, which we define as books intended for youth that are written by and about African Americans. While not disputing that authors from a variety of racial and ethnic backgrounds can adequately create narratives about African American culture, we have chosen this definition because we believe that, in part, literature does reflect the experiences, perspectives, struggles, and triumphs of its creators. "Giving voice," then, sometimes requires focusing on a selected group (e.g., African American writers), as we have opted to do within this volume.

Moreover, we aim to underscore throughout that African American children's and young adult literature, like African American adult literature, comes out of a long-standing tradition of relying on oral and written stories for a range of educational and recreational purposes within African American communities. For these reasons, both bodies of literature contain visual depictions, narrative elements, linguistic patterns, and themes that continually resurface in the imaginations of African American writers.

This volume, which is aimed primarily at literary scholars and literacy researchers, contains original essays that present research conducted by scholars across several disciplines, including education and English. The book is divided into three sections: textual analysis, reader response research and theory, and pedagogical issues. In particular, the textual analysis section provides examples of the ways in which African American children's and young adult literature can be situated within the research literature as well as the various rigorous theoretical frameworks (e.g., feminist thought and critical race theory) that can be applied to this body of literature. The response section examines the ways in which readers reading for different purposes and situated in varying contexts (e.g., after-school programs, community centers, and classrooms) respond to and interpret the books. The final section explores the pedagogical implications (e.g., for in-service and pre-service teachers) related to reading and sharing African American literature with children and adolescents.

By including varied disciplinary perspectives and offering examples from multiple types of research methodologies, this volume is, to our knowledge, the only book ever published about African American literature for youth with these distinct foci. It is our intention that these chapters will inspire others to embrace, evaluate, and examine African American children's and young adult literature for many years to come.

I

TEXTUAL ANALYSIS

1

A Comparative Analysis of *The Brownies' Book* and Contemporary African American Children's Literature Written by Patricia C. McKissack

Jonda C. McNair

Children's literature functions as an important tool in the educative process within schools, and it serves to socialize children and shape their values, cultural norms, and worldviews (Bishop, 1992; Harris, 1990; Johnson, 1990). Children's literature has the potential to expose children to the beliefs and perspectives of racial and ethnic groups outside of their own. Perhaps children's literature that reflects and affirms children's cultural experiences can play an important role in students' educational success. For example, Bell and Clarke (1998) conducted an experimental study with more than one hundred African American children in grades one through four and found that "comprehension was significantly more efficient for stories depicting both black imagery and culturally related themes than for stories depicting both white imagery and culturally distant themes" (p. 470). According to Purves and Beach (1972), research contends that children tend to prefer and are more likely to become engaged with literature that reflects their personal experiences. Indeed, African American children's literature in this case has the potential to increase the educational achievement of African American children.

Many scholars of multicultural education, such as Banks (1994), Delpit (1995), Gay (2000), and Ladson-Billings (1994), have begun to address the significant disparities between the educational achievement of white and black students. In an article that examined the teaching practices of exemplary African American teachers, Mitchell (1998) stated: "national test scores, grades and special education designation demonstrate that the educational achievement and attainment of African American students have long lagged behind that of white students" (p. 104). African American students are less likely to attend college and more prone for failure to complete high school (Mitchell, 1998). Scholars of multicultural education have begun to theorize about pedagogical practices that will allow African American students equal opportunities to achieve academic success. These scholars have found that various factors in the American educational system—such as low teacher expectations, ability grouping, culturally biased standardized testing, and monocultural tradebooks and textbooks—prevent African American children from receiving equal opportunities to succeed.

Beginning in the first half of the twentieth century, scholars of color also expressed concern about the academic success of African American children. For example, Carter G. Woodson (1933/2000), a well-known historian often referred to as the "father of black history," and W.E.B. Du Bois (1919), a renowned activist, author, educator, and historian, were both troubled about the education of African American children. Woodson and Du Bois both believed that the American educational system "miseducated" black children. In his classic book *The Mis-Education of the Negro*, Woodson (1933/2000) wrote: "The education of the Negroes, then, the most important thing in the uplift of the Negroes, is almost entirely in the hands of those who have enslaved them and now segregate them" (p. 22). Similarly, Du Bois (1921) stated, "the education of the Negro child has been too much in terms of white people. All through school life his text-books contain much about white people and little or nothing about his own race" (p. 63). Du Bois was fully cognizant of the power of children's literature to impair black children's developing sense of self.

In an attempt to educate African American children and give them a sense of their beauty, importance, and cultural and historical legacy, W.E.B. Du Bois, along with members of *The Crisis* staff, created *The Brownies' Book*, one of the first periodicals directed primarily at black children. *The Crisis* functioned as the official publication of the National Association for the Advancement of Colored People (NAACP), the largest and oldest civil rights organization in the United States. W.E.B. Du Bois, one of the founders of the NAACP, served as the editor of *The Crisis* for several decades. In regard to *The Brownies' Book*, Du Bois (1919) articulated seven objectives that he hoped to accomplish with its publication:

1. To make colored children realize that being colored is a normal, beautiful thing;
2. To make them familiar with the history and achievements of the Negro race;
3. To make them know that other colored children have grown into useful, famous persons;

4. To teach them delicately, a code of honor and actions in their relations with white children;
5. To turn their little hurts and resentments into emulation, ambition and love of their own homes and companions;
6. To point out the best amusements and joys and worthwhile things of life;
7. To inspire them for definite occupations and duties with a broad spirit of sacrifices. (p. 286)

The Brownies' Book was published monthly from January 1920 through December 1921, with Jessie Fauset, a Harlem Renaissance novelist, serving as literary editor. It was in publication for only two years because of financial difficulties. *The Brownies' Book* contained news pieces, games, fiction, columns, and folk tales that aimed to educate black children. Several well-known Harlem Renaissance literary figures such as Langston Hughes and Nella Larsen submitted selections (Johnson-Feelings, 1996). In describing *The Brownies' Book*, Du Bois (1919) wrote: "It will be a thing of Joy and Beauty, dealing in Happiness, Laughter and Emulation" (p. 285). W.E.B. Du Bois and Jessie Fauset wanted to create suitable reading materials for "children of the sun" that countered negative and demeaning images they were likely to find in mainstream children's literature.

At approximately the same time that *The Crisis* was announcing the debut of *The Brownies' Book*, the poem "Ten Little Niggers" appeared in *St. Nicholas Magazine* (Sinnette, 1965). Considered one of the most highly regarded mainstream children's periodicals of its era, *St. Nicholas Magazine* was in existence from 1873 until 1940, and many well-known authors and illustrators such as Louisa May Alcott, Rudyard Kipling, Eudora Welty, Emily Dickinson, Joel Chandler Harris, Mark Twain, Laura Ingalls Wilder, Norman Rockwell, and Howard Pyle contributed to this periodical. *St. Nicholas Magazine* either ignored the existence of African Americans or, worse, depicted them in a stereotypical and dehumanizing manner.

Stories that ridiculed African Americans were commonplace in the magazine. For example, in the July 1919 issue of *St. Nicholas* there is a drawing of a child, who appears to be black, eating a large slice of watermelon. The caption underneath reads "Satisfied." This drawing was submitted by a fourteen-year-old child and was awarded a gold badge in the magazine's prize competition. As this example illustrates, *St. Nicholas Magazine* rewarded its young readers for reinforcing racial stereotypes. It was out of this context that African American children's literature came into existence and evolved.

From its inception, then, African American children's literature has battled against racism, which remains deeply embedded within American society, just as it was nearly a century ago. In fact, critical race theory, a multidisciplinary epistemology that places race at the center of critical analysis and is concerned with altering the relationship between racism and power, maintains that racism in American society is normal and not aberrant (Bell, 1992; Delgado, 1995). Given such a history, and given the fact that literature reflects the struggles, experiences, and aspirations of its creators, it is not surprising that African American children's literature, as created by African American writers, has developed distinct characteristics and has focused to a large extent on affirming black life, culture, and history. Just as *The Brownies' Book* focused on the aforementioned themes, much of contemporary African American children's literature, such as that written by Patricia McKissack, an African American, also focuses on similar themes. Exploring that connection is the purpose of this investigation.

Scholars of African American children's literature such as Harris (1986) and Johnson (1990) contend that *The Brownies' Book*, in terms of its objectives and underlying ideologies, laid the foundation for a new tradition in children's literature, a tradition that challenged the stereotypical depictions of African Americans in mainstream children's literature. This study attempts to verify their claims by conducting a comparative analysis of *The Brownies' Book* and contemporary African American children's literature written by Patricia McKissack. In her definitive research study of *The Brownies' Book*, Violet Harris (1986) discovered the following eight major themes: "race pride," "duty and allegiance to the race," "intelligent Blacks," beautiful Blacks," "moderation," political and social activism," "knowledge of and respect for African culture," and the "inculcation of specific values such as kindness, truthfulness, egalitarianism, and love" (p. 207). These themes are compared here with themes in African American children's literature written by Patricia McKissack. This study examines specifically the areas of convergence or divergence in terms of themes, ideologies, and goals within these two bodies of work.

Patricia McKissack, like W.E.B. Du Bois and Carter G. Woodson before her, began writing due to her concern over the lack of suitable reading materials featuring African Americans for her eighth-grade students (Bishop, 1992). Her first book, *Paul Laurence Dunbar: A Poet to Remember*, was published in 1984. Since that book, she has authored or co-authored more than one hundred books spanning several genres, including fantasy, biography, nonfiction, and fiction. McKissack has garnered critical acclaim and earned several of the highest awards in children's literature, including a Newbery Honor, a Boston Globe–Horn Book Award, several Coretta Scott King Awards, and the NCTE's Orbis Pictus Award for nonfiction. McKissack's work was selected for this investigation because she is currently active as an author, is well respected as a writer, has such a large body of work, and chooses to write mainly about the African American experience. Thus, analyzing her work seems particularly suitable for exploring the extent to which the themes and underlying ideologies expressed within *The Brownies' Book* are truly foundational within the context of contemporary African American children's literature.

THEORETICAL FRAMEWORK

Because racism has had a considerable impact on the development and creation of African American children's literature, I chose critical race theory as a theoretical framework, since it provides important insights about the significance of race within the context of children's literature. Bell (1995), a legal scholar often identified as the father of critical race theory, states: "critical race theory is a body of legal scholarship . . . a majority of whose members [critical race theorists] are both existentially people of color and ideologically committed to the struggle against racism, particularly as institutionalized in and by law"(p. 898). For the purposes of this study, I define racism as a system of privileges that works to the advantage of whites and to the detriment of people of color.

Critical race theory is an outgrowth of the critical legal studies movement. The critical legal studies movement attempted to demonstrate how "legal ideology has helped to create, support and legitimate America's present class structure" (Crenshaw, 1988, p. 1350). Critical race theorists were concerned that the critical legal studies movement failed to acknowledge racism in its critique (Crenshaw, 1988; Ladson-Billings, 2000). What follows is a description of critical race theory and its application to children's literature.

Underlying critical race theory (CRT) are a number of basic tenets, most of which are applicable to children's literature. The first is that racism is embedded into the fabric of our everyday lives and often appears natural, instead of abnormal, to most Americans. A second feature of CRT is to use storytelling in order to subvert dominant constructions of social reality. Bell (1995) states: "Critical race theory writing and lecturing is characterized by frequent use of the first person, storytelling, narrative, [and] allegory" (p. 899). According to Ladson-Billings (1998), "The primary reason then, that stories, or narratives, are deemed important among CRT scholars is that they add necessary contextual contours to the seeming 'objectivity' of positivist perspectives" (p. 11). Richard Delgado (1987) claims that the practice of exchanging what he refers to as "counterstories" about racial experiences is commonplace among people of color and that these stories are important in that they challenge dominant versions of reality.

A third feature of critical race theory is its contention that liberal legal perspectives must be challenged, since they often neglect to recognize the limitations of the legal system to bring about substantive social change. A fourth feature of CRT is the notion that whites have benefited from civil rights legislation more than people of color. For instance, Guy-Sheftall (1993) found that white women have benefited the most from affirmative hiring policies. Whites, who are much more likely to maintain positions of authority, are largely responsible for enforcing the hiring policies of affirmative action, and it appears as if they selectively enforce them in a manner that maintains white dominance. Although there are differing perspectives among critical race theorists, a common interest is in examining the construction and maintenance of white supremacy and changing the relationship between the legal system and racial power (Bell, 1995; Ladson-Billings, 1998).

Recently CRT has been applied by scholars such as Ladson-Billings (1998) and Tate (1997) within the context of education. In education, critical race theory is useful for providing insights into educational phenomena such as curriculum, pedagogy, and school funding. For instance, critical race theorists are likely to view school curriculum as a social construction that functions as a tool to maintain white supremacy (Ladson-Billings, 1998). Although CRT has been used to examine the abovementioned educational phenomena, few scholars have attempted to apply critical race theory within the context of children's literature.

Because CRT maintains that racism is a "permanent fixture" in American society, it provides an explanation of why African American children's literature has maintained particularly unique characteristics over time. From *The Brownies' Book* to contemporary African American children's literature written by Patricia McKissack, blacks have used the power of the pen to challenge racist and stereotypical notions of African Americans and their cultural and historical legacy (Johnson, 1990). Du Bois (1926) contended that he used his talents as a writer for propaganda in order to gain equal rights for African Americans. In regard to her career as a children's book author, McKissack stated that she writes because she believes there is a need for books about African Americans that document their contributions to the development of American society (personal communication, September 22, 2002).

Many of the crucial tenets of CRT, which borrows from disciplines such as economics and psychology, can provide insights into phenomena that have transpired within the context of literature (Delgado & Stefanic, 2001). For instance, Bell's (1987) theory of interest convergence contends that in order for blacks to make racial advances, these advances must also intersect with the interests of whites. He argues, "reforms resulting from civil rights legislation invariably promote the interests of the white majority" (p. 63). Bell believed that concern over the United States' political and economic interests abroad and at home was the major reason for the "successes" of the 1960s civil rights era.

The increase in publishing of African American children's literature during the late 1960s illustrates Bell's theory of interest convergence. One of the key factors in the publishing of African American children's literature was the passage of the Elementary and Secondary Education Act of 1965, which allocated an enormous amount of funding from the federal government for school districts to purchase books created by African Americans. Therefore, it could be argued that providing literature that affirmed African American children was not the primary motive; instead, economic incentives took precedence in that publishers capitalized on an opportunity for financial gain.

In relation to psychology, critical race theorists maintain that racism serves not only the economic interests of the wealthy, but also the psychological interests of whites. Most whites benefit psychologically from the feelings of superiority associated with having a racial group situated beneath them (Bell, 1992; Delgado & Stefanic, 2001; Feagin & Vera, 1995). Literature can serve to affirm and provide ideological support for the misconception that blacks are inferior and contented with their treatment as second-class citizens, thereby reinforcing the psychological interests of whites. For example, in *The Betrayal of the Negro* (1954), Logan examined the portrayal of African Americans in prominent magazines and northern newspapers during the Reconstruction era and found that derogatory terms such as nigger, pickaninny, mammy, aunt, uncle, darkey, and coon were regularly used in stories, cartoons, and poems. According to Logan, Thomas Nelson Page went so far as to write an article in *Harper's* entitled "All the Geography a Nigger Needs to Know." Blacks were ridiculed and bestowed with bizarre names and titles such as Abraham Lincum, Prince Orang Outan, and Lady Adeliza Chimpanzee. They were depicted as being superstitious, ignorant, happy-go-lucky, and lazy. They apparently used "big words" that they didn't understand and loved watermelon and chicken (Logan, 1954).

These same stereotypes and misrepresentations also appeared in children's literature written during the Reconstruction era. For instance, in the preface to *Diddie, Dumps, and Tot, or Plantation Child-Life* (Clarke-Pyrnelle, 1882), the author states:

> I know not whether it [slavery] was right or wrong (there are many pros and cons on the subject); but it was the law of the land, made by statesmen from the North as well as the South, long before my day, or my father's or grandfather's day; and born under that law a slave-holder, and the descendant of slave-holders, raised in the heart of the cotton section, surrounded by Negroes from my earliest infancy, "I KNOW whereof I do speak"; and it is to tell of the pleasant and happy relations that existed between master and slave that I write this story of Diddie, Dumps, and Tot.

This passage is illustrative of the manner in which children's literature can serve to affirm the psychological interests of whites and provide ideological support for white supremacy. By emphasizing the supposedly "happy relations" between slaves and their masters and not explicitly questioning the right of one human being to own another, the author chooses to appease the consciousness of whites and validate racism.

Critical race theory is particularly relevant within the context of this research study, for several reasons. Several strong parallels can be made between the tenets of critical race theory and literary phenomena. First, critical race theorists argue that the law is a social construction, that it is not colorblind or neutral, and that it functions to recreate the social order status quo. Similarly, literary canons are also social constructions that are not colorblind or neutral and that function to recreate the social order status quo. For instance, *A Light in the Attic* (Silverstein, 1981), *The Very Hungry Caterpillar* (Carle, 1969), and *James and the Giant Peach* (Dahl, 1961) are children's books that most students will be exposed to throughout their schooling, while books by African American authors such as *Honey, I Love* (Greenfield, 1978), *Some of the Days of Everett Anderson* (Clifton, 1970), and *Zeely* (Hamilton, 1967) often remain unknown and ignored by teachers and school curricula.

Second, critical race theory is committed to social justice and aims to alter the relationship between the law and racial power. From the slave narratives of Harriet Jacobs and Frederick Douglass to the poetry of Langston Hughes and Gwendolyn Brooks to the essays of James Baldwin to the novels of Richard Wright and Toni Morrison, African American literature has focused, to a large extent, on racial protest (Jackson, 1989). W.E.B. Du Bois and Patricia McKissack have shown a commitment to social protest and have aimed, through their writing, to alter the relationship between literature and racial power. Du Bois created *The Brownies' Book* during an era in which poems such as "Ten Little Niggers" were appearing in *St. Nicholas*, a reputable mainstream periodical for children (Sinnette, 1965). He wanted to provide black children with positive and realistic depictions of themselves. Similarly, McKissack began writing when she found that there were few suitable reading materials for her eighth-grade students featuring African Americans. Du Bois and McKissack both have created African American children's literature in order to challenge overt and subtle racism within children's literature.

A final argument for the use of critical race theory is the utilization and significance of storytelling on the part of critical race theorists to challenge racial objectivity. One instance of storytelling within the context of children's literature occurred in an article Pinkney (2001) wrote in *The Horn Book*, which was in response to an earlier article written by Aronson (2001). Aronson, a European American children's book editor and author, had criticized children's literature awards such as the Coretta Scott King Award and the Pura Belpré Award, which were created specifically to recognize the talents of authors and illustrators of color. Aronson argued that several decades ago these awards were necessary, but that now they were no longer needed, since the publishing industry was, in his opinion, becoming more diverse and because now African Americans were winning mainstream children's literature awards.

In response to Aronson (2001), Andrea Davis Pinkney (2001), a well-known African American children's book editor and author, began her essay with a story about a presentation of a purportedly comprehensive survey of picture books she had attended only to discover that distinguished African American picture book illustrators such as Tom Feelings, Jerry Pinkney, and the late John Steptoe were excluded although all three have been awarded Caldecott Honors. Pinkney argued that the exclusion of African American illustrators was a subtle form of racism and indicative of a much larger problem within the field of children's literature. Pinkney contended that the Coretta Scott King Award was still a necessity and that the publishing industry was not as diverse as Aronson claimed. For example, Pinkney mentioned that as an editor with over a decade of experience in the children's book publishing industry, she has encountered fewer than ten black editors.

Pinkney (2001) agreed that Christopher Paul Curtis, an African American author, had indeed recently received a Newbery medal, but she also highlighted the fact that it had been twenty-five years since the last Newbery Medal had been awarded to an African American, Mildred Taylor. Andrea Pinkney's article functioned as a counterstory in that she subverted Aronson's version of events, which reflected a dominant perspective. Aronson minimized racism in his article, but by sharing her personal experiences with racism in the field of children's literature, Pinkney challenged his version of the truth.

Because reality is socially constructed, the truth as people of color perceive it is usually quite different from the truth as whites perceive it. Pinkney (2001) noted that most of the other attendees at the picture book presentation were white, and it is likely that most of them, if not all, walked away from the presentation with the perception that it was indeed comprehensive, objective, and informative, whereas Pinkney's perspective was quite different. However, dominant social groups have the power to validate their stories, experiences, and versions of the truth while negating those of social groups with less power, such as African Americans.

Stories have also been used by W.E.B. Du Bois and Patricia McKissack to challenge racial objectivity and racism. For instance, in the author's note of *Red Tail Angels: The Story of the Tuskegee Airmen of World War II*, McKissack (1995) tells a story involving an African American college student taking an

American history course. The student explains to the professor that her father had been a pilot during World War II, only to be told by the professor
that her father was probably just making up a story. Even after having her
father send proof, which she shared with her professor, he never acknowledged her father's participation in World War II as a fighter pilot. The fact
that a college professor could be unaware of the role that African American
fighter pilots played during World War II and furthermore would refuse to
believe it in the face of evidence is presented by McKissack as evidence of
the level of racism in American society. By writing a book about the
Tuskegee Airmen, Patricia McKissack challenged racist and uninformed
misconceptions regarding the role of African Americans in World War II
and affirmed their outstanding accomplishments.

Many of the books written by McKissack, such as *Goin' Someplace Special*
(2001), a story of a young girl who takes a trip to the public library in segregated Nashville, Tennessee, could also be considered counterstories in
that they subvert dominant versions of reality by presenting the differing
perspectives of people of color. W.E.B. Du Bois (1935) argued that Negroes
"ought to study intelligently and from their own point of view, the slave
trade, slavery, emancipation, Reconstruction, and present economic development" (p. 333). In *Goin' Someplace Special*, McKissack interprets segregation from her own point of view in that the reader is given a glimpse into
the manner in which 'Tricia Ann, along with other African Americans
within her community, negotiate their existence in a segregated society
while maintaining their sense of dignity and questioning the injustice of
Jim Crow laws. Critical race theory, which places race at the center of critical analysis, serves as a useful theoretical paradigm by which to highlight
and explore issues related to race within the context of African American
children's literature.

METHODOLOGY/DATA COLLECTION

This research study comprises two parts. The first consisted of a reexamination and content analysis of *The Brownies' Book* to elaborate on and to provide support for the major themes that Harris (1986) discovered in her definitive study of this publication. In order to obtain a representative
sampling of *The Brownies' Book* for content analysis, I selected every fourth
issue of the twenty-four issues that were published. Therefore, I analyzed
the April, August, and December issues from 1920 and 1921. As I read and
reread these six issues, I looked for affirming evidence of the eight themes
that Harris discovered, and I noted recurring themes and underlying assumptions within the publication that were not addressed by Harris, such
as an emphasis on books and reading. I also read issues of *St. Nicholas Mag-*

azine that were published in the years 1919, 1920, and 1921. These issues were examined to obtain examples of the manner in which African Americans were depicted in mainstream children's literature prior to and during the existence of *The Brownies' Book*.

Harris (1986) completed a content analysis of all twenty-four issues of *The Brownies' Book* and generated the following major themes: "race pride, duty and allegiance to the race, intelligent blacks, beautiful blacks, moderation, political and social activism, knowledge of and respect for African culture and the inculcation of specific values such as kindness, truthfulness, egalitarianism and love" (p. 207). The purpose of Harris's study was to determine whether or not *The Brownies' Book* challenged the selective tradition in children's literature. In *Marxism and Literature*, Williams (1977) defines the selective tradition "as an intentionally selective version of a shaping past and a pre-shaped present, which is then powerfully operative in the process of social and cultural definition and identification" (p. 115). The selective tradition refers to the process by which certain images and characterizations are selected and validated over others, even though these images may be inauthentic. Harris contends that the selective tradition, as it operated within the context of children's literature, stereotyped African Americans and their culture.

My own content analysis of *The Brownies' Book* found affirming evidence for all eight of the themes Harris uncovered in her study. For instance, in regard to race pride, which Harris contended was the most prevalent theme in *The Brownies' Book*, I found that one of the ways in which the magazine accomplished this goal was by providing a plethora of information about aspects of American history related to African Americans. Most issues of *The Brownies Book* contained at least one in-depth description of a famous African American, and others sections of the publication incorporated aspects of African American history as well. For example, the April 1920 issue contained a two-page narrative of Sojourner Truth entitled "A Pioneer Suffragette." In the section entitled "As the Crow Flies," which kept readers informed of national and international current events, the text states: "The man who discovered the North Pole, Robert E. Peary, died recently in Washington, D.C., at the age of sixty-four. With him at the time he reached the Pole, was Matthew Henson, a colored man. Mr. Henson is today the only living human being who has stood at the North Pole" (p. 119). Affirming evidence of the remaining seven themes was also found during the content analysis of *The Brownies' Book*.

I also discovered another pervasive theme not mentioned in Harris's (1986) study. The importance of literacy and reading was stressed in many ways throughout *The Brownies' Book*. For example, on the last page of the April 1920 issue, the text states: "We are prepared to recommend books and periodicals for children. Why not begin a library for your boy and girl today?" Similarly, in the August 1920 issue, an advertisement on the last page of the magazine reads: "For the Children's Library . . . Books Books Books." The advertisement lists seven recommended books by authors such as Mary White Ovington and W.E.B. Du Bois. It seems apparent from these advertisements that the editors of *The Brownies' Book* wanted to convey the importance of reading to its readers.

The second part of this study consisted of a content analysis of children's literature written by Patricia McKissack as well as other relevant documents, such as the transcript of an interview with the author. This interview was conducted by telephone on September 22, 2002, and lasted for approximately one hour. This part of the research study entailed the reading and rereading of many children's books by Patricia McKissack, the interview transcript, and scholarly publications such as dissertations and articles. In order to obtain a representative sampling of the books by Patricia McKissack, I examined all of the books that focused on African Americans and categorized them by genre: biographies, nonfiction, historical fiction, and literary folktales. However, the majority of the books were in the genres of biography and nonfiction. The books selected for content analysis were chosen based on the expert opinions of children's literature scholars, book reviews, and dates of publication so as to ensure that they would span McKissack's career as a children's book author. For example, *Paul Laurence Dunbar: A Poet to Remember* (McKissack, 1984) was McKissack's first book, while *Goin' Someplace Special* (McKissack, 2001) is one of her most recent publications. See appendix A for a listing of the books by McKissack that were selected for content analysis.

DATA ANALYSIS

The analysis followed procedures for content analysis as specified by Berg (2001). According to Berg, "the categories researchers use in a content analysis can be determined inductively," and "an inductive approach begins with the researchers 'immersing' themselves in the documents . . . in order to identify the dimension or themes that seem meaningful to the producers of each message" (p. 245). Upon conducting close readings of children's literature by Patricia McKissack and documents related to her work, I generated initial categories based on pervasive, recurring ideas that were apparent in her children's books. These categories were created in order to guide analysis and interpretation of documents related to Patricia McKissack as well as to generate interview questions for her. According to Dey (1993), "The categories that we create become the basis for organizing and conceptualizing our data. Categorizing is therefore a crucial element in the process of analysis" (p. 112). The initial categories were as follows: African American historical figures, attitudes toward black vernacular, community and family relationships, and strong black females. A more in-depth analysis of the interview with Patricia McKissack and her children's literature generated the following additional categories: emancipatory literacy, racial activism, challenges to classism, and challenging dominant perspectives via story-telling. Dey also contends that it is important to create a "set of criteria in terms of which we can decide where and when to assign the categories to the data" (p. 102). For example, any passages that dealt with African Americans, famous or otherwise, who played a significant role in shaping American history or achieved outstanding accomplishments were placed within the category "African American Historical Figures." For instance in *Black Hands, White Sails: The Story of African American Whalers*, the following passage was labeled in this manner:

> Lewis Temple, for example, was an African-American blacksmith who made a very important contribution to the whaling industry . . . he often heard the whalemen talking about how easily their harpoons pulled out of the whale once it had been struck. Temple developed a "toggle" harpoon with barbs that stuck into the whale's body and wouldn't pull out easily. Temple changed the design of the harpoon forever. (McKissack, 1999, p. 56)

Passages that dealt with women being depicted as challenging patriarchal hierarchies or gender stereotypes and taking an active role in challenging the social order status quo were considered relevant in terms of "strong black females." For example, the following passage from the short story "A Home Run for Beth Ann" (McKissack, 1997) was categorized in this respect:

> The idea of cooking wasn't something that interested Beth Ann. Since baseball had come into her life, she had been hardly able to think of anything else. On her eighth birthday during the summer, she had gone to see the Kansas City Monarchs play against the Birmingham Black Barons. For months now, all she'd been able to think about was hitting, scoring runs, and pitching—hard and fast just like the great Satchel Paige. (p. 46)

On a few occasions, as the above example shows, passages could be categorized in multiple ways. The above passage challenges gender stereotypes while simultaneously incorporating African American history related to the Negro baseball leagues and Satchel Paige.

As I read the books, I noted and marked passages based on their relevance to the aforementioned categories. After reading the books several times, I filled out a literary analysis sheet for each one (see appendix B). In order to ensure that my analysis was thorough and in-depth, each time I read a book, I set aside two categories in particular to guide my readings. For example, the first time I read *Color Me Dark: The Diary of Nellie Lee Love*

(McKissack, 2000), I was looking for references to African American historical figures and attitudes toward black vernacular, whereas during the second reading of the same book, my analysis was guided by references to
community and family relationships and strong black females. During
these rereadings, I also noted whether new categories appeared to be emerging within the fifteen books that I chose for the purposes of this research
study. I anticipated that further analysis of these categories would yield
themes that could be compared with Harris's (1986) eight themes.

ESTABLISHING TRUSTWORTHINESS

Four methods to establish trustworthiness were used in this study. The first
was prolonged engagement with the sources of data. This process involved
intensive readings and rereadings of the literature over a period of several
months. For example, the selected picture books and novels written by Patricia McKissack were reread several times during a period of four months
so that I could familiarize myself with them and make observations that I
may not have been able to make had I read the books only once. For example, during my initial reading of McKissack's *Mirandy and Brother Wind*
(1988), a story of a young girl who attempts to catch Brother Wind so he
can be her partner at the cakewalk, I did not consider this book to be protest
literature. However after reading an article by cultural critic and poet June
Jordan (1981) in which she argued against the dichotomizing of protest literature and stated that "affirmation of Black values and lifestyle within the
American context is, indeed, an act of protest" (p. 87), I began to reconsider
my initial interpretation of this book during subsequent rereadings.

The second method was to triangulate the data sources in order to support my interpretations. For instance, if I wanted to assert that in *Flossie
and the Fox* (1986), McKissack challenges the negative associations associated with black English and those who speak it, I could use book reviews
from publications such as *The Horn Book* and *School Library Journal*, scholarly articles such as "Flossie Ebonics: Subtle Sociolinguistic Messages in
Flossie and the Fox" by Milner and Stewart (1997), and comments made by
McKissack about her use of language in this particular book.

Third, in order to determine the reliability of the criteria for placing data
into the aforementioned categories, I asked a colleague specializing in children's literature to serve as a peer debriefer. This colleague was selected
based on her expertise in African American children's literature and her
knowledge of qualitative research methodology. She was given the descriptive criteria for the aforementioned categories and five pages of a children's
book written by Patricia McKissack to categorize. I had meetings with her in
order to compare her categorization of passages with my own. It would be

unreasonable to expect that we would have categorized all five pages identically. However, the purpose of this task was to determine if my descriptions for categorizing data were clear or needed to be refined or revised. A final method for establishing trustworthiness was to conduct a member check by having Patricia McKissack provide feedback via e-mail regarding my interpretations about the major themes and ideologies present within her children's books.

RESULTS

There were three common themes in *The Brownies' Book* and in children's literature written by Patricia McKissack. First, both bodies of work consistently challenged dominant perspectives through storytelling. This was evidenced in at least two ways. The first way was to subvert dominant ways of seeing and telling. For example, there were numerous instances in which information (e.g., about Africa) was provided that directly opposed dominant ways of presenting information on that same topic. Both *The Brownies' Book* and McKissack's children's literature offered positive descriptions of Africa. In *Color Me Dark* (McKissack, 2000), after attending youth services at a local church, the main protagonist, Nellie, states:

> I had never heard of kingdoms in Africa. Far as I knew, Africa was a place where people ran around half naked with bones in their noses. But Reverend McDonald told us something very different. Before slavery time, there were big cities in Africa. They had large trading markets where gold and salt were traded. There were well-respected universities in places called Gao and Timbuktu. They even had libraries. Can you imagine that? (p. 94).

The Brownies' Book, like McKissack, also painted a very different portrait of Africa to its young readers. In fact, one of the eight themes that Harris discovered in *The Brownies' Book* was "knowledge and respect for African culture." One section of *The Brownies' Book* entitled "The Judge" contained discussions between an adult and children about a number of topics. In "The Judge" section of the August 1921 issue, a discussion takes place about Africa. One of the children asks the Judge which continent is the greatest, and he replies "Africa." When the children challenge the Judge as to how this could be, he explains that there are seven reasons, which include the discovery of iron, the beginnings of world trade, and the diversity of Africa's natural products. Such positive descriptions of Africa can be considered subversive, since often in mainstream discourse Africa is considered a "dark" continent inferior to Europe.

The second way of challenging dominant perspectives through storytelling was to provide a plethora of information about aspects of American history related to African Americans that is typically excluded from mainstream discourse. For example, _The Brownies' Book_ and children's literature by McKissack include information about African American abolitionists, inventors, whalers, writers, and musicians. Both bodies of work make it clear that African Americans do indeed have their own stories to tell. In line with the storytelling component of critical race theory, both Du Bois and McKissack use stories as a means by which to give voice to the experiences and perspectives of African Americans.

The second theme common to _The Brownies' Book_ and McKissack's work is social protest against racism. W.E.B. Du Bois was motivated to create _The Brownies' Book_ because of overt racism. Overt racism was prevalent in the era of _The Brownies' Book_ in the form of racial stereotypes in mainstream children's literature and in the form of blatant social injustices that were regularly committed against blacks. Events such as lynchings and race riots were mentioned in the "As the Crow Flies" section of _The Brownies' Book_. McKissack was motivated by covert racism when she, as a teacher, discovered the scarcity of books about famous African Americans she thought her students should know about, such as Paul Laurence Dunbar (personal communication, September 22, 2002). During a telephone interview, McKissack also acknowledged that growing up during the era of legalized segregation impacted her work and made ideas such as freedom and justice ones that she wants to convey to her readers. Both _The Brownies' Book_ and children's literature by McKissack address issues of racism and highlight the ways in which African Americans have protested against racism. For example, in her book _African-American Inventors_ (1994), she provides information about James Forten, who created a device to help ships navigate tumultuous waters, and she highlights the fact that he refused to install this device on any slave ships. The theme of social protest against racism is also in line with one of the tenets of critical race theory. Just as critical race theorists are committed to social protest against racism and use storytelling in order to accomplish this task, so do W.E.B. Du Bois and McKissack.

A third common theme was the importance of literacy. _The Brownies' Book_ encouraged its subscribers to read books and start their own libraries. McKissack not only emphasizes the importance of literacy but also demonstrates the strong historical connection within the African American community between literacy and freedom. For example, in _Christmas in the Big House, Christmas in the Quarters_ (1994), McKissack writes: "A copy of the _North Star_ newspaper, published by the runaway slave Frederick Douglass, is smuggled into the Quarters. The secret reader shares Douglass's words about freedom and the abolitionist movement" (p. 21). McKissack appears to believe, as did the famous abolitionist Frederick Douglass, that people who learn to read are forever free.

In terms of the convergence of *The Brownies' Book* and children's literature by McKissack in regard to ideologies, both are concerned with entertaining and educating children, but there is also an underlying assumption that race does indeed matter and that it should be addressed within the context of children's literature. Du Bois and McKissack realize, as do critical race theorists, that racism is very much a part of American life, and children should be prepared to encounter it in their lives. Because both of these bodies of work have these underlying assumptions related to race, it is logical that one of their common goals is to use literature as a political tool to challenge racism and prepare children to resist it while not letting it destroy their lives.

Another common underlying ideological assumption is centered on the belief that all children, African American children especially, deserve to see accurate and positive representations of the culture, experiences, and history of African Americans in literature. In light of this underlying assumption, it is understandable that another common goal shared by these two bodies of work is to present accurate information about African Americans, which is often excluded in mainstream discourse.

McKissack's work diverged from that of *The Brownies' Book* in the following four ways: attitude toward black vernacular, strong black females, emphasis on the working class, and emphasis on family and community relationships. McKissack embraces black vernacular in several of her stories. She code switches as a writer and switches back and forth between black vernacular and standard English depending on her authorial purpose. *The Brownies' Book* exhibited a preference for standard English and a somewhat negative bias toward speakers of black vernacular. For example, in a biographical sketch entitled "A Pioneer Suffragist," which appears in the April 1920 issue, the following description is provided of Sojourner Truth: "Being uneducated, of course, she spoke in dialect or broken English, which I shall not attempt to reproduce here, though her speech, evidently, lost nothing by its use" (p. 121). Although it is true that Sojourner Truth could not read and write, this passage seems to equate "broken" English with a lack of intelligence or education, as if it is not possible to speak in dialect and be educated at the same time. In all likelihood, *The Brownies' Book* probably avoided black vernacular due to stereotypical misrepresentations of black speech patterns that were prevalent in mainstream culture at that time. However, it should be noted that negative attitudes toward black vernacular continue to pervade American culture (Feagin, 2000). In spite of the negative attitudes toward black vernacular held by many Americans, McKissack chooses to use black vernacular and validate it as an acceptable language form.

In contrast to *The Brownies' Book*, another prevalent theme in McKissack's books is challenging sexism and presenting strong black female protagonists like Flossie, Mirandy, and Nettie Jo. Such self-sufficient characters often challenge gender stereotypes. McKissack states (as cited in Owens, 2000):

> In *Flossie and the Fox*, in *Mirandy and Brother Wind* and in *Nettie Jo's Friends*, I tried to take some universal fairy tale themes, and rewrite them with African American girls or just girls in general who were able to overcome obstacles and solve their problems without the help of a husband, without running away from the problem and not handling it. (p. 143)

The Brownies' Book did include biographical information about famous African American women, such as Phillis Wheatley, Harriet Tubman, and Sojourner Truth. And Harris (1986) noted that information about the women's suffrage movement was provided in the "As the Crow Flies" section. However, black women were not depicted as independent, self-sufficient, and assertive to the extent that they are depicted in this manner by McKissack. Overall, Patricia McKissack's books contain much stronger feminist tones.

In addition, McKissack places an emphasis on the working class and challenges negative attitudes toward them. *The Brownies' Book* demonstrated class prejudices in a number of stories and gave the impression that working-class people should emulate the values and cultural norms of those who are more financially well off. McKissack believes that children should see themselves in books, and that as a black child growing up during the 1950s in the projects, this would have been virtually impossible for her. Arguably, her experiences growing up in a low-income community have impacted her portrayals of working-class people in a positive, nonstereotypical manner (personal communication, September 22, 2002).

Lastly, unlike *The Brownies' Book*, McKissack places a strong emphasis on the importance of family and community relationships. *The Brownies' Book* did not ignore the importance of family and community relationships. In fact, one of the seven objectives articulated by Du Bois (1919) was to "turn their little hurts and resentments into emulation, ambition and love of their homes and companions" (p. 285). However, the emphasis on family and community relationships in McKissack's books—her fiction especially—is much stronger. Many of her characters gain strength through their relationships with family and community members. For example, it is through her relationships with her grandmother and the people in her working-class community that 'Tricia Ann, in the book *Goin' Someplace Special* (2001), is able to accomplish her goal of arriving at the library. The protagonists in McKissack's books also show respect for their elders and are frequently depicted as being active in communal organizations such as the NAACP and the church.

In contrast to *The Brownies' Book*, an underlying ideology within McKissack's books is an awareness of issues of race, class, and gender and how they intersect to affect black people. As a result of this awareness, a goal of McKissack is to challenge racial, gender, and class stereotypes in her children's books. The aforementioned examples of the ways in which McKissack's work diverges from *The Brownies' Book* provide ample evidence of the fact that there are numerous ways in which she makes her own contributions to the field of children's literature.

CONCLUSIONS

This study has implications for the manner in which issues of race are explored and discussed with children within the context of children's literature. In *The First R: How Children Learn Race and Racism*, sociologists Van Ausdale and Feagin (2001) describe the interactions of young children at a day care center and suggest that they are much more knowledgeable concerning issues of race than most adults believe. Literature by and about African Americans such as *The Brownies' Book* and children's literature by Patricia McKissack has the potential to counter the racism and negative stereotypes of African Americans that are so prevalent in mainstream American society. Sharing African American children's literature also provides opportunities for teachers to engage children in discussions about race and racism (Copenhaver, 2000). Sharing African American children's literature will be beneficial for teachers and children of all racial groups, but especially for African American children, because for them racism is unavoidable.

Children's literature has the capability to help children learn to read the word and the world (Freire & Macedo, 1987). Because much of African American children's literature has a strong social justice component, using books written by and about African Americans offers increased opportunities to raise students' social consciousness and engage them in discussions of equity and fairness in regard to issues surrounding race, class, and gender. African American children's literature can also serve as a starting point in helping children learn to examine social justice issues within the context of children's literature written by white authors, since the responsibility for addressing social justice issues should not be placed solely within the context of literature by and about African Americans.

This study is also significant in that it places critical race theory within the context of children's literature. Children's books are social and cultural products that reflect the perspectives, cultural norms, and biases of their creators. They are not created in vacuums and consequently are not free of cultural phenomena such as racism as pre-service teachers often assume (McNair, 2003). Teacher educators can use critical race theory as a valuable tool for helping pre-service teachers see how issues of race are operative within the contexts of children's literature and education. Issues pertaining to race can also be addressed within the illustrations of children's literature. Given that this study did not offer an analysis of the illustrations, more studies of illustrators of African American children's literature are necessary. The illustrations in picture books are just as important as the text, because the two function together to tell the story (Nodelman, 1996). Many of the themes, such as social protest against racism, that were found within *The Brownies' Book* and the children's literature by Patricia McKissack could also be addressed through art. Prominent African American artists such as Jacob Lawrence, Elizabeth Catlett, Betye Saar, and Henry Ossawa Turner have used their artwork to comment on social issues such as racism. Now there is a growing number of African American children's book illustrators, which includes notables such as Kadir Nelson, Pat Cummings, James Ransome, Floyd Cooper, Bryan Collier, Faith Ringgold, and E.B. Lewis. Studies that examine the themes, ideologies, and goals expressed through picture book illustrations created by African Americans are also worthy of scholarly attention.

Another possible way to extend this study would be to incorporate the children's literature of other African American authors such as Nikki Grimes, Angela Johnson, and Jacqueline Woodson. Johnson and Woodson would serve as good choices in order to examine how contemporary authors of African American children's literature are beginning to address controversial issues that affect children, such as mental illness, death, homosexuality, interracial relationships, child neglect, and the incarceration of family members. Books such as these do indeed expand on the objectives and goals that W.E.B. Du Bois articulated for *The Brownies' Book*. It is imperative that there be such continuous and sustained research on the works of African American children's book authors and illustrators.

REFERENCES

Aronson, M. (2001). Slippery slopes and proliferating prizes. *Horn Book, 77*, 271–278.

Banks, J. (1994). *An introduction to multicultural education*. Needham Heights, MA: Allyn & Bacon.

Bell, D. (1987). *And we are not saved: The elusive quest for racial justice*. New York: Basic Books.

———. (1992). *Faces at the bottom of the well: The permanence of racism*. New York: Basic Books.

———. (1995). Who's afraid of critical race theory? *University of Illinois Law Review, 95*, 893–910.

Bell, Y., & Clarke, T. (1998). Culturally relevant reading material as related to comprehension and recall in African American children. *Journal of Black Psychology, 24*, 455–475.

Berg, B. (2001). *Qualitative research methods for the social sciences*. Needham Heights, MA: Allyn & Bacon.

Bishop, R. S. (1992). Profile: A conversation with Patricia McKissack. *Language Arts,* 69, 69–74.

Copenhaver, J. (2000). Silence in the classroom: Learning to talk about issues of race. *Dragon Lode,* 18, 8–16.

Crenshaw, K. (1988). Race, reform, and retrenchment: Transformation and legitimation in antidiscrimination law. *Harvard Law Review,* 101, 1331–1387.

Delgado, R. (1987). The ethereal scholar: Does critical legal studies have what minorities want? *Harvard Civil Rights–Civil Liberties Law Review,* 22, 301–322.

———. (1995). Introduction. In R. Delgado (Ed.), *Critical race theory: The cutting edge.* Philadelphia: Temple University Press.

Delgado, R., & Stefanic, J. (2001). *Critical race theory: An introduction.* New York: New York University Press.

Delpit, L. (1995). *Other people's children: Cultural conflict in the classroom.* New York: New Press.

Dey, I. (1993). *Qualitative data analysis: A user-friendly guide for social scientists.* New York: Routledge.

Du Bois, W.E.B. (1919). The true brownies. *Crisis,* 18, 285–286.

———. (1921). The grownups' corner. *The Brownies' Book,* 2, 63.

———. (1926). Criteria of Negro art. *Crisis,* 32, 290–297.

———. (1935). Does the Negro need separate schools? *Journal of Negro Education,* 4, 328–335.

Feagin, J. (2000). *Racist America: Roots, current realities, and future reparations.* New York: Routledge.

Feagin, J., & Vera, H. (1995). *White racism: The basics.* New York: Routledge.

Freire, P., & Macedo, D. (1987). *Literacy: Reading the word and the world.* South Hadley, MA: Bergin & Garvey.

Gay, G. (2000). *Culturally responsive teaching: Theory, research, and practice.* New York: Teachers College Press.

Guy-Sheftall, B. (1993, April). *Black feminist perspectives on the academy.* Paper presented at the annual meeting of the American Educational Research Association, Atlanta, GA.

Harris, V. (1986). *The Brownie's Book: Challenge to the selective tradition in children's literature.* Unpublished doctoral dissertation. University of Georgia, Athens.

———. (1990). African American children's literature: The first one hundred years. *Journal of Negro Education,* 54, 540–555.

Jackson, B. (1989). *A history of Afro-American literature: Vol. 1.* Baton Rouge: Louisiana State University Press.

Johnson, D. (1990). *Telling tales: The pedagogy and promise of African American literature for youth.* Westport, CT: Greenwood Press.

Johnson-Feelings, D. (Ed.). (1996). *The best of* The Brownies' Book. New York: Oxford Press.

Jordan, J. (1981). *Civil wars.* Boston, MA: Beacon Press.

Ladson-Billings, G. (1994). *The dreamkeepers: Successful teachers of African American children.* San Francisco: Jossey-Bass.

———. (1998). Just what is critical race theory and what's it doing in a nice field like education? *International Journal of Qualitative Studies in Education,* 11, 7–24.

——. (2000). Racialized discourses and ethnic epistemologies. In N. Denzin and Y. Lincoln (Eds.), *Handbook of qualitative research* (pp. 257–277). Thousand Oaks, CA: Sage.

Logan, R. (1954). *The betrayal of the Negro.* New York: Da Capo Press.

McNair, J. (2003). "But the *Five Chinese Brothers* is one of my favorite books!" Conducting sociopolitical critiques of children's literature with preservice teachers. *Journal of Children's Literature, 29,* 46–54.

Milner, J., & Stewart, L. (1997). Flossie ebonics: Subtle sociolinguistic messages in *Flossie and the Fox. New Advocate, 10,* 211–214.

Mitchell, A. (1998). African American teachers: Unique roles and universal lessons. *Education and Urban Society, 31,* 104–122.

Nodelman, P. (1996). *The pleasures of children's literature.* New York: Longman.

Owens, I. (2000). *Toward inclusion: Factors that influence the writings of children's books by African American women.* Unpublished doctoral dissertation. Rutgers University, New Brunswick, NJ.

Pinkney, A. D. (2001). Awards that stand on solid ground. *Horn Book, 77,* 535–539.

Purves, A., & Beach, R. (1972). *Literature and the reader.* Urbana, IL: National Council of Teachers of English.

Sinnette, E. (1965). The Brownies' Book: A pioneer publication for children. *Freedomways, 5,* 133–142.

Tate, W. (1997). Critical race theory and education: History, theory, and implications. *Review of Research in Education, 22,* 195–247.

Van Ausdale, D., & Feagin, J. (2001). *The first R: How children learn race and racism.* Lanham, MD: Rowman & Littlefield.

Williams, R. (1977). *Marxism and literature.* Oxford: Oxford University Press.

Woodson, C. (2000). *The mis-education of the Negro.* Chicago: African American Images. (Original work published 1933.)

CHILDREN'S BOOKS CITED

Carle, E. (1969). *The very hungry caterpillar.* New York: Philomel.

Clarke-Pyrnelle, L. (1882). *Diddie, Dumps, and Tot, or plantation child-life.* New York: Grosset & Dunlap.

Clifton, L. (1970). *Some of the days of Everett Anderson.* New York: Henry Holt.

Dahl, R. (1961). *James and the giant peach.* New York: HarperCollins.

Greenfield, E. (1978). *Honey, I love: And other love poems.* New York: HarperCollins.

Hamilton, V. (1967). *Zeely.* New York: Macmillan.

McKissack, P. (1984). *Paul Laurence Dunbar: A poet to remember.* New York: Children's Press.

——. (1986). *Flossie and the fox.* New York: Dial Books for Young Readers.

——. (1988). *Mirandy and Brother Wind.* New York: Alfred A. Knopf.

——. (1989). *Nettie Jo's friends.* New York: Alfred A. Knopf.

——. (1997). A home run for Beth Ann. In *It's great to be eight: Twelve stories about being eight.* New York: Scholastic.

——. (2000). *Color me dark: The diary of Nellie Lee Love.* New York: Scholastic.

———. (2001). *Goin' someplace special*. New York: Simon & Schuster.

McKissack, P., & McKissack, F. (1994). *African-American inventors*. Brookfield, CT: Millbrook Press.

———. (1994). *Christmas in the big house, Christmas in the quarters*. New York: Scholastic.

———. (1995). *Red-tail angels: The story of the Tuskegee Airmen of World War II*. New York: Walker.

———. (1999). *Black hands, white sails: The story of African-American whalers*. New York: Scholastic.

Silverstein, S. (1981). *A light in the attic*. New York: HarperCollins.

APPENDIX A
CHILDREN'S LITERATURE SELECTED FOR CONTENT ANALYSIS

An asterisk (*) indicates that the book was written by Patricia McKissack in collaboration with her husband, Fredrick McKissack.

Biographies

Paul Laurence Dunbar: A Poet to Remember (1984)
Zora Neale Hurston: Writer and Storyteller (1992)*
Louis Armstrong: Jazz Musician (1991)*
Sojourner Truth: Ain't I a Woman (1993)*

Non-Fiction

Christmas in the Big House, Christmas in the Quarters (1994)*
African-American Inventors (1994)*
Black Diamond: The Story of the Negro Baseball Leagues (1994)
Black Hands, White Sails: The Story of African-American Whalers (1999)*

Literary Folk Tales

Mirandy and Brother Wind (1988)
Nettie's Jo's Friends (1988)
Flossie and the Fox (1986)

Historical Fiction

A Picture of Freedom: The Diary of Clotee, a Slave Girl (1997)
Color Me Dark: The Diary of Nellie Lee Love, the Great Migration North (2000)
Goin' Someplace Special (2001)
"A Home Run for Beth-Ann," a short story from *It's Great to Be Eight* (1997)

APPENDIX B
ANALYSIS SHEET FOR
PATRICIA C. MCKISSACK'S CHILDREN'S LITERATURE

Title _____

Information about a Main/Major Character

Name _____

Age _____

Skin Color _____

Race _____

Sex _____

SES _____

Profession _____

Physical Characteristics _____

Family Status _____

Other _____

Information about a Main/Major Character

Name _____

Age _____

Skin Color _____

Race _____

Sex _____

SES _____

Profession _____

Physical Characteristics _____

Family Status _____

Other _____

Language Use (code switching, standard English, black vernacular, etc.)
Relevant Quotes or Passages

_____

_____

_____

Other

_____

_____

_____

Racial Issues/Racism
Relevant Quotes or Passages

_____

_____

_____

Other

_____

_____

_____

Class Issues/Classism
Relevant Quotes or Passages

_____

_____

_____

Other

_____

_____

_____

Strong Black Females/Sexism

Relevant Quotes or Passages

_____

_____

_____

Other

_____

_____

_____

Community/Family Relationships

Relevant Quotes or Passages

_____

_____

_____

Other

_____

_____

_____

Aspects of African American History

Relevant Quotes or Passages

_____

_____

_____

Other

_____

_____

_____

Counterstories/Narratives as a Challenge to Racial Objectivity

Relevant Quotes or Passages

_____

_____

_____

Other

_____

_____

_____

2

"The Random Brushing of Birds": Representations of African American Women in Biographies

Elizabeth Marshall

> It's not that we haven't always been here, since there was a here. It is that the letters of our names have been scrambled when they were not totally erased, and our fingerprints upon the handles of history have been called the random brushings of birds.
>
> —Audre Lorde

This chapter focuses on biographies written by and about African American women that have been included in the Coretta Scott King Award list published from 1978 to the present. Biography can be read as a unique narrative mode through which raced and gendered experiences of black girls and women are made visible. The biographical accounts of women that appear on the Coretta Scott King list reflect earlier pedagogical efforts to resist derogatory images and storylines while educating children about race (e.g., *The Brownies' Book*). The life histories of African American women also indicate a focus on gender. As bell hooks (1981) writes: "No other group in America has so had their identity socialized out of existence as have black women. We are rarely recognized as a group separate and distinct from black men, or as a present part of the larger group 'women' in this culture" (p. 7). This chapter provides an analysis of the ways in which women authors honored by the Coretta Scott King Award locate and resist the double invisibility of race and gender that hooks names.

Conceived in 1969 by two school librarians and a publisher, the Coretta Scott King Award was established to honor the talents of African American children's authors and illustrators often ignored by the Caldecott and New-bery committees (American Library Association, 2005). Since its inception, eleven biographies about black women have appeared on the list. Six of these biographical narratives, written by and about African American women, are discussed here.[1] Texts include *Mary McLeod Bethune* (Green-field, 1977), *Coretta Scott King* (Patterson, 1977), *Portia: The Life of Portia Washington Pittman, the Daughter of Booker T. Washington* (Stewart, 1977), *Don't Explain: A Song of Billie Holiday* (De Veaux, 1980), *Let It Shine: Stories of Black Women Freedom Fighters* (Pinkney, 2000), and *Talkin' about Bessie: The Story of Aviator Elizabeth Coleman* (Grimes, 2002). These diverse life his-tories provide race- and gender-conscious titles that fill in historical ab-sences and counter stereotypical constructions within cultural texts written for young readers. The authors analyzed in this chapter suggest that making the life stories of African American women visible requires different modes of telling that often challenge the form and content of the "classic" chil-dren's literature canon.[2]

Aapola, Gonick, and Harris (2005) assert that "girls become girls through their negotiation of raced, classed and sexed femininities" (p. 3). Young readers are consistently asked to navigate a range of competing cul-tural lessons embedded with storylines and images. For girls of color, this has often meant a lack of materials that represent their diverse experi-ences. Iris Jacob (2002), editor of *My Sister's Voices: Teenage Girls of Color Speak Out,* writes that "girls of color have a "unique and rarely validated struggle . . . in addition to bearing the weight of being teenagers and fe-male, we also carry the enormous issues of race and ethnicity" (p. xv). The importance of the biographical works analyzed here lies in an educative agenda that reinserts African American girls and women as historical and political actors who fight against interconnected racisms and sexisms within a U.S. context. This analysis does not attempt to portray *the* African American female experience; rather, it seeks to describe the multifaceted ways in which the lives of African American girls and women are repre-sented through biography.

This study provides an introduction to biographies written by black women and the range of pedagogies about African American girlhood and womanhood within those narratives. It seeks to understand the ways in which women use biography to intervene in the children's literary canon and a U.S. context that has refused to acknowledge the experiences and contributions of African American girls and women. The first section pro-vides an overview of the use of biography as a pedagogical tool within African American children's literature. The next section focuses particu-larly on lessons about race and gender within the biographies. Next, Grimes's (2002) *Talkin' about Bessie: The Story of Aviator Elizabeth Coleman* is used to illustrate how biography allows an author to tell an individual's life story and simultaneously reframe historical narratives in ways that disturb traditional Eurocentric versions of American history. This is followed by an overview of the first biographies written by women to win a Coretta Scott King Award. A close reading of Alexis De Veaux's *Don't Explain: A Song of Billie Holiday* (1980) and Andrea Davis Pinkney's collective biography *Let It Shine: Stories of Black Women Freedom Fighters* (2000) completes the chapter.

BIOGRAPHY AS A PEDAGOGICAL TOOL

Since at least the 1930s, scholars and educators have argued for biography as a particularly powerful genre for conveying the histories of African Americans (Collins, 1994; Johnson-Feelings, 1996; Thompson & Woodward, 1972; Thompson, 2001; Woodson, 1933/1990). Black biography has served as an educative tool through which authors, especially women, seek to make visible antiracist pedagogies (Mickenberg, 2002). Dianne Johnson (1990) argues that African American children's literature shares a "pedagogical impulse" (p. 129). Johnson writes: "To teach Black history, to reinforce self-esteem, to interpret realities of the present while offering promise for the future—is manifest throughout the literature" (1990, p. 129). That numerous biographies appear on the Coretta Scott King Award list suggests that they remain important cultural texts through which to teach black history.

All children's and young adult texts contain explicit or implicit ideologies about race, class, gender, and sexuality (Stephens, 1992; Taxel, 1986; Trites, 2000). Like other literature, the biographies for young readers on the Coretta Scott King Award list cannot be separated from larger institutional contexts. In this way, "All literature, published, unpublished, and yet to be written, exists within the political/economic structure of the publishing industry and, too, is part of the dynamics of popular culture, mass media, public education, and adult literature" (Johnson, 1990, p. 129). The women biographers featured here intervene in a tradition of racial and sexual discrimination by creating images of and narratives about black girlhood/womanhood that resist stereotypes or fill in gaps. Authors such as Eloise Greenfield (1977) and Nikki Grimes (2002) recover black women's life stories usually excluded from "traditional" histories. They provide a counterpoint to the very legacy of biography itself—the study of famous, usually white men. In this way, "Remembering is political and inextricably bound to culturally contested issues" (McDowell, 1995/2000, p. 557). Remembering the contributions of African American women provides young readers with black history and also intervenes into institutions such as the public school, where these historical narratives are likely unavailable in the standard social studies curriculum.

PEDAGOGIES OF RACE AND GENDER

The first biographies written by and about women that were honored on the Coretta Scott King Award list appeared during the late 1970s and reflect the influences of the civil rights and women's movements. Specifically, the National Black Feminist Organization in New York was established in 1973. Antiracist and antisexist politics define black feminism. *A Black Feminist Statement* published in 1977 by the Combahee River Collective, a group of black feminists, captures the move to underscore both racial and gender oppression:

> There have always been Black women activists—some known, like Sojourner Truth, Harriet Tubman, Frances E. W. Harper, Ida B. Wells Barnett, and Mary Church Terrell, and thousands upon thousands unknown—who had a shared awareness of how their sexual identity combined with their racial identity to make their whole life situation and the focus of their political struggles unique. Contemporary Black feminism is the outgrowth of countless generations of personal sacrifice, militancy, and work by our mothers and sisters. (Combahee River Collective, 1977/2003, pp. 164–165)

Biographical narratives about Mary McLeod Bethune (Greenfield, 1977), Barbara Jordan (Haskins, 1977), Coretta Scott King (Patterson, 1977), and Portia Washington Pittman (Stewart, 1977) appear in 1978, one year after *A Black Feminist Statement*. In some ways, then, the biographies on the Coretta Scott King Award list reflect larger social movements and provide another avenue through which to focus on the unique political struggles of African American girls and women. Whether or not black women biographers or their subjects in this sample define themselves as "feminist," each narrative in some ways acknowledges how race intersects with larger issues of sexism in the United States.

Specifically, the biographies on the Coretta Scott King Award list draw attention to the ways in which African American women are situated within the multiple and intersecting social hierarchies of race, gender, class, and sexuality. In her biographical sketch of Sojourner Truth, Pinkney (2000) brings the readers' attention to the double bind Truth experiences as an African American woman. "In the 1840s women couldn't vote, couldn't hold political office, and couldn't have custody of their children if they divorced. So while the abolitionists cried out for slavery's end, women's groups—the suffragists—fought to win equality for women. Sojourner took up both causes, for she was black *and* female" (pp. 4–5). The biographies in this sample capture the diverse ways that girls and women experience racism and sexism across time in the United States.

Johnson (1990) interprets the pedagogical aspects of African American literature for youth as a "Response to stereotyping and misrepresentation in mass media in general" (p. 2). The biographies written by women on the Coretta Scott King Award list contain themes commonly seen in African American children's literature, such as freedom, literacy, and name (Johnson, 1990, p. 11). The biographies analyzed here also include lessons that directly address misrepresentations of black girls and women. For example, some of the biographers take on stereotypical representations of African American women as Mammy, Aunt Jemimah, Sapphire, or Jezebelle figures (Jewell, 1993).

The women biographers in this sample deal with the gendered identities of their subjects in a variety of ways. About African American children's literature, Violet Harris (1997) writes: "Authors and illustrators do not necessarily consider other issues—class and gender, for example—less important. Generally, the issues are welded with notions about race" (p. 40). While each biography focuses on a famous woman's life, gendered lessons are located differently in the texts. For instance, earlier biographies such as Patterson's *Coretta Scott King* (1977) and Stewart's *Portia* (1977) emphasize more traditional lessons of femininity that stress a woman's role as wife, mother, or daughter. In contrast, Alexis De Veaux's *Don't Explain* (1980) foregrounds pedagogies that underscore sexual exploitation and sexisms within and outside of the black community. That is, there is no one lesson of black femininity adopted within these texts. Rather the biographies mark how black girlhood and womanhood is "informed by class, geographical location, religious backgrounds, etc." (hooks, 1992, pp. 42–43).

REVISING CULTURAL MEMORIES

The women's biographies discussed here are literary hybrids that draw on elements of fiction and fact, poetry and prose as a way to tell previously untold or silenced life stories. The authors of these works often incorporate cultural materials such as photos, documents, and illustrations into their biographical accounts to capture the diverse experiences of their subjects. This range of biographical structures and literary elements highlights the complexity of writing about identity and suggests that black women's life histories require unique narrative modes of telling. Wagner-Martin (1994) writes:

> The writing of women's biography is also caught in a web of genre conflicts. What rules of biography exist are sporadic, but most assume that *biography* means an adulatory recounting of events in the life of a male subject. So far as structure is concerned, then, the narrative begins with a subject's ancestry and birth, follows the events of his life, and ends with his death. As the structures of recent women's fiction suggest, women's lives often break away from

conventional patterns; sometimes the breaking away is, indeed, the story worth telling. (p. 30)

The life stories of African American women recounted in the biographies analyzed here often veer from conventional frameworks. For instance, several of the subjects were born into slavery, making it difficult for the writer to pin down an exact date of birth. The life histories of African American women invite biographers to create textual innovations. Thus, authors use poetry (De Veaux, 1980; Grimes, 2002) and picture book formats (Greenfield, 1977; Grimes, 2002) or produce collective rather than individual biography (Pinkney, 2000).

Nikki Grimes's *Talkin' about Bessie* (2002) provides an example of the use of textual innovation. Grimes tells Coleman's story through a picture book format and a series of fictionalized eulogies written as poems. In the beginning of the biography, she writes: "The form of the following story is fictional, but the story itself is based on fact." Grimes disrupts the chronological imperative of biographical narratives and begins with the funeral of her subject rather than with her birth.

Grimes's voice as the sole interpreter of Coleman's life disappears after her preface. Coleman's story is told through different narrators. "Somewhere on the South Side of Chicago, in a private parlor twenty souls gather to mourn the death of Bessie Coleman and share their memories of her" (Grimes, 2002). Grimes argues: "The characters in this oral history portray actual friends, relatives, and associates of Bessie Coleman. However, the voices, styles of speech, and characterizations are all imaginary devices used to bring Bessie's true story to life. In addition, several composite characters have been created in order to maintain the chronology of events."

Grimes (2002) uses poetry as a form for the different narrators to remember Coleman. Narrators include family members, classmates, her flight instructor, and several news reporters. Her teacher recalls, "When it came to knowledge, Bessie was a miser, / hoarding facts and figures like gold coins she was / saving up to spend on something special." A white woman for whom Coleman did laundry remembers that "there was somethin' disturbin' about her. I think / it was her eyes. She'd never look *down*, you know?" Robert Abbott, creator of the newspaper *The Chicago Defender* recollects that Bessie "planned to be / the first Colored woman in the world to fly. / The problem was, no flight school / in our color-minded nation / would accept a woman, or a negro." And news reporter 2 remembers Coleman's 1922 flight "And what a sight she was! / The 'gritty and progressive' woman who once worked cotton, / striding regally in uniform and goggles, waving to / us, her royal subjects, who showered her with applause." The juxtaposition of different people's memories of the famous aviator and the use of poetry rather than prose invite the reader to make her own connections about Coleman's personality and life. Grimes lays out the facts of Coleman's story and at the same time refuses to interpret them for her readers.

Grimes's biography of Bessie Coleman makes it clear that "biographies are not transparent containers of facts" (Tridgell, 2004, p. 27). Rather, the biographer picks and chooses how she will write her subject's life, and that crafting often draws on storytelling techniques. As Wagner-Martin (1994) points out, "The story told by biography is, in some respects, as much fiction as the narrative created by the fiction writer" (pp. 8–9). Biographers are charged with telling a compelling life story, and as they construct a narrative, the line between fiction and fact blurs in part because lived experience cannot be whittled down to one truth. Rather, as Alison Booth (2004) points out, "Identity is constructed of stories" (p. 53). Grimes's poetic picture book biography exposes the complexity of life narrative as well as the author's role in the selection of facts and the shaping of story.

In the process of providing a context and a frame for an individual's life, biographers like Grimes also engage with cultural memories. As Rhiel and Suchoff (1996) suggest, "Cultural memory represented by biography is always shaped in a contested, critical cultural field" (p. 2). The ways in which a life might be told are myriad, and authors might make a number of arguments about a subject. Interpretations of a particular life are tied to an author's investments and the time period in which she or he writes. Alexis De Veaux (2007), author of *Don't Explain: A Song of Billie Holiday*, comments: "I try to look at the intersections between literature and history. I don't think that a book is written in a vacuum. I think it's written within its own particular social or political moment." Thus, two biographers may include the same "facts" about someone's life but organize them in a way that frames a biographical subject in two distinct ways. For instance, in her picture book biography of Mary McLeod Bethune, Eloise Greenfield (1977) highlights different elements of Bethune's history than does Pinkney (2000), who provides more explicit details about racism and explicit gender politics in her later biographical sketch of the famous educator. Reading biographical narratives, then, requires the reader to recognize that each author crafts an argument about a subject's life; she doesn't simply relay a set of "objective" facts.

As authors on the Coretta Scott King Award list bring black women's perspectives and life experiences to the fore, they also work as "cultural historians" (Wagner-Martin, 1994, p. 9). Through the role of cultural historian, African American women reorganize and challenge a tradition in which their experiences have been written out of mainstream U.S. histories, or told from a white perspective. As bell hooks (1992) writes, "Looking and looking back, black women involve ourselves in a process whereby we see our history as counter-memory, using it as a way to know the present and invent the future" (p. 131). In this way, women biographers recognized by the

Coretta Scott King Award offer a critical pedagogy in their works that provides an "oppositional space" (hooks, 1992, p. 77) for teaching about black girlhood and womanhood.

In this space, biographers capture the diverse ways in which their subjects have agitated for change. As Zinn and Dill (1996) write: "Women of color have resisted and often undermined the forces of power that control them. From acts of quiet dignity and steadfast determination to involvement in revolt and rebellion, women struggle to shape their own lives" (p. 328). The ways in which biographers tell the stories of famous black women can be read less as essentialist narratives of African American womanhood or of a linear historical progression, but rather as a dynamic set of narratives in which authors provide diverse approaches to capturing famous black women and their work to combat racism and sexism.

That is, the biographies on the Coretta Scott King Award list challenge the idea that American history is limited to a set of agreed upon interpretations. According to Rhiel and Suchoff (1996): "We no longer view the present as the end point of an agreed-upon narrative of progress, a view of history that fueled traditional biography's emphasis on great men and great deeds. With multiculturalism comes an insistence that biography has limited the fullness of our culture's memory, but biography can also be a means of challenging and recasting that memory" (p. 3). These texts seek to capture a life story and at the same time revise "whitewashed" cultural memories.

Specifically, one of the central concerns of African American children's literature lies in the relationship between the lived realities of black Americans and the "American Dream" (Johnson, 1990, p. 11). Thus, black girlhood and womanhood as represented in these biographies call for analyses that "Insist upon the primary and pervasive nature of race in contemporary U.S. society while at the same time acknowledging how race both shapes and is shaped by a variety of other social relations" (Zinn & Dill, 1996, p. 325). In *Talkin' about Bessie*, for instance, Grimes (2002) begins her biography of Bessie Coleman, who "overcame obstacles of poverty, as well as racial and sexual discrimination, to become the world's first licensed female pilot of African descent," by underscoring for the reader the institutionalized racism in the United States and in the South in particular.

Bessie Coleman was born in Atlanta, Texas, at a time when segregation—with its Jim Crow laws and racist organizations like the Ku Klux Klan—was a way of life in the South, and lynchings of African-American men were commonplace. So-called separate-but-equal schools did little to prepare African-American children to compete in the world of business and academics, because many whites considered African-Americans to be mentally inferior, and descendents of African slaves were only expected to be field hands or factory workers. As a result, there was little talk of technology in the cotton fields of Bessie's world.

Certainly, in 1892, when Bessie was born, few African-American people even dreamed of mastering machines that could fly.

Like Grimes, each biographer tells a life history and in the process inserts vivid countermemories of racial discrimination and related oppressions that challenge historical narratives often contained in standardized social studies textbooks and in children's trade books. The American history remembered in the Coretta Scott King Award biographies written by and about black women is one of slavery, lynchings, segregation, sexual exploitation, and an ongoing fight for basic civil rights.

PORTIA WASHINGTON PITTMAN AND CORETTA SCOTT KING

The first biographies written by and about women honored by the Coretta Scott King Award might best be described as recovery projects that feature the life histories of women often left on the sidelines of history. Initial award winners include *Mary McLeod Bethune* (Greenfield, 1977), *Coretta Scott King* (Patterson, 1977), and *Portia: The Life of Portia Washington Pittman, the Daughter of Booker T. Washington* (Stewart, 1977). These narratives share elements of prior "culturally conscious" (Sims, 1982) biographies. Audrey Thompson (2001), in a more in-depth discussion, writes that "Early biographies written for African-American children often drew their readers' attention to discrepancies and errors in standard historical accounts" (p. 85).

Two of these biographies, *Portia Washington Pittman* (Patterson, 1977) and *Coretta Scott King* (Stewart, 1977), stick to a linear chronological structure and place their subjects in the center of key historical moments. As Violet Harris (1997) observes, "Rather than present individuals, groups, or historical events as footnotes or as only peripherally important, the authors often place them near or at the heart of events" (p. 29). The biographies of Washington Pittman and King, however, are not straightforward histories. Rather, these texts serve as dual life narratives that also tell the story of Booker T. Washington and Martin Luther King. This strategy allows Stewart (1977) and Patterson (1977) to place in the foreground lessons of racial uplift and pedagogies about black girls and women in relation to the family.

In the opening paragraph of *Portia*, Stewart states: "Portia always knew that there was going to be something special about her life. . . . She was born the first child and only daughter of Booker T. Washington and though the Washington name was as yet unknown, in his lifetime Booker was to become one of the most famous men recorded in American history" (Stewart, 1977, p. 1). The book then provides a synopsis of Booker T. Washington's freedom narrative (King, 2003, p. 16), *Up from Slavery* (1901). Portia enters back into the text only later in the chapter in the context of Washington's life, as his daughter (p. 18).

Patterson's (1977) *Coretta Scott King* is also a biography of two people. The first four chapters deal with Coretta Scott King's early life and present a portrait of a young girl painfully aware of racial inequities. Patterson recalls a time when Coretta was splashed with mud from a school bus headed for a whites-only school. "Coretta stamped her feet in anger and brushed the mud from her new dress. This was a part of the children's segregated way of life. White students rode to a neat brick school. Coretta and other black students walked to a one-room frame building" (p. 16).

In chapter 5 entitled "Martin!" Coretta Scott meets Martin Luther King and marries. The rest of the biography chronicles Coretta Scott King in relationship to "her husband's work for civil rights" (Patterson, 1977, p. 57). Coretta Scott King's participation in civil rights activism before she met Martin Luther King is overshadowed throughout the text by the accomplishments of her husband. The lessons about femininity in this biography stress King's commitment as supportive wife and caring mother. In one scene in which she receives threatening phone calls, Patterson writes: "Coretta sat in a chair, holding her baby. She tried to think calmly. Their lives were at a crossroads. She could help her husband with his work. On the other hand, she could ask him to leave the city. Coretta made her choice. 'I must stand beside my husband. We will stay' " (p. 46). The final chapters discuss the ways in which Coretta Scott King continued her "husband's legacy."[3]

Patterson (1977) and Stewart (1977) focus on how their subjects define themselves and their commitments to combat racism through the work of the men in their lives. Wagner-Martin (1994) states: "Biography all too often works to link women with male patrons, as if responding to the unasked questions, 'What man has been responsible for this woman's accomplishment?' " (p. 23). Patterson and Stewart present one approach to telling a woman's life story. The interpretation of women's lives as recognizable only in relation to famous men may be tied to the time period in which the texts were written. If biographies are meant to be pedagogical training materials for young readers, then these texts reveal particular lessons intended for young female readers to emulate. That is, while these texts call women out from the sidelines of history, writing a woman's life through her male counterpart also relies on pedagogies of femininity that deemphasize issues of gender equity and in turn elide the distinct contributions women make.

DON'T EXPLAIN: A SONG OF BILLIE HOLIDAY

De Veaux's (1980) *Don't Explain: A Song of Billie Holiday* is one of the most challenging narratives in its unflinching portrayal of racism and sexism. It is also one of the most innovative texts in the sample. De Veaux is a poet, playwright, novelist, and professor of women's studies at SUNY Buffalo. As the title of the book suggests, De Veaux's biography represents one version of Holiday's life story. In *Don't Explain*, De Veaux uses poetry to improvise within biographical conventions. She writes: "I'm interested in the relationship between history and literature, so I like to investigate how African American women and women of color construct our visions of history while appropriating literary forms. I see our contemporary literatures as agents of social change, critical to our different but similar struggles for self-determination and peoplehood" (De Veaux, 2007). De Veaux's biography of Holiday is a radical departure in form and content from the biographies of Washington Pittman and King. Like Grimes's (2002) multifaceted narrative, De Veaux relies on the elliptical form of poetry as well as other genres to depict Holiday.

Holiday's life story is told through a series of poems as well as the inclusion of sheet music, photos, a bibliography, and a discography of recordings by Holiday. It is one part biography, one part history of American jazz, and one part African American history. As bell hooks (1992) argues, "Much creative writing by contemporary black women authors highlights gender politics, specifically black male sexism, poverty, black female labor, and the struggle for creativity" (p. 46). De Veaux's (1980) creative nonfiction fits into this category as she focuses on the racial, economic, and sexual oppressions that Holiday confronts.

In contrast to the life stories of Bethune, Washington Pittman, and King, in which education holds the key to empowerment, school is a luxury for Holiday, who quits in the fifth grade. Holiday's mother, Sadie, works in a factory and Billie takes a job, too. "And for 15¢ at 8 years old Billie scrubbed / white marble steps plus bathrooms or / ran errands for 5¢ or 10¢ either one. / In the meantime she left school / in the 5th grade / to grow up a big boned-big breasted / grown up child / men mistook for a woman in those / days in the South" (De Veaux, 1980, p. 5). Throughout the biography, De Veaux underscores how others sexualize Holiday.

When Holiday is ten, a neighbor rapes her. "Mr. Dick took Billie into a back room / he put her to bed / see Mr. Dick get into bed / with Billie Mr. Dick that was his name" (De Veaux, 1980, p. 6). De Veaux does not shy away from articulating the sexual oppression that Holiday faces from a black man. In this way, De Veaux has ties to fiction writers such as Toni Morrison and Alice Walker, who also refuse to shy away from sexual abuses that black women face from both white and black men.[4] In addition she points out how the white cops refuse to believe Holiday's story. De Veaux (1980) describes Holiday's interactions with the police: "Billie was already crying and bleeding so / the police took Billie / and Mr. Dick and Sadie / down to the police precinct / and Mr. Dick was in his 40s Billie was 10 / and the police sergeant did not / believe Billie / was only 10 / none of the police did when they looked / at her / well formed big breasts and big bones and / nobody believed / she was only 10 / with a body like that / Billie enticed Mr. Dick they thought" (p. 7).

The failure of the police to arrest "Mr. Dick" for rape, De Veaux implies, is tied to stereotypes of black female sexuality. The police view Holiday as a young Jezebelle, who entices men. Here, De Veaux makes visible the raced and gendered politics of sexual exploitation in ways that make the reader confront the material reality of Holiday's experiences. Stereotypes of African American female sexuality allow Holiday to be read not as a little girl but as a hyper-sexualized black female body. This interpretation works to absolve all of the men from recognizing or taking a responsibility for the rape.

Through Holiday, De Veaux (1980) articulates and counters stereotypical representations of black women. In one scene, Holiday is asked to wear black greasepaint because she's "too light skinned" (p. 58). The biography changes from stanzas to a script format.

THE MANAGERS	LADY DAY
	What the heck is this
	you giving me?
Black greasepaint to	
darken	
your face.	
	I AIN'T USING IT SUCKA.
	I AIN'T NO DAMN
	MAMMY
	RAG DOLL SO GET OUT
	OF HERE. (p. 59)

In order to keep her job as well as the employment of Count Basie and his band, Holiday wears the greasepaint and plays the part of Mammy for the entertainment of white audiences. " 'There's no business like show business,' she said / 'You have to smile / to keep from throwing up' " (p. 60). De Veaux writes that for Holiday this is the ultimate heartbreak. "A Black woman in blackface. / This was the tragedy. / Not the life she lived. / Or the men she loved. / Or the women after men left. / Not that. / But the narrow attitudes of entrepreneurs / and birds of prey / who carved the jazz / feasted on the song / ate without saying Grace" (p. 60).

De Veaux (1980) comments on the "triple consciousness" that Holiday experiences: "Slowly the Jazz Queen / had begun to learn a painful lesson: / She was a well known experimental / vocalist / an artiste / whose sound had changed the orbit of music / and she was Black / was the wrong color and the wrong sex and / she was not to be / granted the status or respect she deserved" (p. 66). Throughout the text, Holiday finds herself defined by racialized gender stereotypes. For instance, in Hollywood in the late 1940s,

Holiday learns that she is expected to act according to derogatory popular cultural images. De Veaux writes: "Hollywood had its own image of the Black woman. / After all / weren't all sassy Black women / mammies mulattos and maids?" (p. 99).

In 1939, Holiday sings "Strange Fruit," a "haunting tale of the South / and lynchings of black women / and men and the smell of burning flesh" (De Veaux, 1980, p. 69). De Veaux highlights Holiday's activism through her music. "For the first time in her career / Lady Day sang a protest song. / She spit feeling into its radical meaning. / She rode the lyrics breathless / this untamed jocky / Fought / Cajoled / Seduced / Wrenched / And freed a defiant song in a dangerous time" (p. 72). Against popular opinion, Holiday persisted and recorded "Strange Fruit." "And until she did she would not give up. / Perseverance. / That's what she had perseverance. / Step and keep stepping. / Over obstacles over nonbelievers over / no matter what" (p. 74).

De Veaux (1980) consistently emphasizes Holiday's social location as black and female in ways that bring structural issues to the fore. For instance, De Veaux points out how racial and gendered meanings are embedded in the law, as when Holiday is arrested on her deathbed. "The Law crawled under her door. / Under her bed. Between her clothes. Beneath her sheets. / The unmerciful Law of the United States. / The blank gray face of crawling laws / and restrictions and jails / and convictions. / That same shameless Law / that could not find Southern lynchers in the night / could not find decent jobs for the men up north / found Billie strapped to a hospital bed / and arrested her" (pp. 146–147).

De Veaux presents Holiday's flaws but refuses to portray her as simply a victim. Rather, she stresses how the everyday realities of racism and sexism caused Holiday to cope in the ways that she did. The lessons of femininity in this text are complex, and De Veaux refuses to moralize about Holiday's heroin abuse or to ignore Holiday's sexualities. De Veaux makes Holiday an example of resistance, a figure who provides an "oppositional gaze" for young readers.

LET IT SHINE: STORIES OF
BLACK WOMEN FREEDOM FIGHTERS

Andrea Pinkney's *Let It Shine* (2000) is a collective biography.[5] In the introduction she writes: "I decided to focus the collection on ten women whose individual lives wove together one incredible story—a story of the challenges and triumphs of civil rights that spanned American history from the eighteenth century to the present day" (p. xi). As a subgenre of biographical writing, collective biography creates a particular kind of subject, one that is part of a larger history. "To tell one's story, to attend to a collective telling of the past, is to take trauma in hand and begin the healing or reparation" (Booth, 2004, p. 53). This collection of biographies makes amends for previous narratives by placing black girls and women at the center of American history.

Unlike other biographical collections, where black women are "tokens of diversity" (Booth, 2004, p. 199)—as woman in collections of African Americans or as black in compilations about famous women—Pinkney dedicates *Let It Shine* solely to black women civil rights and freedom fighters. Subjects range from Sojourner Truth to nurse/midwife Biddy Mason to Congresswoman Shirley Chisholm. Pinkney writes about women in their own right, not simply as mothers, wives, or sisters but as political figures who change the course of history.

According to Booth (2004), "Collections of lives can rarely disguise their didactic purpose. A collective biography requires an additional rhetorical frame besides that of a biography: the definition of the category or principle of selection" (p. 10). Pinkney (2000), for example, includes a brief apology, a convention of collective biography, about the women she didn't include. Missing from her collection are the "hundreds of women who, through their bravery, have changed the face of America. Since *all* of their stories cannot be told in a single book, I chose the women whose stories I found most compelling" (p. xi).

Pinkney (2000) also uses the rhetorical frame of the preface to lay out her pedagogical purpose. She writes:

> It is my hope that the stories of the women presented here offer a window into their tremendous power. And I hope their lives reflect something in each of us—the courage to fight for what we believe is right, the willingness to stand up under fire and disadvantage, the serenity to carry on when self-doubt, weariness, and the ignorance of others stand in the way of progress, and the fortitude to keep one's eyes on those prizes that will lead to a better world. (p. xi)

Let It Shine connects to an activist strain within African American children's literature. As Johnson (1990) argues: "Literature is not just good stories, but stories that acculturate and that have the power to politicize" (p. 55). Pinkney's reconstructions of black women's life histories emphasize political activism and a commitment to social justice.

Pinkney (2000) defines herself as a female freedom fighter. "'Black empowerment' was more than a slogan in our home. It was a deeply held belief that my parents, through their example, instilled in their three children—to brand myself a product of the civil right movement is no overstatement. . . . I *had* to write this book" (p. x). Through her own coming-of-age story in which famous civil rights activists as well as parents guided her to social action, Pinkney exemplifies how young women might be taught to be freedom fighters, to carry on the tradition of social justice through the power of example. According to Booth, "In exemplification, the preface asserts that biographies shape character and that female biographies model girls or women" (2004, p. 54). As *Let It Shine* suggests, collective biographies often aim to educate through exemplary characters. In this case, the collection seeks to provide examples of and lessons about certain traits, such as determination, outspokenness, generosity, "smarts," and religious commitments.

The range of past and contemporary "sheroes" in *Let It Shine* and how Pinkney (2000) remembers her subjects link the past with the present. Addressing a range of freedoms for which women have fought, Pinkney states: "We understood that as it pertains to the pursuit of racial justice, *freedom* means so much more than freedom from slavery. These women fought for many freedoms—freedom from sexism, oppression, the fear of being silenced. Freedom to choose housing, ride public transportation, and express themselves both in newspapers and on television" (p. xi).

Additionally, the biographical sketches often end with a comment about the women's contemporary legacy. For instance, she writes that civil rights activist Dorothy Height's "commitment to racial equality has given black women an undeniable presence on the face of American justice" (p. 69). As she charts the ongoing contributions of each subject, Pinkney refuses to relegate racial discrimination to the past or ignore the ways it informs the everyday gendered experiences of black girls and women.

Most of the short biographical sketches in *Let It Shine* follow a general pattern. The subject experiences racial or sexual oppression that curtails her girlhood/adolescence; confronts injustice in her everyday life; resists, usually against a white male figure; succeeds in her quest for freedom; commits herself to working for others; and finally earns public recognition that results in an ongoing legacy. Nurse/midwife Biddy Mason, for instance, is born into slavery and bought and sold several times during her girlhood. At age eighteen, "John Smithson gave her and her two friends Hannah and Ella away as wedding gifts to his cousin Rebecca and Robert Marion Smith, Rebecca's new husband. That's when Biddy promised herself she would someday do something to stop the injustices of slavery" (Pinkney, 2000, p. 10). Robert Smith fathers Mason's three children. Smith moves Mason to California, a free state, where she "encountered all kinds of free black people" (p. 11). When Smith decides to bring Mason and her daughters back to slave territory to sell them at a profit, she refuses. With the help of other free blacks, Mason presents Smith with legal papers "that made it clear to Smith that Biddy Mason—and all of his slaves—were now residents of California, and as such, they were free men and women" (p. 12).

With her newfound freedom, she works to improve "conditions for the black residents of the city and its surrounding areas" (Pinkney, 2000, p. 13) and also works as a nurse and midwife. Later, she buys property on which she builds homes to rent to black families and that she donates to neighborhood causes. "By owning land she could help other black people find affordable places to live, housing that didn't discriminate on the basis of skin color"(p. 14). Pinkney concludes Mason's life story by commenting on her ongoing legacy: "Today Biddy Mason's memory stands as strong as the buildings that were built under her charge" (p. 15). The outlines of the lives of each of the freedom fighters—such as Ida B. Wells, Ella Baker, and others—follow this trajectory in one way or another.

Several themes emerge across the collection, including the importance of education, words (spoken or written) as weapons, parents as guides or examples, and religion. One of the strongest themes in *Let It Shine* is that of speaking up and out about injustice. Writes Pinkney, "The real accomplishment of these amazing women is that they *spoke out* fearlessly. No matter what, these freedom fighters let their lights shine on the darkness of inequality" (2000, p. xi). Readers are taught about the power of voice to overcome oppression. Ida B. Wells learns "to speak out and breathe freely under the haze of racism" (p. 32); Mary McLeod Bethune "had a special calling—she could inspire people with her strong, steady voice" (p. 42); Dorothy Height learns as a young girl "that the words *she* spoke—and the fortitude with which she spoke them—had the power to change people's lives" (p. 61); and "Fannie Lou Hamer—proud, black, and loud—stated her case. She told the American public about the horror, bloodshed, and humiliation African Americans in the South had suffered" (p. 91). As each woman "speaks *out* fearlessly," she provides an example for young readers of the ongoing power of words, and of the ways in which ordinary women became extraordinary heroes.

This speaking out includes women's struggles with gender as well as race. For example, through several of her subjects, Pinkney (2000) underscores the complex gender relations within the civil rights movement. Dorothy Height is quoted as saying: "Black women are the backbone of every institution, but sometimes they are not recognized as even being there, even in the civil rights movement" (p. 69). Similarly, about Congresswoman Shirley Chisholm, Pinkney writes: "As much as Shirley enjoyed sharing her political views with other African Americans, she discovered that sexism was just as prevalent among black men as it was among white men. In 1964 when Shirley decided to run for office in the New York State Assembly, the Unity Club men told her that as a woman, she could certainly take part in club activities but running for public office was best left to men" (p. 100). *Let It Shine* provides a range of lessons about black girlhood and womanhood in which the intersections of race, class, and gender play out in diverse ways and in which young women "'Act up' and flourish" (hooks, 1992, p. 50).

CONCLUSION

The women biographers on the Coretta Scott King Award list place the fingerprints of African American girls and women back onto the handles of history. The biographers analyzed in this essay specify how race marks the coming-of-age experiences of African American women in ways that critique romanticized ideas and monolithic paradigms about feminine coming-of-age. Here, the girlhoods of African American women are cut short by racial and sexual oppression. A majority of the girls in these biographies fit the description of a "woman-child—a girl who had to grow up quickly because of hurt and hardship" (Pinkney, 2000, p. 29). Sojourner Truth, Harriet Tubman, and Biddy Mason are born into slavery. Others, such as Fannie Lou Hamer and Billie Holiday, spend their early girlhoods working to help support their families. Other girls become surrogate mothers to their siblings so that their mothers can work in white homes. In *Talkin' about Bessie*, Elizabeth Coleman's brother, Nilhus, tells the reader: "Overnight, my big sister became a second mother, / who cleaned and swept and cared for us, / while Mama kept another's house crosstown" (Grimes, 2002). All of the women chronicled here, including Coretta Scott King, Mary McLeod Bethune, and Portia Washington Pittman, experience racial injustice at an early age.

The Coretta Scott King Award list provides a forum for biographers to write about African American women in ways that often exceed the form and content of the "classic" children's literature canon. The women's biographies honored by the award offer a unique set of pedagogical materials in which race- and gender-specific lessons converge in a variety of ways. Overall, the biographers on the list share Dorothy Sterling's (1972) belief that "History must be completely rewritten, not just revised with supplements tacked on to the end" (p. 184). The biographies by and about women included in the Coretta Scott King Award list present historical accounts and cultural memories that rewrite traditional narratives to include the unique struggles, contributions, and triumphs of African American girls and women.

NOTES

1. The biographies in this sample are limited to those by and about African American women that have received a Coretta Scott King Award for writing. Thus, this study does not address Haskins, (1977, 1983), McKissack and McKissack (1992), Schroeder (1996), or Rockwell (2000).

2. For early critiques of racism in Newbery titles, including biographies, see MacCann and Woodard (1972), pp. 78–106. See also, Taxel (1986) and Pirofski (2001) for information on representations of race in the American children's literary canon.

3. African American historian Barbara Ransby (2006) has recently complicated this representation of Coretta Scott King as traditional helpmate to her husband.

4. De Veaux's biography of Holiday was published during an ongoing "gender debate" around African American women's representations of black men. Authors such as Toni Morrison and Alice Walker have been accused of being "traitors" to the race. See King (2003, p. 148) for a brief overview.

5. Alison Booth (2004, pp. 213–223) provides a related history of nineteenth-century collective biographies or "prosopographies" of African American women as a way to counter misrepresentations of black women at the World's Columbian Exposition in Chicago.

REFERENCES

Aapola, S., Gonick, M., & Harris, A. (2005). *Young femininity: Girlhood, power, and social change.* New York: Palgrave.

Alexis De Veaux. (2007). Retrieved 9/23/07 (paragraphs 14&1) from FemmeNoir: A web portal for women of color website: www.femmenoir.net/new/content/view/228/154/1/1/.

American Library Association. (2005). Coretta Scott King Award. www.ala.org.

Booth, A. (2004). *How to make it as a woman: Collective biographical history from Victoria to the present.* Chicago: University of Chicago Press.

Collins, C. J. (1994). African-American young adult biography: In search of the self. In K. P. Smith (Ed.). *African-American voices in young adult literature: Tradition, transitions, transformation* (pp. 1–29). Lanham, MD: Scarecrow Press.

Combahee River Collective. (2003). A black feminist statement. In C. R. McCann & S. K. Kim (Eds.), *Feminist theory reader: Local and global perspectives* (pp. 164–171). New York: Routledge. (Original work published in 1977.)

De Veaux, A. (1980). *Don't explain: A song of Billie Holiday.* New York: Harper & Row.

Greenfield, E. (1977). *Mary McLeod Bethune.* Illus. J. Pinkney. New York: Thomas Crowell.

Grimes, N. (2002). *Talkin' about Bessie: The story of aviator Elizabeth Coleman.* Illus. E. B. Lewis & B. Moser. New York: Scholastic.

Harris, V. (1997). Children's literature depicting blacks. In Harris, V. (Ed.), *Using multiethnic literature in the k-8 classroom* (pp. 21–58). Norwood, MA: Christopher-Gordon.

Haskins, J. (1977). *Barbara Jordan.* New York: Dial.

———. (1983). *Lena Horne.* New York: Coward-McCann.

hooks, b. (1981). *Ain't I a woman: Black women and feminism.* Cambridge, MA: South End Press.

———. (1992). *Black looks: Race and representation.* Cambridge, MA: South End Press.

Jacob, I. (Ed.). (2002). *My sisters' voices: Teenage girls of color speak out.* New York: Henry Holt.

Jewell, S. K. (1993). *From mammy to Miss America and beyond: Cultural images and the shaping of U.S. policy.* New York: Routledge.

Johnson, D. (1990). *Telling tales: The pedagogy and promise of African American litera-ture for youth*. Wesport, CT: Greenwood Press.

Johnson-Feelings, D. (1996). *The best of the Brownie's Book*. New York: Oxford University Press.

King, L. (2003). *A students' guide to African American literature 1760 to the present*. New York: Peter Lang.

Lorde, A. (1990). Foreword. In J. Braxton & M. McLaughlin (Eds.), *Wild women in the whirlwind: Afra-American culture and the contemporary literary renaissance*. New Brunswick, NJ: Rutgers University Press.

MacCann, D., & Woodard, G. (1972). *The Black American in books for children: Readings in racism*. London: Scarecrow Press.

McDowell, D. (2000). Black feminist thinking: The "practice" of "theory." In W. Napier (Ed.), *African American literary theory: A reader* (pp. 557–579). New York: Routledge. (Original work published 1995.)

McKissack, P., and McKissack, F. (1992). *Sojourner Truth: Ain't I a woman?* New York: Scholastic.

Mickenberg, J. (2002). Civil rights, history, and the left: Inventing the juvenile black biography. *MELUS*. www.findarticles.com/cf_dls/m2278/2_27/92589726/print.jhtml.

Patterson, L. (1977). *Coretta Scott King*. New York: Garrard.

Pinkney, A. D. (2000). *Let it shine: Stories of black women freedom fighters*. Illus. Stephen Alcorn. New York: Harcourt.

Pirofski, K. I. (2001). *Multicultural literature and the children's literary canon*. www.ed-change.org/multicultural/papers/literature.html.

Ransby, B. (2006). Coretta Scott King was more than civil rights widow. *The Progressive*, http://progressive.org/media_mpransby020106.

Rhiel, M., & Suchoff, D. (Eds.). (1996). *The seductions of biography*. New York: Routledge.

Rockwell, A. (2000). *Only passing through: The story of Sojourner Truth*. Illus. R. G. Christie. New York: Random House.

Schroeder, A. (1996). *Minty: A story of young Harriet Tubman*. Illus. J. Pinkney. New York: Dial.

Sims, R. (1982). *Shadow and substance: Afro-American experience in contemporary children's fiction*. Urbana, IL: National Council of Teachers of English.

Smith, V. (1987). *Self-discovery and authority in Afro-American narrative*. Cambridge, MA: Harvard University Press.

Stephens, J. (1992). *Language and ideology in children's fiction*. New York: Longman.

Sterling, D. (1972). The soul of learning. In D. MacCann & G. Woodard (Eds.), *The Black American in books for children: Readings in racism* (pp. 175–187). London: Scarecrow Press.

Stewart, R. A. (1977). *Portia: The life of Portia Washington Pittman, the daughter of Booker T. Washington*. New York: Doubleday.

Taxel, J. (1986). The Black experience in children's fiction: Controversies surrounding award winning books. *Curriculum Inquiry*, 16 (3), 245–281.

Thompson, A. (2001). Harriet Tubman in pictures: Cultural consciousness and the art of picture books. *The Lion and the Unicorn*, 25, 81–114.

Thompson, J., & Woodward, G. (1972). Black perspective in books for children. In D. MacCann & G. Woodard (Eds.), *The Black American in books for children: Readings in racism* (pp. 14–27). London: Scarecrow Press.

Tridgell, S. (2004). *Understanding our selves: The dangerous art of biography.* New York: Peter Lang.

Trites, R. S. (2000). *Disturbing the universe: Power and repression in young adult literature.* Iowa City: University of Iowa Press.

Wagner-Martin, L. (1994). *Telling women's lives: The new biography.* New Brunswick, NJ: Rutgers University Press.

Washington, B. T. (1901). *Up from slavery: An autobiography.* New York: Doubleday.

Woodson, C. G. (1990). *Mis-education of the negro.* Trenton, NJ: Africa World Press. (Original work published 1933.)

Zinn, M. B., & Dill, B. T. (1996). Theorizing difference from multiracial feminism. *Feminist Studies, 22* (2), 321–331.

3

Following Tradition: Young Adult Literature as Neo-slave Narrative

KaaVonia Hinton

They were not slaves. They were people. Their condition was slavery.

—Julius Lester

In the Pulitzer Prize–winning *Beloved* (Morrison, 1987/2004), Sethe tells her daughter, Denver, of the power of memories, of lived experiences that subsist long after the inhabitant of the experience dies. Sethe explains that her experiences continued to be real for her long after she obtained freedom: "if you go there—you who never was there—if you go there and stand in the place where it was, it will happen again; it will be there for you, waiting for you. So, Denver, you can't never go there. Never. Because even though it's all over—over and done with—it's going to always be there waiting for you" (p. 36). These memories, "the pictures of what [slaves] did, or knew, or saw [are] still out there" (p. 36). Like Sethe, contemporary African American writers are reflecting on the experiences of slaves and (re)telling their stories.

Recently published books for young adults have put slavery at the center, emphasizing the humanity, resilience, and guile of enslaved men, women, and children. These stories constitute neo-slave narratives (Rushdy, 1997; Beaulieu, 1999), a contemporary genre of fiction. Several examples of young adult literature from this genre are examined here. The examples selected are nonclassical or noncanonized works that feature protagonists from age twelve to twenty (Hinton-Johnson, 2003).

TOWARD A DEFINITION OF THE NEO-SLAVE NARRATIVE

While original slave narratives are narratives written by people who actually lived during the antebellum period and were enslaved, neo-slave narratives are written by contemporary authors who retell or reenvision the slave experience in America. Often loosely basing their work on historical documents and court cases, the writers of neo-slave narratives create imaginative depictions of the lives of former slaves (Lee, 2001). The genre includes such works as Octavia Butler's *Kindred* (1979), Sherley Anne Williams's *Dessa Rose* (1986), Toni Morrison's *Beloved* (1987/2004), Charles Johnson's *Middle Passage* (1998), J. California Cooper's *Family* (1991), Michelle Cliff's *Free Enterprise* (1993), and Phyllis Alesia Perry's *Stigmata* (1998), to name a few.[1]

Rushdy (1999) and Beaulieu (1999) discuss many of the novels mentioned above as neo-slave narratives. In an entry in *The Oxford Companion to African American Literature*, Rushdy (1997, pp. 534–535) maintains that the neo-slave narrative exists in at least four forms: (1) historical novels about slavery written in either first or third person (e.g., Toni Morrison's *Beloved* and Alex Haley's *Queen*); (2) novels about slavery's impact on contemporary society, or "palimpsest narratives" (e.g., Octavia Butler's *Kindred* and Gloria Naylor's *Linden Hills*); (3) narratives that trace family history to the importation and enslavement of ancestors, or "genealogical narratives" (e.g., Alex Haley's *Roots*); and (4) narratives that adhere to the form of traditional slave narratives, usually written in first person from the perspective of an enslaved person (e.g., Sherley Anne Williams's *Dessa Rose* and Charles Johnson's *Middle Passage*).[2]

Later, in a chapter in *The Cambridge Companion to the African American Novel*, Rushdy revises his analysis, describing only three forms of neo-slave narratives: (1) historical novels, (2) pseudo-autobiographical slave narratives, and (3) "novels of remembered generations" (2004, p. 90). The genealogical narrative form is omitted in this discussion, as Rushdy (2004) uses what he cites as seminal neo-slave novels, *Jubilee* (1966/1999) by Margaret Walker, *The Autobiography of Miss Jane Pittman* (1971/2005) by Ernest Gaines, and *Corregidora* (1975) by Gayl Jones, as the basis of his chapter.

Beaulieu (1999) defines neo-slave narratives as "contemporary fictional works which take slavery as their subject matter and usually feature enslaved protagonists." These narratives "depend on the historical reclamation efforts of [antebellum] slave narrative scholars and contribute to attempts to revise history to include the perspective of enslaved Americans" (p. xiv). Though Beaulieu (1999) and Rushdy (1999) argue that slavery has been the subject of fiction since the publication of antebellum slave narratives in every period in literary history except possibly the Harlem Renaissance, in the majority of their books they reach for an answer that will

satisfactorily explain what they call "the emergence" of such stories during
the twentieth century. They both attribute the emphasis on slavery in literature during contemporary times to at least two social movements: the civil
rights and black power movements. According to both scholars, these
movements called for a reexamination of how African Americans were positioned in history books, a return to primary sources such as slave testimonies, and a renewed sense of pride and interest in African heritage. While
African American students demanded black studies programs, African
American historians and others began to challenge historical texts, which
led to the publication of new scholarly historiographies. Rushdy (2004) describes his efforts as a discussion of the "social, intellectual, and institutional transformations in American life during and since the mid-1960s"
that created an opportunity for a literary focus on slavery (p. 88).

Beaulieu (1999) focuses specifically on the texts of contemporary women
writers and argues that the black feminist movement in conjunction with
the civil rights and black power movements created a climate that encouraged the exploration of slavery in fiction. Groundbreaking historiographies
that focus on the female slave emerged as a result of black feminist efforts
to create a space for the voices of women.

Beaulieu (1999) maintains that Toni Morrison, J. California Cooper,
Sherley Anne Williams, and others tell the female-centered slave story, a
story that describes circumstances unique to enslaved females. Discussions
of neo-slave narratives are incomplete if they are not grounded in an understanding of antebellum slave narratives such as Harriet Ann Jacobs's *Incidents in the Life of a Slave Girl* (1861/2000). Jacobs's narrative emphasizes
the horrific conditions of women forced to contribute to the longevity of
slavery. As Roberts (1997) explains, "female slaves served as both producers
and reproducers" during slavery (p. 25). According to the law, slave
women's children followed the condition of the mother. Therefore, all children born of slave women were counted as slaves and added to the property of the slave owner. This was the case regardless of whether the children
were fathered by free white or black men. Roberts (1997) maintains that
slave owners "expect[ed] natural multiplication to generate as much as 5 to
6 percent of their profit" (p. 24).

Further, Roberts (1997) explains that the motive behind raping slave
women was not only to increase the economic value of the slave owner's
property, but it was also a tool used to deter black women from resisting
and failing to remember that they were property. Using the research of
scholars and antebellum slave narratives by Harriet Ann Jacobs and Frederick Douglass, for example, to support her claim, Beaulieu (1999) argues
that because of the enslaved female's position as mother, the enslaved female's narrative operates under a paradigm that differs from that of an enslaved male's. Thus, Beaulieu's (1999) is a gendered discussion of neo-slave

narratives, a thesis that describes black women's sense of humanity, identity, and epistemology during a time when they were required to be silent and feign complacency.

SLAVERY AND LITERATURE FOR YOUTH

As in literature written in the adult African American literary tradition, slavery has also been an enduring subject in literature for young people. Julius Lester's *To Be a Slave* (1968/2000), named a Newbery Honor book in 1969, is the first noteworthy contemporary young adult work written in the tradition of the neo-slave narrative. Using quotes from actual slaves, the book describes the experiences of enslaved Americans. The book's purpose, to make the voices of enslaved people audible, to present the humanity of those forced to be slaves, and to educate readers about connections between the past and present, is consistent with the work that some of the adult neo-slave narratives take up. *To Be a Slave* is important because of its use of the oral tradition and its "acknowledgement of the authenticity of the slaves' voices and memories" (Rushdy, 2004, p. 92). Neo-slave narratives often value the oral tradition, suggesting that oral stories, lived experiences expressed orally, are superior to "literary documents," "documented research," and academic scholarship (Rushdy, 2004, p. 92).

Virginia Hamilton's *The House of Dies Drear* (1968/2006), with its emphasis on the Underground Railroad, and certainly her *Anthony Burns: The Defeat and Triumph of a Fugitive Slave* (1988) are also novels following in the tradition of the neo-slave narrative. More recent works such as Mary Lyons's *Letters to a Slave Girl: The Story of Harriet Jacobs* (1996) and Mildred D. Taylor's *The Land* (2001) might also be read as neo-slave narratives, as these books focus on the experiences of blacks during slavery and reconstruction.

In Rita Williams-Garcia's *Like Sisters on the Homefront* (1995), the story of the family's lineage—from slavery to freedom, as told by the oldest member of the family before she dies—is so important that it changes the direction of the protagonist's life. As Rushdy (2004) points out, this literary device, ancestral storytelling used to jar the protagonist, is not new: Hurston's *Their Eyes Were Watching God* (1937/1990) and Ellison's *Invisible Man* (1952/1995) both use it. Like these precursors, Williams-Garcia's use of the family story highlights the connection between past and present. However, unlike novels such as *Corregidora*, a neo-slave narrative similar to *Like Sisters on the Homefront* in that it depicts a black female deeply affected by the experiences of her enslaved *female* ancestors, memories of slavery passed down by a maternal figure do not "haunt" or "limit the possibilities for the life of the contemporary" characters; rather, such memories empower them (Rushdy, 2004, p. 95).

A number of novels written about slavery by black writers seem to follow the tradition of the neo-slave narrative. Four works in particular are of interest because of the experimental forms and text structures the authors use to tell stories of enslavement. Rushdy (2004) writes: "one of the remarkable things about contemporary African American narratives of slavery is how experimental the authors have been in developing diverse forms to tell a story that many acknowledge as the most difficult in their careers" (p. 90). This chapter examines *I, Dred Scott* (2005) by Sheila P. Moses, *Slave Moth* (2004) by Thylias Moss, *Day of Tears* (2005) by Julius Lester, and *Copper Sun* (2006) by Sharon Draper, which are written in the tradition of the neo-slave narrative. Elements analyzed are the alternative structure of each novel, its emphasis on slave women's stories, and its form as suggested by Rushdy's (2004) work.

I, DRED SCOTT

I, Dred Scott (Moses, 2005) is the fictional account of Dred Scott, a slave born in Virginia. After moving with his master to Missouri, Scott was sold to a doctor. He eventually sued his owners for his family's freedom, arguing that they became free when his owners took them to live in states that prohibited slavery. Of the four novels discussed here, *I, Dred Scott* is more traditional in terms of reflecting the form and narrative structure of antebellum slave narratives. Following the tradition of neo-slave narratives about enslaved women, Moses purposely creates a space for the enslaved woman by developing the character of Scott's wife, Harriett. Though little historical information is available about Scott, and almost none about his wife, Moses chooses to describe Scott's marriage to Harriett, the birth of their children, and Scott's love for his family in an effort to depict them not as slaves but as human beings.

Moses characterizes Harriett as argumentative, shrewd, and resourceful. It is Harriett who learns that slaves are suing owners who have taken them into free states. Angered because their owner will not allow Scott to purchase their family's freedom, Harriett explains the significance of the Missouri Compromise to her husband. Together, Scott and Harriett file a suit against their owner, beginning a legal case that will go on for eleven years. Though Harriett and Scott file the lawsuit together, Harriett's gender and race render her invisible. Scott's view of this seems somewhat anachronistic and feminist: "Slave men had no rights, but slave women had even less. I reckon Harriett's name should have been on every last one of those papers from start to finish," concludes Scott (Moses, 2005, p. 53).

Similar to Douglass's *Narrative of the Life of Frederick Douglass, an American Slave, Written by Himself* (1845/1986), Moses's pseudo-autobiographical account begins: "I was born in Southampton, Virginia, where 'bout 1799" (Moses, 2005, p. 1). Unlike Douglass's book, which Beaulieu (1999) argues follows a literacy-identity-freedom paradigm that allows Douglass to take on a public identity under the auspices of fighting for the abolishment of slavery, *I, Dred Scott* suggests an alternative paradigm. Scott's narrative seems to be more in line with Harriet Ann Jacobs's narrative, which expresses her connection to family, particularly to her children. As Beaulieu (1999) points out, black women writers like Moses "have recreated the [slave narrative], shifting its focus from literacy and public identity to family" (p. 13). The Dred Scott Moses depicts is a family man who is more concerned with obtaining the freedom of his wife and their two daughters, Eliza and Lizzie, than he is concerned with being able to read and write or move north to become an orator for the abolitionist cause.

In fact, Moses suggests that Scott does not go north to join abolitionists because of his commitment to his family and respect for his wife's determination to oppose whites who viewed Scott as a commodity: "Harriett always wanted me to hide when white folks came by. She had heard a lot of white folks talking about taking me north to make money. They believed some whites in the North would pay a whole lot of money just to see the slave whose case went all the way to the Supreme Court. . . . Said they would even pay me a thousand dollars a month. That money did not mean nothing to Harriett as bad as we needed it" (p. 72). Public scrutiny is resisted to the point of Harriett's initial refusal to allow photographers to take Scott's picture.

Reviews of *I, Dred Scott* were mixed. Critic Anne L. Tormohlen (2005) of the *School Library Journal* writes: "Moses fails to give a real sense of her subject; Scott never expresses emotion inwardly or outwardly" (p. 139). It can be argued, however, that Moses purposely depicts a man who is quite emotional and loving in an attempt to counter traditional slave narratives by men such as Frederick Douglass. Douglass (1845/1986) depicted himself as an individual so absorbed with developing his own identity that he had little interest in elaborating on emotional ties or mentioning his marriage to Anna Murray, the woman who helped him escape slavery. Conversely, Scott announces his wedding and explains, "For the first time in my life, I had someone to love me. I had me someone to love" (Moses, 2005, p. 35).

Echoing Tormohlen, a critic for *Kirkus Reviews* (2004) argues, "Scott's narrative voice seems disembodied; there's too little character development and historical context to make Dred Scott seem like a real person. Much is told, but there's no drama in the telling" (p. 1206). In contrast, Hazel Rochman (2004), in a review published in *Booklist*, says of *I, Dred Scott*: "An excellent curriculum addition, this book will resonate with adults as well as teens" (p. 1284). Few critics, however, have recognized Moses's attempt to write a story using some of the conventions of traditional slave narratives, such as the use of a first-person narrator and an emphasis on the focal character's journey from slavery to freedom. Instead, they read the book as "historical fiction written in journal format" (Tormohlen, 2005, p. 139). The book is much more than that. The novel not only adopts some of the conventions of antebellum slave narratives but also seeks to "fill in the gaps" around gender that are inherent in original slave narratives, textbooks, and historiographies (Aljoe, 2006).

Moses told a reporter for *USA Today* that she saw a plaque with Dred Scott's name on it while in Missouri conducting research for a book she was writing about Dick Gregory. "That little plaque aroused my curiosity," Moses says. "I started doing research, and the more I did, the more I began to think about Dred Scott. Who was he? What was he like?" she told the reporter. "I know he was a father and a husband," Moses says. "He had a heart with a rhythm and a beat just like the people who enslaved him. He must have felt something. That has been left out of the history books. I felt it was my job to tell his story, the story he never got to tell for himself" (Minzesheimer, 2005). These are the types of questions and concerns other neo-slave narrative authors have asked themselves about their subjects, as is implied by Sherley Anne Williams (1986) in an author's note: "*Dessa Rose* is based on two historical incidents. A pregnant black woman helped to lead an uprising on a coffle. . . in 1829 in Kentucky. . . . In North Carolina in 1830, a white woman living on an isolated farm was reported to have given sanctuary to runaway slaves. . . . How sad, I thought then, that these two women never met" (p. 5).

Moses has also written a book for adults about Scott, but according to the article in *USA Today*, she has not found a publisher for it. She did much to prepare before writing *I, Dred Scott*. "To get the voice right, Moses read slave narratives and listened to interviews with elderly former slaves conducted as part of the Federal Writers Project in the 1930s" (Minzesheimer, 2005). It is no surprise that she read one of the most celebrated neo-slave narratives of the 1980s, *Beloved*, as part of her preparation. She also, as evident in the book's author's note, visited Scott's grave and studied legal documents describing the case. Moses also "recalled the stories and voice of her grandmother, Lucy Jones, who was born in the 1880s in North Carolina not far from where Scott was born nearly a century earlier" (Minzesheimer, 2005).

The fact that Moses makes Harriett an important and influential part of her husband's life is significant when considering the book's connection to other neo-slave narratives. Following the tradition of such novels as *Beloved* and *Dessa Rose*, books inspired by the lives of real people, this fictionalized account goes beyond the court case, establishing a context and awareness of events in the Scotts' lives prior to the court battle up until contemporary times, as implied in the foreword written by John A. Madison Jr., Dred and Harriett's great-grandson (Hinton, 2005a). The year after the Supreme

Court decided that the Scotts would remain slaves until death, Dred, Harri-ett, and their two daughters, Lizzie and Eliza, were sold to their former own-ers, the Blows, who freed them. This detail introduces another area of focus presented in the neo-slave narrative: the complexity of relationships be-tween slaves and whites. While complex relationships between slaves and whites are alluded to in *I, Dred Scott*, such relationships are depicted rather vividly in *Slave Moth* (Moss, 2004).

SLAVE MOTH

The forms that Rushdy (1997, 2004) discusses are evident in the young adult novels mentioned here, but he admits that the neo-slave narrative is not limited to three or four forms. The forms he cites can be expanded, and other genres set during slavery should be explored. Thylias Moss's *Slave Moth* (2004) allows for such an opportunity. The book might be the first neo-slave narrative written in verse. In sixteen poems, Moss—who has won both a Guggenheim and a MacArthur fellowship—introduces Varl, a witty slave girl living on Peter Perry's plantation in Tennessee. Doris Lynch (2004), a reviewer for *Library Journal*, points out that some of the poems work against the otherwise cohesiveness of the book, as "sustaining a sin-gle voice throughout an entire book is difficult" (p. 160). Conversely, Tonya C. Hegamin (2004), a *Black Issues Book Review* critic, applauds the book, claiming that "Moss's outstanding narrative in verse transcends many boundaries of slavery discourse" (p. 54).

Similar to *I, Dred Scott*, *Slave Moth* is written in the first person, as if Varl is offering an autobiographical account of her life, from birth to the mo-ment she decides to seek freedom. Though nonlinear, the book also shares (and revises) a number of the conventions found in traditional slave nar-ratives. Varl's narrative does not focus on the quest for literacy because Mamalee—her mother, who teaches slaves and is a slave herself—has al-ready taught her to read and write.

A sophisticated user of written and oral language, Varl shares with Doug-lass the uneasiness that literacy causes once someone who is oppressed be-comes knowledgeable of an existence larger than her or his own. Through-out the book runs the sentiment Douglass (1845/1986) eloquently de-scribes: "I would at times feel that learning to read had been a curse rather than a blessing. It had given me a view of my wretched condition, without the remedy. . . . Freedom now appeared, to disappear no more forever. It was heard in every sound, and seen in every thing. It was ever present to tor-ment me with a sense of my wretched condition" (pp. 84–85).

Slave Moth is an example of a neo-slave narrative that emphasizes "the in-teriority or psychology of . . . slaves and new world slavery" (Aljoe, 2006,

p. 674). For Varl, cloth becomes the tool she uses to record intimate thoughts. As moths often do, Varl relies on the fabric she wraps tightly about herself, to nourish her insatiable appetite for self-expression and self-ownership. Once her secret is discovered, it fuels her decision to free herself physically.

As in the other young adult books discussed here, the stories of several women, black and white, are intertwined with Varl's. The women's stories both reify and revise depictions of women found in traditional and neo-slave narratives, such as the educated slave woman's experiences as chattel, her journey to freedom, her relationships, and the precarious position of the slave owner's wife, who was also often treated as property. Varl's literacy affords her (and Mamalee) a certain kind of power over Ralls Janet, her owner's wife, who hated "what she took to be the ranking: Peter Perry, Mamalee, / me, Ralls Janet in the hierarchy of intelligence" (Moss, 2004, p. 6). Troubling the notions of freedom and ownership, Varl believes early on in her narrative that she is already free mentally, a freedom Ralls Janet may never experience: "can't read or / write or impress her husband who is also her master / with her own thinking. Won't let her learn. She was placed / above learning" (p. 62). Varl knows that, unlike Mamalee, who stays on Peter Perry's land in order to one day forcefully claim it as her own, she must obtain physical freedom.

> If you get up there high enough, high
> as the roof, if you hang on
> to a bird, bat, luna moth, climb in
> a hot-air balloon . . .
> (would you be free up there, free in the air
> above Tennessee? Or property there, too?),
> you see how Mamalee . . .
> has shaped the rows of corn
> to grow into the letters of her name,
> a deed spelled out. Entitlement. . . .
> but I don't feel the bond that she feels.

(Moss, 2004, p. 18)

The forced relationships between black women and white slave owners are also explored in *Slave Moth*, particularly concerning Varl's belief that her owner is in love with her and perhaps Mamalee. Varl listens as "two traveling men" tell an intriguing story that involves a slave owner who, rather than pursuing any of the white women in the area, decides to buy a young slave woman, Clarie Lukton, whom he repeatedly rapes. Clarie gives birth to a number of her owner's children before murdering him. The story is reminiscent of the relationship between Alice and Rufus in Octavia Butler's *Kindred*. Rufus has "loved" Alice since they were children, so he finds it difficult to accept that she does not want a relationship with him. Refusing to take no for an answer, he eventually purchases her, forcing her to have a sexual relationship with him. They have children, and Alice tries to convince Rufus to free them, but he uses the children's potential freedom as a pawn to get Alice to willingly have sex with him. Surprisingly, he wants her to love him. When he realizes that Alice does not intend to do this, he tells her he has sold their children. Knowing she cannot run away, she does the only thing she can do to obtain physical and psychological freedom: she takes her own life.

As the travelers tell Clarie's story, Varl is initially puzzled by Clarie's sudden retaliation to ongoing sexual abuse. After further thought, however, Varl surmises that Clarie "found in herself emancipation / that let her act in a way that was hard for her to choose. . . . / But as soon as somehow / she saw a self in herself, she refused" (Moss, 2004, p. 75). It is this revelation concerning Clarie Lukton's sense of identity, self-hood, that brings Varl closer to pursuing her own freedom. Of course the pursuit of freedom is an important aspect of neo-slave narratives. Similar to *Slave Moth*, Julius Lester's *Day of Tears* (2005), which won a Coretta Scott King Award in 2006, also troubles the notion of freedom.

DAY OF TEARS: A NOVEL IN DIALOGUE

In an opening letter to the reader, Julius Lester writes in *Day of Tears* (2005), "For most of my life, I have felt that the spirits of slaves were lined up inside me, waiting for me to tell their stories. . . . The characters . . . wanted to talk." *Day of Tears* is similar to what Rushdy (1999) calls an "ambiguously first-person narrative," in which "the author undermines the coherent subject of narration by developing a series of other voices which sometimes supplement and sometimes subvert the voice of the 'original' narrator" (p. 231).

The book reads like a play and begs to be performed. An opening cast of characters prefaces the book's action. There are "stage directions," chapter titles announcing the setting, and interludes similar to soliloquies interspersed throughout the book (Hinton, 2005b). Flashing back and forward from the present, each character gives his or her version of how their lives were forever changed as a result of the day of tears. The book includes thirteen chapters and fourteen interludes. Multiple voices and perspectives give a varied depiction of slavery. There is the voice of the benevolent master or mistress, the abolitionist, the devoted mammy figure, the subversive slave, and the loyal slave who discourages others from pursuing freedom. Yet the central character, Emma, helps to give the book unity. Many of the characters are based on real people, and both the plot and subplots are influenced by real events.

The Day of Tears, an actual occurrence, is the name given to the day a Georgian plantation owner made history by orchestrating the largest slave auction to ever take place. It rained for two days, merging God's tears with those of over 400 slaves who were auctioned and separated from their loved ones forever. The ambitious slave-seller loses his voice during the auction, ruining his career. Jeffrey's master is unable to buy his lover Dorcas, but he remains faithful to her and is devastated after the Civil War when he learns she is married to someone else. The vignettes that make up the novel are important because they are taken from actual slave stories and testimonies, providing information about slavery that was not a part of traditional slave narratives. The presence of vignettes from the point of view of several different characters suggests questions, as many neo-slave narratives do, about authorship, authenticity, and perspective. The question of who has the right to tell stories is an underlying theme in neo-slave narratives.

During the auction, Emma is sold unexpectedly, though she later escapes and eventually finds freedom in Canada. Emma shares the story of the Day of Tears with her granddaughter, who is writing a report on American slavery. In this way, *Day of Tears* is reminiscent of neo-slave narratives that recognize American slavery as a part of a particular family's experiences. Emma emphasizes the goodness of white abolitionists and others, like her slave owner's daughter, for whom her own daughter was named, in an effort to argue that the repercussions of slavery adversely affect blacks and whites. Equally important is Emma's insistence that some white people were quite supportive of blacks. Emma's response to her slave owner's daughter is similar to Sethe's appreciation for Amy Denver in Morrison's *Beloved* (1987/ 2004). During Sethe's escape from slavery, she goes into labor and is aided by Amy, a white indentured servant. Grateful for Amy's help, Sethe decides to name her newborn Denver in Amy's honor.

Most of the reviews for *Day of Tears* were favorable, though a reviewer for *Publishers Weekly* pointed out the intrusiveness of the interludes: "Some of the flashback sections (particularly that of the "slave-seller") interrupt the flow of events" (2005, p. 63). Blair Christolon (2005) of *School Library Journal* says *Day of Tears* is "A thought-provoking and telling look at the many sides of slavery" (p. 49).

COPPER SUN

Sharon Draper's *Copper Sun* (2006) is already being compared to *Roots* by Alex Haley (1976), though the novel ironically follows in the tradition of books such as *Dessa Rose* (Williams, 1986) and *Beloved* (Morrison, 1987/ 2004), novels Beaulieu (1999) argues "are responsible for repositioning the black woman in slavery, according her new status as a whole woman with a gender identity completely her own" (p. 25). As Beaulieu (1999) points out, Haley's *Roots*, "the story of village life, enslavement, and freedom from a male point of view," might have partially influenced black women writers to tell fictional stories about enslaved black women, as the work does little to depict enslaved women's lives (p. 146). *Copper Sun* tells a similar story from a woman's perspective.

In an essay titled "Alex Haley, Me, and a Kid Named Kyrus: A Tale of Cosmic Connections," Draper (2001) describes the influence *Roots* had on her teaching and writing: "I cherished [*Roots*] and all it meant," she writes. "I used excerpts from the book . . . and videotapes . . . in my classroom. We discussed issues of fairness and racism and bigotry and redemption. . . . It was multicultural, cross-curricular teaching and learning at its best, and I didn't even know it. I just knew [the students] were thriving and enjoying the learning process with no pain and much gain. Alex Haley helped me do that" (p. 27).

Interestingly, her description of Haley's story could serve as the description of her own *Copper Sun*: "The film, and the book on which it was based, detailed the horrors of the hold of the slave ship, the shame of the auction block, the pain and confusion of families split apart, and the realities of forced labor under terrible conditions. But it also showed the unquenchable will to live, the determination to survive and overcome, and power of the human spirit" (Draper, 2001, p. 26).

An excerpt from Harlem Renaissance poet Countee Cullen's "Heritage" opens the novel, bringing to mind one of his earliest books of poetry, *Copper Sun*, while illuminating the book's theme: what is Africa to me? Similar to some of the earlier antebellum slave narratives, such as Olaudah Equiano's (1789/2004), the opening chapters reveal Amari's loving community before "milk-faced" strangers ravage the village, killing the very young and old while kidnapping others. Readers follow along as Amari is taken to the Ivory Coast, survives the Middle Passage, and is sold in the Carolinas to serve as a birthday gift for young Clay Derby. Draper abruptly introduces another narrator, Polly, an ambitious white indentured servant purchased haphazardly by the Derbys. In alternating chapters, Amari and Polly tell how their stories connect. When Polly is forced to teach Amari English and appropriate ways to interact on the plantation, the two become close, eventually escaping together (Hinton, 2006). The relationship between Polly and Amari is typical of neo-slave narratives that examine the necessity of "interracial coalitions," such as those seen between Amy and Sethe in *Beloved* and Rufel and Dessa in *Dessa Rose* (Rushdy, 1999).

Copper Sun revises historical assumptions about African culture, enslaved black women, and white free and indentured women. In American society, particularly southern society, mythmaking around race had occurred for some time but seemed to escalate around the Civil War (Dessens, 2003).

Since African culture has been described as barbaric and uncivilized, Draper (2006) depicts Amari's village in a way that counters this misconception. Polly's earlier chapters in the book reveal negative, offensive beliefs she has about blacks, but as her character develops and her relationships with Amari and Teenie, the master's cook, grow in depth, she realizes her assumptions about blacks are ill informed.

Similar to Moss, Draper (2006) chooses to emphasize the lack of rights white women had, particularly indentured servants. Early in the novel, Clay Derby tells Polly, "Let me warn you, girl. Women don't need to be reading, so just keep that ability to yourself" (Draper, 2006, p. 82). One of Polly's greatest struggles is her desire for something unobtainable for a poor, indentured white woman: membership in the "cult of true womanhood" to which Mistress Derby belongs. A blurry, yet simultaneously distinct line exists between the enslaved and the white woman's places in the home. Mrs. Derby has little freedom to do more than what her husband and society deem appropriate if she is to maintain her status as a "lady." When Teenie, Lena, Amari, and other slaves discuss the matter, Lena insists, "but she ain't no slave" (p. 124). Teenie's quick rebuttal is summative: "Pretty close to it. . . . He decide where she go, who she talks to, what she wear—everything. She just sleep in a better bed than you do!" (p. 124).

One of the interesting ideas concerning the neo-slave narrative is the author's freedom to explore topics original slave narrative authors could not, as they were concerned with earning the endorsement of abolitionists (Sekora, 1997, p. 673). According to Beaulieu (1999), "The revival of the slave narrative as genre, freed from its rigid nineteenth-century conventions and its obligation to flatter white audiences, is the most significant development in late-twentieth-century American literature" (p. 143).

Draper (2006) charters territory few traditional slave narratives dared when she explores a consenting sexual relationship between Mrs. Derby and her "bodyguard" that results in the birth of a black daughter. Amari, Polly, and Teenie attempt to hide the baby and, indirectly, Mrs. Derby's relationship with her personal slave, but their efforts are discovered, and Mr. Derby threatens to sell Amari, Polly, and Teenie's son, Tidbit. In retaliation, one of the slaves puts a sedative in Mr. Derby's son's drink while Teenie poisons Mr. Derby, an act of defiance essential in neo-slave narratives.

Throughout the novel, Amari hopes for death: while joined to a coffle headed for the Cape Coast, while smothered amidst the bodies of hundreds of slaves, and while repeatedly being raped on the deck of the ship. It is a woman named Afi who tells her that hope must keep her alive. Amari finds that hope when mere coincidence steps in and the man the Derbys have asked to sell Amari, Polly, and Tidbit happens to be an abolitionist at heart. He gives them money and food and encourages them to run north.

Amari eventually makes it safely south, to Fort Mose in the Spanish colony of Florida. The reason Amari must live rests in her adoption of Tidbit and in the birth of her own child. In this way, Draper's historical novel is similar to the neo-slave narratives of Morrison (1987/2004) and Williams (1986); it features a young woman representative of "the repositories and carriers of the African American communities' histories and memories" (Aljoe, 2006, p. 674).

Historical texts that put black slave women at the center were scarce when Angela Y. Davis published *Women, Race, and Class* in 1981, but several other books soon followed: Jacqueline Jones's *Labor of Love, Labor of Sorrow: Black Women, Work, and the Family, from Slavery to the Present* (1985) and Deborah Gray White's *Ar'n't I a Woman? Female Slaves in the Plantation South* (1999). According to Beaulieu (1999), "These works challenged prevailing notions of enslaved women as one-dimensional figures capable of little more than rudimentary wifely or mothering roles" (p. 6). As a result of revisionist historical works, a number of contemporary black writers (women and men) began to imagine what life was like for slaves.

I, Dred Scott (2005), *Slave Moth* (2004), *Day of Tears* (2005), and *Copper Sun* (2006) can be read as neo-slave narratives, narratives written during contemporary times that explore slavery in a way that antebellum slave narratives did/could not. These young adult texts share an intertextual relationship with the original slave narratives and neo-slave narratives identified by scholars such as Rushdy (1999, 2004) and Beaulieu (1999). Each of the novels adopts some of the conventions of the original slave narratives while revising the genre in light of recently published revisionist historiographies. Reading select young adult books as neo-slave narratives offers several opportunities for in-depth study, including giving close and critical attention to antebellum slave narratives, examining links between slavery and contemporary society, and exploring the sophisticated ways that texts about slavery written for young people follow in the tradition of books such as *Incidents in the Life of a Slave Girl* (Jacobs, 1861/2000) and *Narrative of the Life of Frederick Douglass* (Douglass, 1845/1986) as well as recent novels like *Beloved* (Morrison, 1987/2004) and *Dessa Rose* (Williams, 1986).

NOTES

1. While many of these titles are taught in high schools, here a distinction is made between novels adopted for secondary classroom use and those originally (and actually) marketed to young adults.

2. All examples are from Rushdy (1997).

REFERENCES

Aljoe, N. N. (2006). Neo-slave narrative. In E. Beaulieu (Ed.), *Writing African American women: An encyclopedia of literature by and about women of color: Vol. 2* (pp. 673–675). New York: Greenwood Press.

Beaulieu, E. (1999). *Black women writers and the American neo-slave narrative: Femininity unfettered.* New York: Greenwood Press.

Butler, O. (1979). *Kindred.* Boston: Beacon Press.

Christolon, B. (2005). [Review of the book *Day of tears: A novel in dialogue*]. *School Library Journal, 51,* 49.

Cliff, M. (1993). *Free enterprise.* New York: Penguin.

Cooper, J. C. (1991). *Family.* New York: Doubleday.

Davis, A. Y. (1981). *Women, race, and class.* New York: Random House.

Dessens, N. (2003). *Myths of the plantation society: Slavery in the American South and the West Indies.* Gainesville: University Press of Florida.

Douglass, F. (1986). *Narrative of the life of Frederick Douglass, an American slave: Written by himself.* New York: Penguin. (Original work published 1845.)

Draper, S. (2001). Alex Haley, me, and a kid named Kyrus: A tale of cosmic connections. *Obsidian, 3* (1), 26–35.

———. (2006). *Copper sun.* New York: Atheneum.

Ellison, R. (1995). *Invisible man.* New York: Knopf. (Original work published 1952.)

Equiano, O. (2004). *The interesting narrative of the life of Olaudah Equiano, or Gustavus Vassa, the African, written by himself.* New York: Random House. (Original work published 1789.)

Gaines, E. (2005). *The autobiography of Miss Jane Pittman.* New York: Dial. (Original work published 1971.)

Haley, A. (1976). *Roots: The saga of an American family.* New York: Doubleday.

———. (1993). *Queen.* New York: Morrow.

Hamilton, V. (1988). *Anthony Burns: The defeat and triumph of a fugitive slave.* New York: Knopf.

———. (2006). *The house of Dies Drear.* New York: Simon & Schuster. (Original work published 1968.)

Hegamin, T. C. (2004). [Review of the book *Slave moth: A narrative in verse*]. *Black Issues Book Review, 6,* 54–55.

Hinton, K. (2005a). [Review of the book *I, Dred Scott: A fictional slave narrative based on the life and legal precedent of Dred Scott*]. *Voice of Youth Advocates, 28,* 46.

———. (2005b). [Review of the book *Day of tears: A novel in dialogue*]. *Kliatt, 39,* 15.

———. (2006). [Review of the book *Copper sun*]. *Voice of Youth Advocates,* 484.

Hinton-Johnson, K. (2003). *Expanding the power of literature: African American literary theory and young adult literature.* Unpublished doctoral dissertation, Ohio State University, Columbus.

Hurston, Z. N. (1990). *Their eyes were watching God.* New York: Perennial Library. (Original work published 1937.)

Jacobs, H. A. (2000). *Incidents in the life of a slave girl, written by herself.* Harvard University Press. (Original work published 1861.)

Johnson, C. (1998). *Middle passage.* New York: Simon & Schuster.

Jones, G. (1975). *Corregidora*. New York: Random House.

Jones, J. (1985). *Labor of love, labor of sorrow: Black women, work, and the family from slavery to the present*. New York: Basic Books.

Lee, V. (2001). Class lecture, June 12. The Ohio State University.

Lester, J. (2000). *To be a slave*. New York: Penguin. (Original work published 1968.)

———. (2005). *Day of tears: A novel in dialogue*. New York: Hyperion.

Lynch, D. (2004). [Review of the book *Slave moth: A narrative in verse*]. *Library Journal*, 129, 93.

Lyons, M. (1996). *Letters to a slave girl: The story of Harriet Jacobs*. New York: Simon & Schuster.

Minzesheimer, B. (2005). *I, Dred Scott* puts a face on a name from history. *USA Today*. www.usatoday.com/life/books/news/2005-02-02-dred-scott_x.html.

Morrison, T. (2004). *Beloved*. New York: Random House. (Original work published 1987.)

Moses, S. P. (2005). *I, Dred Scott: A fictional narrative based on the life and legal precedent of Dred Scott*. New York: McElderry Books.

Moss, T. (2004). *Slave moth*. New York: Persea Books.

Naylor, G. (1985). *Linden Hills*. New York: Ticknor & Fields.

Perry, P. A. (1998). *Stigmata*. New York: Anchor.

Review of the book *Day of tears: A novel in dialogue*. *Publishers Weekly*, 252, 63. (2005).

Review of the book *I, Dred Scott: A fictional slave narrative based on the life and legal precedent of Dred Scott*. *Kirkus Reviews*, 72, 1206. (2004).

Roberts, D. (1997). *Killing the black body: Race, reproduction, and the meaning of liberty*. New York: Pantheon.

Rochman, H. (2004). [Review of the book *I, Dred Scott: A fictional slave narrative based on the life and legal precedent of Dred Scott*]. *Booklist*, 1284.

Rushdy, A.H.A. (1997). Neo-slave narratives. In W. L. Andrews, F. S. Foster, & T. Harris (Eds.), *The Oxford companion to African American literature* (pp. 533–535). New York: Oxford University Press.

———. (1999). *Neo-slave narratives: Studies in the social logic of a literary form*. New York: Oxford University Press.

———. (2004). The neo-slave narrative. In M. Graham (Ed.), *The Cambridge companion to the African American novel* (pp. 87–105). New York: Cambridge University Press.

Sekora, J. (1997). Slavery. In W. L Andrews, F. S. Foster, & T. Harris (Eds.), *The Oxford companion to African American literature* (pp. 670–673). New York: Oxford University Press.

Taylor, M.D. (2001). *The Land*. New York: Dial.

Tormohlen, A. L. (2005). [Review of the book *I, Dred Scott: A fictional slave narrative based on the life and legal precedent of Dred Scott*]. *School Library Journal*, 51, 139.

Walker, M. (1999). *Jubilee*. New York: Houghton Mifflin. (Original work published 1966.)

White, D. G. (1999). *Ar'n't I a woman? Female slaves in the plantation South*. New York: Norton.

Williams, S. A. (1986). *Dessa Rose*. New York: Quill William Morrow.

Williams-Garcia, R. (1995). *Like sisters on the homefront*. New York: Lodestar.

4

Arna Bontemps, Langston Hughes, and the Roots of African American Children's Literature

Michelle H. Martin

Carter G. Woodson, the founder of Negro History Week (which later became Black History Month), wrote in the *Journal of Negro History* in April 1926: "If a race has no history, if it has no worth-while tradition, it becomes a negligible factor in the thought of the world, and it stands in danger of being exterminated" (p. 239). By the same token, if a literary genre has no history—or enables contemporary readers to believe it has none—that genre, too, becomes "a negligible factor" within the literary world at risk of extinction. Arna Bontemps and Langston Hughes, whom critics such as Violet Harris (1990) and Katharine Capshaw Smith (2004) have labeled the "fathers" of African American children's literature, have played a key role in the development of two parallel literary genres: African American literature and children's literature. But because children's books are more often than not excluded from the African American studies canon, and because historical African American texts are often overlooked within the canon of children's literature, the works that Langston Hughes and Arna Bontemps composed for children and young adults have routinely been marginalized within and excluded from both genres. Clearly, if the current generation of college students in general and pre-service teachers in particular learn nothing of the work of these two talented writers and their black contemporaries who wrote for children, future readers and teachers of these genres will likely remain ignorant of their work.

Recovering and teaching the children's and young adult texts of Arna Bontemps and Langston Hughes are important because, in pursuit of their craft, these two likeminded artists, more than any other black children's authors of their time, transgressed professional as well as literary boundaries that ran along the black–white color line, as they wrote for a mixed-race audience from 1932 until Hughes's death in 1967 and Bontemps's death in 1973. Hence, the first section of this essay will explore the backgrounds of these two men and the similarities between them that made their life-long collaboration so natural; the second will discuss the professional innovations that they brought to the genre; the third will delve into these authors' expansion of literary boundaries within children's literature. The final section briefly looks ahead to the future of the genre in light of their contributions.

LIKEMINDED ARTISTS: BONTEMPS AND HUGHES

The forty-three-year friendship and professional collaboration that developed between Langston Hughes and Arna Bontemps began late in 1924 during the height of the Harlem Renaissance when writer Countee Cullen, friend of both Hughes and Bontemps, introduced them to one another in New York. It is easy to see why they became fast friends. They had much in common: "the firmness of their commitment to African and Afro-American culture throughout the world, the creation of a vital and productive art among Negroes, the effort to fulfill the splendid promise of an often-despised minority. This mission," suggests Charles H. Nichols, who compiled and edited the 1925–1967 letters between Bontemps and Hughes, "drew them into a lasting bond of mutual interests and deep affection" (1980, p. 1). Both artists were born in 1902—Hughes on February 1 in Joplin, Missouri; Bontemps on October 13 in Alexandria, Louisiana—and they resembled one another "in color, height, hair texture and in their invariably deferential manner" to such an extent that people often assumed they were brothers, though each "insisted jokingly he was slimmer than the other" (Nichols, 1980, p. 8). In fact, Bontemps mused that when he first arrived in New York and journeyed to Countee Cullen's parents' house bearing a letter of introduction, Countee's father opened the door, saw Bontemps standing there, and "yelled to his son, 'It's Langston Hughes!' " (Jones, 1992, p. 60).

While both Hughes and Bontemps felt a steadfast devotion to the working class and the poor throughout their careers, they were born into middle-class, mixed-race families to fathers who sharply scorned the black folk tradition and black vernacular speech. "It should be observed, however, that each of the men bore a special, marginal relationship to the Black middle class. Hughes's work sometimes met with their censure. And Arna Bontemps moved deftly among a three-layered society—the Black masses, the Creole society of Louisiana, and the larger white world" (Nichols, 1980, p. 4). Both Hughes and Bontemps were teachers for a time, Hughes at the Lab School in Chicago, and Bontemps at Oakwood College in Alabama as well as Harlem Academy prior to becoming the Fisk University librarian (Bontemps, 1998). Both were persecuted for liberal or leftist views at some point during their careers: Bontemps, for instance, resigned from his teaching position at Oakwood College after only three years in part because the school's Seventh-Day Adventist administration ordered him to burn his personal library (Jones, 2000) and considered the title of his first novel, *God Sends Sunday* (1931/2005), blasphemous (Bishop & McNair, 2002). Hughes, on the other hand, was "denounced (erroneously) as a communist in the U.S. Senate" in 1948 (Johnson, 2003, p. xiv).

Despite being the center of such controversies throughout their writing careers, they remained gentle men committed to social change accomplished not through violence but through art. In the introduction to *The Pasteboard Bandit* (1997), Alex Bontemps, son of Arna, comments on the relationship between Hughes and his father: "They had different contacts and different interests, so at a professional level they were very helpful to one another. But also, their temperaments were almost made for one another. My father was a very patient and very genuinely affable person, and so was Langston. There was no ego, never any tension, and I think that's why they bonded and held together for so long" (Bontemps & Hughes, 1997, p. 7).

Furthermore, both Hughes and Bontemps began to write while they were still very young and determined early in their lives to pursue careers in writing. Hughes even published his first pieces of writing in publications intended for children and young adults. His first *public* publication appeared in 1921 in *The Brownies' Book*, a magazine that W.E.B. Du Bois and Jessie Fauset created expressly for black children, or "Children of the Sun." But his *very* first publication appeared in his junior high school magazine in Lincoln, Illinois, after his classmates, whom he hardly knew, elected him class poet. Puzzled by their election of him for this office soon after his having moved to their school, Hughes (1940) reasoned that since whites in the 1910s assumed that all Negroes could sing and dance, his white classmates must have felt confident that he would make a good class poet. Hughes's biographer, Arnold Rampersad (1986), however, believes that Hughes's teachers probably recognized his writing talents and therefore encouraged him to assume this role.

In 1916, after graduating from eighth grade, Hughes moved to Cleveland, Ohio, where he attended Central High School. There he studied English with Ethel Weimer, who taught her students the work of living poets while most of her contemporaries would teach only historical poets such as Byron, Shelley, Donne, and Shakespeare. She also strongly influenced his conception of poetry, setting him on the path to blurring the distinctions between verse (rhyming and lighthearted) and "serious" poetry. This nurturing of his poetic aspirations inspired Hughes to publish some of his early poems in the school's monthly magazine.

Like Hughes, Bontemps also had early encouragement concerning his writing abilities, though certainly not from his father, who staunchly insisted that Negroes could not expect to earn a living from writing. Most of his relatives, in fact, considered too much reading and studying unhealthy for a boy. "Even during Arna's early boyhood . . . both parents had decided to restrict the number of books their son could check out of the library at one time" (Jones, 1992, p. 48). Bontemps was nurtured artistically, however, by a teacher at San Fernando Academy who offered him "special help" in writing when he was in tenth grade there.

Clearly, the drive to become successful writers, despite obstacles, formed in these young men early in their lives. Even more relevant to the purposes of this essay is that as adults, both of them recalled feeling disappointed and cheated as children by the absence of literature for black youth, which certainly contributed to their desire to create *positive* images of black children in stories not just for black youth but for all children. Besides, though Hughes remained a bachelor all his life, Bontemps eventually had six very good reasons to write for children, and their names were Joan, Poppy, Constance, Camille, Paul, and Arna Alexander (nicknamed Alex).

TRANSGRESSING PROFESSIONAL BOUNDARIES

Langston Hughes and Arna Bontemps were professional pioneers in children's literature both individually and collaboratively, and this pioneering manifested itself in their publishing strategies, in the decisions they made about settings and sociopolitical ideas in their collaborative works, and in the awards that their children's books won. During an era when most black children's writers were publishing exclusively with black presses, Arna Bontemps and Langston Hughes were the first authors of black children's literature to place the majority of their work with mainstream, white publishing houses and to bring children's texts into print with the intention of appealing to *all* children. Du Bois, who along with Augustus Granville Dill established the publishing arm of the NAACP that published *The Crisis* magazine, sought the financial support of an African American readership for their publications and sought "New Negro" readers of a range of ages. Katharine Capshaw Smith (2004) explains in *Children's Literature of the Harlem Renaissance* that many *Crisis* articles were cross-written to appeal to child and adult readers simultaneously but also sometimes to address less-literate adults through the more-literate young people in their lives. Though NAACP publications targeted a mixed-age audience, their purpose was clearly not to address a white or mixed-race audience, even if some whites did read them. By contrast, a multiracial and even a multinational audience is exactly what Hughes and Bontemps had in mind for their children's literature.

Furthermore, the publishing venues that they chose assured at some level that their work would reach a wider audience than those who published exclusively or primarily with black publishing houses like Carter G. Woodson's Associated Publishers. Their first collaborative work, *Popo and Fifina: Children of Haiti* (1932), was published with Macmillan, a major New York publishing house. Most of the other works that Hughes and Bontemps wrote for children they placed with Morrow; Knopf; Lippincott; Harper; Doubleday; Dodd, Mead; Franklin Watts; and Houghton Mifflin. Not only were most of these publishers in the mainstream economically, but they also had substantial trade divisions that gave Hughes and Bontemps literary exposure that went beyond the classroom textbook market—the market that Associated Publishers primarily served. Both authors were keenly aware of the economics involved in post-Depression publishing and "sensitive to the formidable presence of White children in their reading audience" (Smith, 2004, p. 233). As Smith comments:

> When Jane Dabney Shackelford met Bontemps at the Chicago Exposition of 1940, he advised her, "Do not write books for Negroes alone because Negroes do not buy books. Write for all (people) readers." . . . Ever aware of the economic impact of the Depression on black communities, Bontemps recognized that the buying power within the children's marketplace rested largely with white children and their parents, and he appeared anxious about the images of African America offered to white readers. According to R. Baxter Miller, Bontemps was concerned with "integration and high arts as well as the need for White acceptance." (2004, p. 233)

Clearly, the economics of dealing with major white publishing houses that reached a much wider audience than did black publishing houses helped Hughes and Bontemps to cross the color line in ways that black writers of the pre–Harlem Renaissance era would likely have found impossible. But the content of Hughes and Bontemps's children's literature had perhaps even more influence on the cross-racial success of their work than did economic factors, for had their work spoken too exclusively to black readers or dealt too directly with United States race relations, they would have been dismissed as "too political" and would have been unable to publish with mainstream presses, particularly early in their careers.

Popo and Fifina (1932), the first of their collaborative works, set the ideological stage for their children's literature and laid the groundwork for how their future work for children—both collaborative and individual—would proceed. Underlying the setting, themes, and carefully crafted literary elements of *Popo and Fifina* is an ideology that places children of color at the center of positive family and social dynamics. Popo and Fifina's family is poor but happy, and their parents place a high value on taking pride in one's work and doing every job as well as one can, even if a laborer or artist is very young. In this book and in *The Pasteboard Bandit* (1997), set in Mexico, Bontemps and Hughes address racial and cultural issues indirectly. "By unsettling biases about international cultures, the books uncover and challenge the reader's participation in a binary representational system that renders all minorities 'other'; implicitly, the rejection of the binary system would allow readers to resist stigmatizing African Americans as 'other' as well" (Smith, 2004, p. 235). Hence, setting the story in the non-U.S. African diaspora makes black and white readers alike examine their assumptions about what it means to be a child of color—especially what it means to be a child of color in a society that values rather than dismisses blackness. Many of the ideas evident in this early work concerning cross-cultural understanding also surface in their later children's literature.

While these collaborators published with mainstream white publishing houses and created stories that would appeal to a multiracial and international audience, Bontemps transgressed an additional boundary through his literary partnership with Jack Conroy, a "worker-writer" (Wixson, 1998, p. 402), with whom he published five books, three of which were for children. During the early 1930s when Conroy and Bontemps became friends, most labor unions were still segregated, and only the most radical, leftist unions "sought to join Black and White workers on equal terms" (Wixson, 1998, p. 402). Conroy was a part of this movement. Despite the unlikelihood of a college-educated, Harlem Renaissance writer teaming up with the son of a coal miner who quit school at age thirteen and became a factory laborer, Conroy and Bontemps established a strong friendship that turned into a productive writing collaboration. And the creativity evident in their American tall-tale children's picture books *The Fast Sooner Hound* (1942), *Slappy Hooper, the Wonderful Sign Painter* (1946), and *Sam Patch, the High, Wide, and Handsome Jumper* (1951) suggests that both Bontemps and Conroy brought a particular perspective to each composition that contributed to its success. Though this collaborative writing relationship is in itself unusual for pre–civil rights movement America (though less unusual within the arts), Bishop and McNair (2002) point out that characterization in these three books was also remarkable, since "the protagonists of these books were all White, and Bontemps was the senior author" (p. 112).

In addition to breaking new ground in terms of cross-racial literary ties, Bontemps is also credited with several "firsts" in children's literature. In 1949, he won a Newbery Honor for *The Story of the Negro* (Bontemps, 1948), becoming the first African American to receive this award (Bishop &

McNair, 2002). In this book, Bontemps tells the story of African Americans from their origins in a variety of African countries through the Middle Passage, into their cultural evolution from slaves to freedmen, all the way up to the black power movement. A groundbreaking work for its time, *The Story of the Negro* also won the Jane Addams Children's Book Award, which the Jane Addams Peace Association grants "annually to the children's books published the preceding year that effectively promote the cause of peace, social justice, world community, and the equality of the sexes and all races as well as meeting conventional standards for excellence" (Jane Addams Peace Association, n.d.).

A strong writer in an incredible array of different genres, Bontemps also garnered recognition for his fiction. *Sad-Faced Boy* (1937), Bontemps's first novel about the Dozier brothers from Alabama—Slumber (the title character), his younger brother, Little Willie, and his older brother, Rags—"was the first urban novel for young people by an African American writer" (Bishop & McNair, 2002, pp. 111–112). In this novel, the brothers run away from home and hop a freight train to Harlem to visit their Uncle Jasper Tappin. Arriving during the heyday of the Harlem Renaissance, these rural boys stand amazed at everything they see. In time, though, the Dozier brothers recover from their sense of awe enough to form a band that they enjoy and find surprisingly lucrative. Like all of the children's literature of Arna Bontemps and Langston Hughes, even when the protagonists make substantial blunders, the humor remains good-natured, the characters learn from their mistakes, and the text never associates blunders with racially linked dimwittedness or character flaws, as is common of writers of the early twentieth century who wrote *about* but not *for* black children.

EXPANDING LITERARY BOUNDARIES

The literary innovations of Arna Bontemps and Langston Hughes were linguistic, thematic, and generic in nature. Young readers of the early twentieth century were accustomed to reading nearly unintelligible broken English spoken by docile, idiotic black characters who often longed for the days of slavery when masters took care of slaves and slaves did their masters' bidding, delighting in what little praise they may have received for a job well done. And many black writers such as poet Effie Lee Newsome, Jane Dabney Shackelford, and Gertrude Parthenia McBrown wrote against this plantation tradition by depicting well-spoken, literate, and usually middle-class young black characters whose experiences were often more universal than specific to African Americans. Much less common, however, were texts that accurately represented black dialect and respectfully portrayed the folk traditions of working-class African Americans. This is one of the literary niches that Arna Bontemps and Langston Hughes filled. In Arna Bontemp's *Sad-Faced Boy* (1937), for instance, when the three boys show up on Uncle Jasper Tappin's doorstep—years after he has last seen them—and announce who they are, then prove it by showing him "the letter what you writ to us," Uncle Jasper Tappin responds: "Well, dog my cats, I reckon you is the boys then. My-oh-me, but look how big—mighty near big as menfolks. Come on inside here and talk to me. Do your mama know you is way up here in Harlem?" (Bontemps, 1937, p. 20). Despite having been transplanted to the big city, Uncle Jasper Tappin still maintains his southern speech patterns—the style of speech that most of Bontemps's immediate relatives did not speak but to which Arna's Uncle Buddy from Louisiana regularly exposed him throughout his childhood and young adulthood, much to the chagrin of Paul, Arna's father. In the context of this story, linguistic humor like "Dog my cats" never serves to ridicule African American characters but instead provides almost anthropologically accurate documentation of the way someone from Uncle Jasper Tappin's background would have spoken in the 1920s. This same respect for the black working class is also evident in Bontemps's later publications.

In *Lonesome Boy* (1955), Bubber and his Grandpa are identified as African American not just by Feliks Topolski's whimsical black-and-white watercolor and pen-and-ink sketches but also by their language. When Bubber tells Grandpa that he likes to blow his trumpet not just in the school band but on the river boat dock, and even in trees down in the swamp, Grandpa looks worried and tells him, "I wouldn't do it if I was you" (Bontemps, 1955, p. 4). When Bubber tells Grandpa he's never heard him play the trumpet, Grandpa shakes his head and responds, "My blowing days are long gone. . . . I still got the lip, but I ain't got the teeth. It takes good teeth to blow high notes on a horn, and these I got ain't much good. They're store teeth" (Bontemps, 1955, p. 4). In this intergenerational dialogue, readers experience accurate speech patterns and colloquialisms of less-educated African Americans of the 1950s, but readers also get an intimate, insiders' view as Grandpa discusses with his grandson the trials of wearing false teeth. The language helps to validate folk culture in ways that were rare in mid-twentieth-century children's literature, and the content of this particular conversation illustrates the closeness between Bubber and his Grandpa, who seems to serve as Bubber's primary parent and advisor, even though Bubber ignores most of his wise advice. Furthermore, this dialogue focuses on the power of music. Created by African Americans, jazz is considered the only genre of music indigenous to the United States, and given the particulars surrounding Bubber's playing jazz and Grandpa's playing it before him, it is easy to read this passage as Grandpa's attempt to impart to his grandson some cultural wisdom about music and life that is firmly grounded in African American culture.

In a similar vein, in some of his juvenile poetry, Langston Hughes uses not just the language and cadences of black colloquial speech, but African American musical forms as well. This is evident in "Homesick Blues," from *The Dream Keeper and Other Poems* (1932), Hughes's first book of poetry for children, the last verse of which is quoted here:

> Homesick blues, Lawd,
> 'S a terrible thing to have.
> Homesick blues is
> A terrible thing to have.
> To keep from cryin'
> I opens ma mouth an' laughs. (p. 62)

The intentional lack of subject-verb agreement, the blues song format, addressing the sacred about a secular situation, as well as the mixture of bitter and sweet sentiments expressed in the poem place it firmly within the African American tradition. It is also significant that Hughes chose blues for this poem, since blues and jazz were considered "lower" forms of art during this era—music embraced by the common folk and criticized by many in the black middle class as vulgar. In using this form for a children's poem, Hughes suggests that blues are good for and relevant to everyone—an apt message, since very young children were also subject to the racism expressed in this poem. The speaker is attempting to return to the South on a boxcar because, as an African American, he would not have been welcome on a passenger train, and neither would black children. Herein lies the speaker's reason for laughing to keep from crying.

With this same optimism, Hughes emphasizes in his more upbeat poems many of the positive aspects of African American life that the Harlem Renaissance brought to the forefront. "Negro Dancers," also from *The Dream Keeper and Other Poems* (1932), establishes a musical beat that brings the dance steps of the Charleston to life.

> Me an' ma baby
> Got two mo' ways,
> Two mo' ways to do de Charleston!
> Da, da,
> Da, da, da!
> Two mo' ways to do de Charleston!
> Soft light on the tables,
> Music gay,
> Brown-skin steppers
> In a cabaret. (p. 60)

Though the speaker mentions "white folks" in the next verse of the poem, they appear only as spectators and outsiders to this dance display—as was often the case when whites came to Harlem clubs to watch black entertainers. The "brown-skin" steppers are obviously the focal point in this poem, and they are clearly being celebrated—with language, but in this case, with music as well.

Though accurate black vernacular and the validation of black folk culture were innovations that set the children's literature of Langston Hughes and Arna Bontemps apart from the work of their contemporaries, some of the themes they depicted in their children's texts also broke new ground. In *Popo and Fifina: Children of Haiti* (1932), the message that the poor can have strong family values and positive family dynamics comes through clearly. Though barefoot and scantily clad, Popo and Fifina play together like any other children, but they also help their parents perform daily chores, such as washing clothes, collecting firewood, and carrying drinking water to the tin-roof shack in which they live. Throughout the narrative, Hughes and Bontemps emphasize the physical strength of Mama Anna and Papa Jean, but also the care and attention that they dedicate to raising their children. These family dynamics echo the theme that everyone, regardless of age or socioeconomic status, has something of value to contribute.

This theme also surfaces in many of the nonfiction works that Hughes and Bontemps wrote for children. Some of these do excellent "recovery" work on forgotten African American heroes, both men and women. Others tell of the lives of black people who are regular folk but who have contributed to the improvement of society or of humankind in some particular way. For instance, in Hughes's *Famous American Negroes* (1954), he details the life and work of well-known African Americans such as freedom fighter Frederick Douglass and the agricultural chemist best known for inventing peanut butter, George Washington Carver. The other titles in this series, *Famous Negro Music Makers* (1955) and *Famous Negro Heroes of America* (1958), also recount the lives of African Americans with whom many of their young readers would already have been somewhat familiar. Hughes's "First Book" series, however, tells stories of many African Americans who had fallen out of historical record. Hughes writes about Estevanico, a Negro explorer born in Morocco, in *The First Book of Negroes* (1952), and he writes about musicians Jelly Roll Morton, Fats Waller, and Willie "The Lion" Smith in *The First Book of Jazz* (1955).

Though some of their contemporaries who wrote for children and young adults chose not to address the negative aspects of their second-class citizenship in America, both Hughes and Bontemps directly confront this issue in some of their work. In Hughes's *Black Misery* (1969), for example, the young speaker articulates some of the instances of discrimination he has experienced. Some of these are without malice but result when children must grow up in a racist society: "Misery is when somebody meaning no harm called your little black dog 'Nigger' and he just wagged his tail and wiggled"

(Hughes, 1969, p. 173). Others result from ethnocentrism and ignorance: "Misery is when your pals see Harry Belafonte walking down the street and they holler, 'Look, there's Sidney Poitier' " (p. 173)—the subtext of which is that all black people look alike—and "Misery is when you start to help an old white lady across the street and she thinks you're trying to snatch her purse" (p. 175)—the subtext of which is that all young black males are criminals. The beauty of *Black Misery* is that the number of "miseries" that Hughes includes emphasizes the frequency with which they occur in the lives of African American children. The text's understated tone also suggests that African American children are so strong that despite being insulted, ostracized, and confined by racist rules of society every day of their lives, they carry on and do what they must do to succeed. Furthermore, the final "misery" in Hughes's book drives home the national and historic significance of racist laws and social practices for individual African American children. Accompanying a sketch of a lone black child entering a school on a path lined by uniformed U.S. marshals who hold back angry hecklers is this text: "Misery is when you see that it takes the whole National Guard to get you into the new integrated school" (p. 176).

Bontemps also directly addresses the harshness of African American life in some of his texts, particularly in his historical nonfiction. In *The Story of the Negro* (1948), Bontemps does not gloss over the cruelty of the Middle Passage and slavery. One reviewer, Ruth Hill Viguers (1984), wrote of Bontemps's book:

> This is an unusual book, and one that all one-world-minded people should take under consideration. It is the story of the Negro race, from the liberation of the Egyptians in 1700 B.C. to an informed and unprejudiced word picture of the status of the American Negro today. It tells, dramatically but without bias, the ghastly story of the slave ships, the underground railway, the insurrection in Haiti, the years that preceded the American Civil War. . . . The freshness, the impact in the story is partly due to Mr. Bontemps's complete detachment. He establishes continuity in time for the history of the Negro race. He gives it a place in the development of civilization in a way that keeps the atmosphere always free of prejudice and propaganda. It is a story that must have developed slowly in a scholarly and balanced mind. (p. 36)

The simplicity and matter-of-factness of which Viguers writes is a trademark of Bontemps's work, and because of it, readers perceive Bontemps's historical writings as history and not as drama. In addition, the painstaking research that this librarian integrated into his literary works for children and young adults also contributes to its credibility and usefulness as supplements to 1940s textbooks, which excluded African American history. Clearly, the approach that Hughes and Bontemps took to both history and fiction served to offer a well-rounded picture for young people of the joy as well as the pain of the black experience.

In addition to linguistic, cultural, and thematic innovations, Hughes and Bontemps also took a fresh approach to genres within children's literature. During the early twentieth century, the most common genre of children's literature written by African American authors was nonfiction about important black historical figures. Though both Hughes and Bontemps wrote many texts of this sort, they wrote a wide variety of other genres as well. Bontemps, for instance, wrote "the first comprehensive anthology of African American poetry selected for young people," *Golden Slippers* (1941) (Bishop & McNair, 2002, p. 112). *Golden Slippers* includes the poetry of authors who were well-known children's writers, like Georgia Douglas Johnson and Effie Lee Newsome, but it also includes poetry by many black artistic "stars" such as Countee Cullen, W. C. Handy, Jessie Fauset, William Stanley Braithwaite, and of course, Langston Hughes.

Bontemps also wrote in a genre still rare for African American children's authors: fantasy. In the posthumously published *Bubber Goes to Heaven* (1998) (originally titled *Bubber Joins the Band*), young Bubber dies and goes to heaven after falling out of a tree he has climbed while on a raccoon hunt with his uncles. After singing in the angel choir, befriending a pretty girl angel, and enjoying several wonderful meals, Bubber wakes up with a broken leg in his bed at home under the watchful eye of his Uncle Demus and Aunt Sarah. In *Lonesome Boy* (1955), the young musician, Bubber, who ignores his Grandpa's advice to "mind *where* you blow that horn, boy," gets picked up by an elusive chauffeur who transports him to a mansion in the woods surrounded by twisty, moss-covered trees. Bubber plays passionately, and the people dance wildly, but in time, he realizes that the dancers for whom he is playing have no faces. When they and the house disappear completely, Bubber finds himself alone in a pecan tree, blowing his horn to the wind. When he finally returns home and relates his experiences to Grandpa, the elder tells him that he, too, once played for a devil's ball and tried to prevent his grandson from suffering the same fate.

True to Bontemps's commitment to cultural enhancement through the literature he wrote for children, his works of fantasy that feature black characters do not simply entertain. They also teach important, culturally significant lessons such as: use the wisdom of your elders, for they have already traveled the road that you are on; and there is an appropriate time and a place for everything—even music.

The three picture books that Bontemps wrote with Jack Conroy, all of which incorporate elements of fantasy, combine a distinctly American genre of traditional story—the tall tale—with some contemporary elements to create compelling stories. *The Fast Sooner Hound* (1942) tells the story of a

sooner hound that can easily outrun the Cannon Ball, the fastest train on
the tracks. In *Slappy Hooper, the Wonderful Sign Painter* (1946), the title character paints signs so real that they actually come to life, wreaking havoc in
the small town where he displays his artistic and commercial talents. And
in *Sam Patch, the High, Wide, and Handsome Jumper* (1951), based on a leg-
end, the protagonist stages jumping competitions with Hurricane Harry
time and time again until Sam triumphs with the most terrific jump of all.
As mentioned earlier, this collaboration with Conroy broke new ground
racially, but their collaborative literary folktales also ventured into uncom-
mon ground generically by making use of fantasy and "magic realism," a
term coined in the 1940s.

Hughes, too, helped to expand the repertoire of genres available to
African American children's authors. One of his first publications was a play
that appeared in *The Brownies' Book* in July 1921 called *The Gold Piece: A Play
That Might Be True*. In this drama, still one of the least common genres
within children's literature, a young married couple who find a gold piece
on the street decide to sacrifice their own materialistic desires to help an old
woman's son regain his sight. Here again, despite writing in a nontraditional genre and also writing about characters who appear to be white,
Hughes's community-minded message about the responsibility young people have to help others comes through.

In another generic innovation, Hughes blends fiction and nonfiction effectively to create a multilayered story about a young boy in *The First Book
of Negroes* (1952). Terry Lane, a young resident of Harlem and the protagonist of the primary story, learns about the Jim Crow South, Fisk University,
African Pygmies, and many other details about historical and contemporary
Negroes, many of which he learns through his grandmother's stories. As
Terry learns, so do young readers. Hughes uses a different type of artistic
blend in *The First Book of Rhythms* (1954), creating visual depictions of
rhythms that one usually thinks of only as auditory, and describing rhythms
in unusual settings, such as in the motion of the planets and even in ath-
letics. Although Hughes claimed to be unmusical, his informative texts
about music certainly have great potential for expanding young readers'
conceptions of music.

In fact, all of Bontemps and Hughes's innovations in the children's literature that they wrote are about the potential for change: potential for
changing the white literary establishment's perspective on African American
children's literature; changing American readers' view of black children's
authors of the early twentieth century; and stretching adult perceptions of
what was good for and pleasurable to young readers. Hughes and Bontemps
actively embraced professional and literary innovations in their attempts to
change the topography of children's and young adult literature for African
American writers who would follow them and to change the genre overall

for African American children, who needed to see themselves honestly and positively represented in literature for young people.

LOOKING TOWARD THE FUTURE

If what Carter G. Woodson said in 1926 is true, then excluding historical African American children's literature from the African American literary canon and from the canon of historical children's literature not only weakens the study of both genres, but it also robs contemporary readers of some worthwhile texts that we cannot afford to lose from the historical record. Langston Hughes and Arna Bontemps composed a vast body of work for young people in an impressive array of genres, but they were also so forward-thinking that they actually wrote for a multiracial, multinational audience that was still coming into existence. Hopefully, the recovery work that is now being done on the children's literature of Langston Hughes, Arna Bontemps, and other African American children's writers who came out of the Harlem Renaissance will be a catalyst for the same type of resurgence that Alice Walker brought to the works of Zora Neale Hurston. This we owe to our children.

REFERENCES

Bishop, R. S., & McNair, J. (2002). A centennial salute to Arna Bontemps, Langston Hughes, and Lorenz Graham. *New Advocate, 12* (2), 109–119.

Bontemps, A. (1937). *Sad-faced boy.* Boston: Houghton Mifflin.

———. (1948). *The story of the Negro.* New York: Albert Knopf.

———. (1955). *Lonesome boy.* Boston: Beacon Press.

———. (1998). *Bubber goes to heaven.* New York: Oxford University Press.

———. (2005). *God sends Sunday.* New York: Harcourt Brace Jovanovich. (Original work published 1931.)

Bontemps, A. (Ed.) (1941). *Golden slippers: An anthology of Negro poetry for young people.* New York: Harper & Row.

Bontemps, A., & Conroy, J. (1942). *The fast sooner hound.* Boston: Houghton Mifflin.

———. (1946). *Slappy Hooper, the wonderful sign painter.* Boston: Houghton Mifflin.

———. (1951). *Sam Patch, the high, wide, and handsome jumper.* Boston: Houghton Mifflin.

Bontemps, A., & Hughes, L. (1993). *Popo and Fifina: Children of Haiti.* New York: Macmillan. (Original work published 1932.)

———. (1997). *The pasteboard bandit.* New York: Oxford University Press.

Harris, V. (1990). African American children's literature: The first one hundred years. *Journal of Negro Education, 59* (4), 540–555.

Hughes, L. (1921, July). The gold piece: A play that might be true. In D. Johnson (Ed.), *The collected works of Langston Hughes: Vol. 11* (pp. 26–30). Columbia: University of Missouri Press.

——. (1932). The dream keeper and other poems. In D. Johnson (Ed.), *The collected works of Langston Hughes: Vol. 11* (pp. 41–83). Columbia: University of Missouri Press.

——. (1940). *The big sea*. New York: Alfred Knopf.

——. (1952). The first book of Negroes. In S. C. Tracy (Ed.), *The collected works of Langston Hughes: Vol. 12* (pp. 223–250). Columbia: University of Missouri Press.

——. (1954). Famous American Negroes. In S. C. Tracy (Ed.), *The collected works of Langston Hughes: Vol. 12* (pp. 13–108). Columbia: University of Missouri Press.

——. (1954). The first book of rhythms. In D. Johnson (Ed.), *The collected works of Langston Hughes: Vol. 11* (pp. 251–276). Columbia: University of Missouri Press.

——. (1955). Famous Negro music makers. In S. C. Tracy (Ed.), *The collected works of Langston Hughes: Vol. 12* (pp. 109–197). Columbia: University of Missouri Press.

——. (1955). The first book of jazz. In D. Johnson (Ed.), *The collected works of Langston Hughes: Vol. 11* (pp. 277–321). Columbia: University of Missouri Press.

——. (1958). Famous Negro heroes of America. In S. C. Tracy (Ed.), *The collected works of Langston Hughes: Vol. 12* (pp. 199–309). Columbia: University of Missouri Press.

——. (1969). Black misery. In D. Johnson (Ed.), *The collected works of Langston Hughes: Vol. 11* (pp. 173–176). Columbia: University of Missouri Press.

Jane Addams Peace Association. (n.d.). Jane Addams Children's Book Awards. http://home.igc.org/~japa/index.html.

Johnson, D. (Ed.). (2003). *The collected works of Langston Hughes: Vol. 11. Works for children and young adults: Poetry, fiction, and other writing*. Columbia: University of Missouri Press.

Jones, J. C. (2000). Arna Bontemps (1902–1973). In E. S. Nelson (Ed.), *African American authors, 1745–1945: A bio-bibliographical critical sourcebook* (pp. 36–43). Westport, CT: Greenwood Press.

Jones, K. C. (1992). *Renaissance man from Louisiana*. Westport, CT: Greenwood Press.

Nichols, C. H. (Ed.). (1980). *Arna Bontemps–Langston Hughes letters, 1925–1967*. New York: Dodd, Mead.

Rampersad, A. (1986). *The life of Langston Hughes: Vol. 1. 1902–1941*. New York: Oxford University Press.

Smith, K. C. (2004). *Children's literature of the Harlem Renaissance*. Bloomington: Indiana University Press.

Tracy, S. C. (Ed.). (2001). *The collected works of Langston Hughes: Vol. 12. Works for children and young adults: Biographies*. Columbia: University of Missouri Press.

Viguers, R. H. (1984). The spice of life: The story of the Negro. In G. J. Senick (Ed.), *Children's Literature Review: Vol. 6* (p. 81). Detroit: Gale.

Wixson, J. (1998). "Black writers and white!": Jack Conroy, Arna Bontemps, and interracial collaboration in the 1930s. *Prospects, 23*, 401–430.

Woodson, C. G. (1926). Negro history week. *Journal of Negro History, 11* (2), 238–242.

5

A Triumphant Mulatto: Racial Construction in Mildred Taylor's *The Land*

Gregory J. Hampton

There are no tragic mulattoes in Mildred Taylor's *The Land* (2001). In this prequel to her novel *Roll of Thunder, Hear My Cry* (1976), Taylor complicates the traditional tropes of biracial characters struggling with racial identity and self-hatred with highly motivated and self-assured individuals who are not limited by their racial ambiguity. Paul Edward Logan is an extraordinary character, unafraid to embrace his mixed heritage despite the unavoidable racial obstacles he faces in post–Civil War America. Paul takes full advantage of every asset that is made available to him by his white ex-slave-owning father and forward-thinking ex-slave mother. Tough love and friendship are the ammunition that Paul uses to quickly mature beyond naïve perceptions of race relations in America. As a result, Paul moves toward fulfilling his seemingly impossible dreams of owning his own land, which happens to be in the racially hostile environment of the American South.

The Land may have the trajectory and several elements of a narrative invested in the tale of a tragic mulatto, but it veers away from this all too familiar vector toward something far less tragic and much more hopeful and empowering. In many respects, "the land" has been used to define race relations and locations in America. This is especially true in antebellum America but also holds true during the nadir period after the Civil War. The ownership of land has always symbolized citizenship in America. It was the device used by "our founding fathers" to decide who voted and who did not, who had a voice and who remained silent. Land defined the "haves" and the "have-nots" in American history. As a result, symbolically, land acted as a mythical divide along racial lines. Black people were not to own

81

land or property (along with humanity and dignity); they were supposed to be property and on paper synonymous with the land itself. The character Paul Edward Logan disrupts this American mythology and asks readers to reconsider the ambiguity of racial and geographical divides in America.

Paul's story is a coming-of-age narrative that presents an allegory of both self-discovery and self-declaration. As Paul "works the land" by cutting timber, he also clears any obstacles that might obscure his vision of himself and how he wishes to be perceived by characters in the narrative. Quite literally, the trees that Paul works so hard to clear from the land are obstacles to his dreams and identity. Every tree that Paul clears from the landscape acts as evidence that the racial divide in America is an illusion, propagated by a forest of lies and wounds that only the land itself can heal. By toiling over the land, Paul demonstrates that being black or white is of little significance, as the land does not discriminate. The trees are misconceptions about black and white America that Paul cuts down with the help of his racially mixed team of friends and family. Thus, both the quest to own land and the actual ownership of land is medicinal to Paul because it places him in a position of existence and authority that cannot be negated legally or metaphorically. The ownership of land acts as Paul's declaration of humanity and manhood.

The character Paul Edward Logan is examined here with the intent to reveal the critical work done in Taylor's novel with regard to race relations in America, the relationships between familial bonds and survival, and the rethinking of literary tropes. The first section examines the manner in which tough love is used as a device to prepare and protect Paul from the conflicts that will threaten him outside of his immediate familial network. Although the love that is exhibited by his family members and closest friends may not always be perceived as "loving" or "gentle," it functions as a complicated and productive method of preparing the protagonist for the physical and mental dangers of growing up in an overtly racist American society. The next section explores the friendship between Paul and Mitchell Thomas and its role in helping Paul develop into adulthood. The final section discusses Paul's familial bonds and the manner in which they help him subvert the image of the tragic mulatto. It will be suggested in this section that Paul is a refiguring of the traditionally female literary trope known as the "tragic mulatto" and a complication of the traditional male slave trope, the "heroic mulatto," popularized by the slave narrative of Frederick Douglass. The study concludes with reasons as to why this work is significant.

TOUGH LOVE

In the United States before and after the Civil War, it was imperative that people of color be aware of their location in the racial hierarchy of American society. To overstep racial boundaries of behavior and privilege, in northern or southern states, could easily equate to severe punishment or death for the person of color, enslaved or free. Thus, in situations where racial boundaries were especially blurred, it became necessary that the racial identity of children and adults be carefully negotiated. It was the responsibility of black mothers to inform their biracial or multiracial children of racial protocol. Explaining to children why they were not equal to their white father's white children surely posed some difficulty for black mothers. However, such difficulties must have been overcome by any means necessary if their children were to be safe from crossing any inappropriate boundaries of racial identity and privilege. For a child of light complexion, as in the case of Paul Edward Logan, it was the responsibility of the parents to teach the rules of racial inequality as an act of love for that child, however harsh or painful.

Although Paul and his sister Cassie are the product of a black and Indian slave mother and a white slave-owning father in East Texas, the children are not allowed to be confused by their racial identities.

> Now, I always called my daddy "Mister Edward," just as Cassie and my mama did. . . . It seemed peculiar to me at first that I called my daddy a formal name while Robert and Hammond and George called him "Daddy." But my mama had broken both Cassie and me when we were still little from ever calling Edward Logan "Daddy." She had broken that misspeaking with bottom-warming spankings whenever we did. (Taylor, 2001, p. 41)

Despite the assistance that Paul received from his mother, he does go through a relatively brief but difficult stage of learning to navigate the racial boundaries located around his family members. Because Edward Logan insisted that his white sons (Robert, Hammond, and George) treat Paul as a brother and not as property, Paul experiences some confusion as he enters adolescence. This disorientation, however, is not to be confused with the condition associated with the tragic or doomed protagonist made famous in Harriet Beecher Stowe's nineteenth-century novel *Uncle Tom's Cabin*. According to Roth (2005), Stowe portrayed her "central black character as a docile child in hopes of discouraging white readers from looking upon even a physically strong, responsible black slave like Tom as worthy of the manly rights afforded white men in antebellum society" (p. 106). Paul's experiences in *The Land* are far from those of the tragic Uncle Tom. Rather, Paul is a hero of the likes of Ulysses and Brer Rabbit—characters famous for their ability to understand the gaze of the surrounding world and manipulate that gaze to their advantage.

As an award-winning novel (Coretta Scott King Award) under the category of children's literature, *The Land* evokes an unusually critical discussion of the employment and deployment of race in Reconstruction America. The text is unusual for a number of reasons, the most important being the presence of multicultural protagonists at the center of the narrative. In a survey of multicultural protagonists in children's historical fiction, only 447 out of 1,605 works featured a protagonist of color (Agosto, Hughes-Hassell, & Gilmore-Clough, 2003). Furthermore, Taylor's main protagonist is more than African American; Paul Edward Logan is a person who identifies as black, white, and Native American, but more importantly has the ability, if not the desire, to pass as white. Taylor's protagonist represents one of the greatest fears of white America at the turn of the twentieth century, a blurring of the color line. It appears that Paul's identity might be read as a response to the persona discussed in W.E.B. Du Bois's *Souls of Black Folk*: "It is a peculiar sensation, this double-consciousness, this sense of always looking at one's self through the eyes of others, of measuring one's soul by the tape of a world that looks in amused contempt and pity" (Du Bois, 1903/1999, p. 11).

Although there is no mention of Du Bois's double consciousness theory in Taylor's novel, Paul develops a fully functional ability to see through the eyes of both the oppressor and the oppressed. The character has a wisdom that is well beyond his years and experience. For Paul, the concept of manhood is inextricable from his racial identity and the difficult decisions that he is forced to make while still in his childhood.

Like Du Bois, Paul learns at an early age (almost twelve years old) that his racial identity is something to be worn with caution and pride. Du Bois, after having his valentine card peremptorily refused with a glance, becomes aware of his racial difference. For the juvenile Du Bois, the "sky was bluest when I could beat my mates [white classmates] at examination-time, or beat them at a foot-race, or even beat their stringy heads" (Du Bois, 1903/1999, p. 10). Through his understanding and acceptance of his racial identity, Paul also learns that race does not have to define and in many cases confine his life. In other words, Paul Edward Logan is an extraordinary mulatto character because he embraces what Beverly Tatum calls "complexity of identity."

> The concept of identity is a complex one, shaped by individual characteristics, family dynamics, historical factors, and social and political contexts. Who am I? The answer depends in large part on who the world around me says I am. Who do my parents say I am? Who do my peers say I am? . . . As social scientist Charles Cooley pointed out long ago, other people are the mirror in which we see ourselves. (Tatum, 1997, p. 18)

Paul was fortunate enough to possess a mirror that reflected very clearly his racial complexity. Paul's father, Edward Logan, made no apologies for his white privilege and social status, just as his mother made no excuses for her status or her pride in her own Native American father, Kanati, which "means the lucky hunter" (Taylor, 2001, p. 42).

As mentioned earlier, tough love is one of the teaching devices that Paul's mother and father employ in his upbringing and the establishment of what will become the foundation of his racial identity. The dynamics found in Paul's family are unusual but not unheard of in American history. For example, in his historical text *From Slavery to Freedom* (1994), John Hope Franklin notes: "Frequently, old, repentant men atoned for their youthful waywardness by freeing their mulatto children and giving them land and money" (p. 140). Of course, Franklin was referring to antebellum America, and Taylor's narrative takes place after the period of legal slavery, but Edward Logan's treatment of his black mistress and children was not deemed socially or politically acceptable in his particular context.

In many respects, Edward Logan disrupts most, if not all, widely accepted performances of white men in postbellum America. Despite Edward Logan's context, he chooses to love, raise, and educate Cassie and Paul in close proximity to his white family, before and after the death of his white wife. Furthermore, the love that he demonstrates is an aware and responsible love. He does not negate the fact that his two black children are black in a racially hostile American South. When he has company to his house for dinner, Paul and Cassie are expected to eat in the kitchen and Paul's mother is expected to serve the meal. However, when Paul expresses his disdain for this practice to his father, Edward Logan says, "You might not like it, but when I sit down to supper with just my family, I expect all my children on this place to be sitting down at the table with me" (Taylor, 2001, p. 60). Logan makes it very clear to everyone in his family that despite his apparent colorblindness, he understands the world in which he lives. He understands and is aware of the privileges that he possesses as a white man and the disadvantages his son Paul will have to face as a black man.

Edward Logan makes great efforts to teach Paul the lessons of racism himself before Paul has to learn them from much more dangerous sources. Logan goes as far as whipping Paul on a Christmas Eve in front of some white guests because Paul struck two white males in defense of his horse and himself. Logan tells him, "I'm going to teach you a hard lesson and I'm going to teach it to you right now. You get those clothes off, or I'll cut right through them. . . . Who said it was about fair?" (Taylor, 2001, p. 83).

After the beating, Logan finds Paul in the woods and explains how the whipping was an act of protection more than a brutal punishment. "All your life I've protected you. Don't you know that? But I just can't protect you in the same way I do Robert, George, and Hammond. I know how white men treat colored men, how white folks treat colored folks, and I know maybe I've been wrong in not making you understand earlier that the way I treat you is not the way every white man is going to treat you" (Taylor, 2001, p. 85).

Despite the brutality and embarrassment that Paul suffers at the hand of his father, Paul's mother refuses to provide any words of sympathy. In fact, Paul's mother seems to be pleased with the lesson and its methodology. "I been telling you and telling you those brothers of yours are white and you ain't. I been telling you that the day was gonna come when things wouldn't be the same between you and them. . . . I been telling you but you ain't been listening. . . . Now the day's come. Merry Christmas" (Taylor, 2001, p. 90). Paul's mother has no illusions about the role that she plays in the life of Edward Logan. She also understands that despite her long-standing liaison with Edward Logan, she is a black mother responsible for the safety and future of her black children. Thus, from her perspective, it was very important that Paul learn he has two families, one black and one white.

Before the conclusion of his narrative, Paul must learn that, despite the love he has for "his family's land," because he is black he will have no legal right to the land owned by his white father. In her article "Whiteness as Property," Cheryl Harris (1998) reminds us: "The legal legacy of slavery and the seizure of land from Native American people is not merely a regime of property law that is (mis)informed by racist and ethnocentric themes. Rather, the law has established and protected an actual property interest in whiteness itself, which shares the critical characteristics of property and accords with the many and varied theoretical descriptions of property" (p. 103). Because of his racial heritage (African, European, and Native American), Paul Edward Logan will not be allowed to share in his father's land or white privilege. Paul's plight is ironic because Edward Logan's land was stolen from the people of Paul's grandfather, Kanati. In a conversation between white father and black son, the theft of land is discussed without shame or regret.

"This land," I said, "it belonged to his people first."
"That's a fact," my daddy agreed. "Maybe that's where you get part of your love for the land. (Taylor, 2001, p. 42)

For whatever reason, Edward Logan does not respond to the irony of Paul's situation. As a result, he must embark on a quest for his own piece of property and racial identity. Luckily for Paul, his father wants him "to have an education and a trade" (Taylor, 2001, p. 43). Apparently Edward Logan understands that as a black man, Paul probably will not be able to possess something that cannot be taken away from him by white men, except education. Furthermore, horse training is not enough of an education in the eyes of Edward Logan. He wants Paul to know "how to build something fine and of quality" (p. 44). He wants Paul to learn carpentry, the vocation of "The Lord Jesus Christ Himself" (p. 44). He wants his son to be mentally prepared for the obstacle that he will undoubtedly have to face in a racist

America. Education, a trade, and a love of reading assist Paul in the achievement of his goals.

FRIENDSHIP

Mitchell Thomas is the character who proves to be more of a brother to Paul than any of his white biological siblings. Mitchell is the black friend who runs away with Paul to achieve his dreams of owning an identity equal or greater to that of his father, Edward Logan. The bond between Mitchell and Paul begins with a covenant. Quite simply, if Mitchell promises to cease his random thrashing of Paul and instructs him in the ways of self-defense, in return, Paul will teach Mitchell to read, write, and figure.

The initial conflict between the two boys is rooted in the fact that Paul's ambiguous appearance is as disturbing to black people as it is to white people.

> "I wanna know exactly how come you don't like me. I mean, I got some of your reasons figured, but far as I can tell, I never done anything to you."
>
> He looked at me square and said matter-of-factly, "I got no use for white niggers." (Taylor, 2001, p. 16)

The response that Paul receives from Mitchell suggests that, despite his actions, Paul's appearance is potentially threatening to the "normative" black person. The fact that Paul looks white, and might be mistaken for white (i.e., receive the privileges of a white person), evokes feelings of jealousy and rage among blacks unable to cross those same racial boundaries. Mitchell perceives Paul as having a power that he does not. Thus, whether Paul is aware of his ability or not, he is defined as a "special" black person who must be aware of his potentially privileged status, "white nigger."

Consequently, when Paul proves to Mitchell that he perceives himself as just another struggling black adolescent, the image of an uppity "white nigger" is disassociated with Paul's character. When Paul takes the blame for Mitchell's mishap with one of Edward Logan's horses, the friendship begins. Mitchell becomes Paul's guide/guard to growing up as a black male in the American south.

> It was during the summer before Robert and I were supposed to go off to school that I came to the realization that I had two families. In part it was Mitchell who brought me to this realization, and the things he said to me; in part it was all the little things of my life and a matter of growing up. (Taylor, 2001, p. 46)

The friendship between Paul and Mitchell is crucial to Paul's development into adulthood; however, Paul's character is not solely dependent on Mitchell's guidance. Mitchell like Paul, stumbles through adolescence for most of the narrative and also benefits from the friendship by escaping from the cruelty of his own father.

When Mitchell attacks a white horse trader in hopes of procuring money owed to Paul for winning a horse race, he demonstrates his commitment to their friendship and his elevation above superficial racial prejudice.

> "Look, I got your money from that Ray Sutcliffe. Jus' took what was yours. Only thing was, ole Ray Sutcliffe, he wasn't ready t' give it up. I waited 'til he gone off alone and I jumped him. I had t' knock that fool down." (Taylor, 2001, p. 122)

Mitchell's willingness to assault a white man to get Paul's money is symbolic of his commitment to friendship and his own desire to escape the restrictions of adolescence. The two escape a potential East Texas lynch mob via a southeast-bound train under the skirts of four white women. Paul and Mitchell ironically escape to the Deep South with the help of a benevolent white woman who seems to contradict every doctrine of southern etiquette. The passage of the two friends foreshadows their complex experiences with race on their quest for land and love.

On his way to Vicksburg, Paul wakes up from a nap to find himself on the land of his dreams. Paul is told by an elderly ex-slave that the land was owned by a southern ex-plantation owner who was forced to sell portions of it after the war. "Man done bought it from my Old Master Morris Granger. Old Master done had t' sell a bunch of his land for taxes, or so that's what folks say. After the war he ain't had no money" (Taylor, 2001, p. 160). The man owning the section of land that Paul was admiring was a white northerner named J. T. Hollenbeck. Hollenbeck informs Paul that to purchase any of the surrounding land, he has to speak with the son of Morris Granger, Filmore Granger. Hollenbeck warns Paul, "I don't know whom Filmore Granger despises more, white Yankees or free Negroes" (Taylor, 2001, p. 162). Unfortunately for Paul, an overtly racist Filmore Granger will act as the primary obstacle to his goal of procuring his own land.

Refusing to pass as white on his arrival in Vicksburg, Paul uses his carpentry skills and shrewd business sense to obtain a less valuable piece of land in order to raise the money for the Granger land. With the help of a white furniture store owner named Luke Sawyer, his friend Mitchell, and the Perry family, Paul patiently moves toward his goals.

Paul persuades Mitchell to help him clear trees from a parcel of Filmore Granger's land in exchange for the ownership of that land. As Granger is a blatant racist, it comes as no surprise that the work is unbelievably grueling and that the deal goes awry. Before the land is cleared, however, Mitchell is murdered by a poor white scavenger, but Paul takes on his widow and unborn child as his own new family. When Paul falls short of the deed price, Paul's sister is able to give him access to funds from land purchased by his mother. *The Land* has an almost fairy-tale ending with Paul and Mitchell's widow, Caroline, living happily ever after. Paul and Caroline eventually become the grandparents of Cassie Logan, the protagonist in Taylor's novel *Roll of Thunder, Hear My Cry* (1976).

Taylor successfully complicates the history of Cassie Logan's family in *The Land* via her examination of Paul Edward Logan's beginnings. In a narrative designed for adolescent readers, Taylor's prose clearly overshoots her primary target to hit the hearts and minds of any and all readers. For this reason, *The Land* initiates a conversation with more mature and canonical texts that reveal it to be reminiscent of the classic slave narrative. The idea that Taylor may have borrowed and then complicated some themes from a much older genre is not as remarkable as the fact that reading *The Land* as a (re)visionary slave narrative works for a contemporary juvenile audience. Taylor reveals truths about antebellum America and Reconstruction that were not as accessible to young readers before her novel.

FAMILIAL BONDS AND THE HEROIC MULATTO

Frederick Douglass's *Narrative of the Life of Frederick Douglass, an American Slave: Written by Himself* (1845/1993) was a text that necessarily possessed very lucid form and function. Borrowing from the genres of biblical texts, epic poetry, and the sentimental novel, the document's primary goal is to inform sympathetic white northern readers about the evils of the institution of American slavery in order that they might assist in its abolition. To achieve this goal, Douglass very carefully constructs a narrative that reveals some of the horrors and suffering that he and his fellow slaves experienced in antebellum Maryland.

Ultimately, Douglass is successful in extracting a great deal of sympathy from the readers of his autobiography because he takes great care in not offending the sensibilities of his predominantly female and Victorian audience. In other words, Douglass does not tell the whole truth of the "Life of Frederick Douglass," because to do so would have undoubtedly offended the sensibility of a large section of his reading audience. Instead, Douglass writes himself as an idealistic hero who bides his time as a youthful slave and eventually earns his right to freedom by overcoming physical and intellectual obstacles. More importantly to his white audience, Douglass does this while maintaining the advantage of moral high ground over his enemies in every chapter of his life.

Douglass's escape to freedom is not dissimilar to the escape of young Paul Edward Logan to his independence, except for assistance in the way of familial bonds. Frederick Douglass, like the great Trojan War hero Ulysses, overcomes the obstacles of his life autonomously. The idea of independently achieving one's freedom from the institution of slavery was crucial in Douglass's writing of himself in the minds of his white audience. Being without familial bonds gave Douglass no reason, noble or otherwise, to stay within the confines of slavery. Furthermore, the process of severing those familial bonds in the narrative acted as excellent material for gaining sympathy from readers. When Douglass experiences his first relocation as a slave, he speaks of his feelings about being separated from his family and home.

> The ties that ordinarily bind children to their homes were all suspended in my case. I found no severe trial in my departure. My home was charmless; it was not home to me; on parting it, I could not feel that I was leaving any thing which I could have enjoyed by staying. My mother was dead; my grandmother lived far off, so that I seldom saw her. I had two sisters and one brother that lived in the same house with me; but early separation of us from our mother had well nigh blotted the fact of our relationship from our memories. (Douglass, 1993, p. 55)

Douglass's indifference about being separated from his family speaks to the inhumanity of the institution of slavery as well as the strength and bravery that it must have instilled in the adolescent Frederick Douglass. The story of a person severed from mother, father, and siblings and put out alone to face the cruelty of slavery is a narrative with all the ingredients for an epic tale of a boy who grows into a heroic man. Thus, both Taylor's and Douglass's narratives entail a quest for manhood or masculinity.

Where the classic masculine slave narrative attempts to define manhood in a traditionally narrow fashion, *The Land* allows Paul Edward Logan a more progressive and realistic understanding of what it is to be a man. Near the end of his narrative, Douglass has his infamous battle with Mr. Covey in order to mark "the turning-point in his career as a slave" (Douglass, 1993, p. 79). Douglass brawls with Covey for an unbelievable two hours, which is clearly symbolic of a struggle between not two men but two political ideologies. Douglass fights for the abolition of slavery and Covey fights for traditional southern values, which include white supremacy and the enslavement of African Americans. Douglass depicts Covey as a pitiful, self-deceiving representation of the slave-owning South. "Mr. Covey's *forte* consisted in his power to deceive. His life was devoted to planning and perpetrating the grossest deceptions. Every thing he possessed in the shape of learning or religion, he made conform to his disposition to deceive. He seemed to think himself equal to deceiving the Almighty" (Douglass, 1993, p. 73).

Covey is the symbol of conflict in Douglass's narrative. The character, more than any other in the narrative, provides Douglass with the justification to escape slavery, and to desire the abolition of the institution even after he gains his freedom. More importantly, the defeat of Covey at Douglass's hands begins to explain the famous quote: "You have seen how a man was made a slave; you shall see how a slave was made a man" (Douglass, 1993, p. 75). These words suggest the making of a man through physical and mental struggle. Douglass's physical battle with Covey marks one of two tasks that he is charged with on his quest to freedom and manhood.

The second task is nonviolent and much more detrimental to the institution of slavery than thrashing the pitiful Mr. Covey. Frederick Douglass starts a Sabbath School where he teaches the doctrines of Christianity and literacy. By spreading literacy to slaves, Douglass ruins the boundaries of ignorance established by the institution of slavery and potentially creates more free-thinking slaves. Thus, by physical battles and intellectual resistance, Douglass achieves both his manhood and freedom by the end of his narrative.

Paul Edward Logan's manhood is constructed in a slightly more complicated fashion than that of Frederick Douglass. Although it is true that Paul does introduce literacy to his friend Mitchell, the reasons are much less noble than those of Douglass. Paul also has to confront the physical battle of clearing forty acres of trees in one year, but as stated before, this is not a battle that Paul has to face alone. Paul's manhood is dependent on his ability to provide for himself and those he cares for, to place himself on the same or higher intellectual level than any white man in the narrative, including his father, and to love his friends and family responsibly.

Paul's character thoroughly disrupts the image of the lonely and confused tragic mulatto in that he is supported by family members and friends every step of the way toward his well-pondered goals. As a result, Paul's construction of manhood is dependent upon communal values and the desire to create a stable and secure home. Paul, unlike Frederick Douglass, is not written to run free and alone like an epic hero, partly because he is never legally a slave vying for his humanity, and partly because his character does not have to contend with Victorian sensibilities that are not ready to imagine the possibility of a complex black male identity. As family is at the core of most of Paul Logan's experiences and desires, his notion of manhood is inextricable from familial bonds.

Consequently, the formulation of Paul's masculinity is similar to the formulation of femininity in the traditional feminine slave narrative. Paul relies more on his ability to mentally outwit instead of physically overpower those who would hinder his progress. In both his escape from the guardianship of his white father and his final success in completing the labor for his land, Paul readily accepts the assistance of both family and friends. Although Paul does not rescue his mother and his sister, Cassie, by the end of the narrative, it is evident that they don't need rescuing. Neither exists in a state of slavery; nor do they depend on Paul to provide for them. Paul's mother is content with her very secure and voluntary relationship with Edward Logan, and Cassie is happily married to Howard Milhouse in Atlanta, Georgia. Both the mother and sister are independent and seemingly content with the paths of their lives.

It is Paul's surrogate family that is in need of his help by the end of the narrative. The wife and unborn child of Mitchell Thomas are analogous to the children/relatives who cannot be left behind in the feminine slave narrative tradition. It is important to note that Caroline is in no way written as a character that needs to be taken care of or provided for. Caroline is a strong and independent woman supported by her paternal Perry family. The necessity for rescue or the providing of security for Caroline rests solely on Paul's conscience.

> "I promise you, Mitchell," I said, and I felt as if Mitchell had squeezed the words right out of me with his final moments of strength, for once the words were spoken, the promise made, he fell back flat and his hand slipped away. (Taylor, 2001, p. 306)

After making a final bargain with his dying friend, Paul promises to protect and provide for Mitchell's widow. Paul's promise to marry Caroline is equivalent to him refusing to let his family be dismantled by systems of oppression analogous, if not synonymous, with the institution of slavery.

It is also important to note that although Paul does initially set out to hunt down Mitchell's murderer, Digger Wallace, he does not take his revenge in a traditionally masculine fashion. While out hunting for Wallace, Paul is intercepted by Caroline's father, Sam Perry, and is dissuaded.

> Sam Perry and Tom Bee talked to me through the rest of that night, and I began to focus on Caroline, on Caroline and her baby, and on my promise to Mitchell, instead of my own grief. They talked until there was nothing left to say. That next morning at daybreak we left the ridge and headed back to the forty. (Taylor, 2001, p. 314)

Sam Perry and Tom Bee helped Paul understand that to take his revenge on Digger Wallace would not only jeopardize his life, for killing a white man, but would also bring grief to the people who loved him. Fortunately, Paul rejects the traditionally masculine route of taking "an eye for an eye" and seeks the more difficult path, ultimately the more practical path of refocusing his energies on his family and friends. Paul does not kill Wallace because his death, much like his life, would yield no value. Digger Wallace, like Mr. Covey in Frederick Douglass's narrative, only serves as a stepping stone to Paul's path to enlightenment and a practical performance of black masculinity.

CONCLUSION

Like Ulysses, Paul Edward Logan finally finds his way home after a long journey filled with hard-fought battles and daunting tasks. Paul's home entails much more than the land that he has successfully procured by the end of the narrative. Paul's home is a place in the world that he has earned with a great deal of hard work and sacrifice. His home is a group of friends and family who have supported him under the direst of situations; the love and memory of his ancestors and friends populate the soil he will live on. Consequently, Paul Logan's home transcends a deed to a parcel of land or the land itself; the term that becomes the title of Mildred Taylor's novel ultimately evokes the notion of "homeland." A homeland is a location synonymous with notions of family, ancestors, friends, sacrifice, and love. In an epilogue, Paul reminds the reader how much he is aware of the connections between family and land.

> I won't deny that I miss the family of my youth. I loved my mama, and Cassie, of course. I loved my daddy, and I loved my brothers too. And I loved Mitchell. . . . There are times I think of my daddy's land and my childhood there. I think on it, but I don't dwell on it, for I know that I have been blessed to have a family now of my own, and I have been blessed to have the land. (Taylor, 2001, p. 369)

For Paul, the land that he is able to obtain symbolizes a rite of passage. With his land, he will be able to ascend to a level of masculinity equal to his father's and to gain the admiration and pride of his mother. Paul's very mature contemplations mark the end of his quest toward adulthood and entrance into manhood.

Paul's ability to embrace his ambiguity as a mulatto does not interfere with his ability to perform a practical black masculinity. This is not a common characteristic noted in children's literature breaching the subject of racial miscegenation. In fact, there are few images and little, if any, analysis of self-assured biracial children in children's literature during or immediately following the Civil War. Mildred Taylor successfully revises the slave narrative tradition by way of empowering one of the tradition's most infamous tropes. By refiguring the concept of mulatto and positioning such a character as both heroic and masculine, Taylor has reinvented what it means to be biracial or "ambiguously identified." There can be no better location to introduce such a novel notion as making the ambiguous acceptable than in a literature targeting young readers. By writing Paul Edward Logan as an identifiable protagonist, Taylor does more than disrupt American mythologies of racial divides; she disrupts the mythology of national and cultural divides. *The Land* does the work of transforming a traditionally African American trope into a universally identifiable icon.

REFERENCES

Agosto, D. E., Hughes-Hassell, S., & Gilmore-Clough, C. (2003). The all-white world of middle-school genre fiction: Surveying the field for multicultural protagonists. *Children's Literature in Education*, 34 (4), 257–275.

Douglass, F. (1993). *Narrative of the life of Frederick Douglass, an American slave: Written by himself*. New York: Bedford Books of St. Martin's Press. (Original work published 1845.)

Du Bois, W.E.B. (1999). *The Souls of Black Folk* (H. L. Gates Jr. & T. H. Oliver, Eds.). New York: W. W. Norton. (Original work published 1903.)

Franklin, J. H. (1994). *From slavery to freedom: A history of African Americans* (7th ed.). New York: McGraw-Hill.

Harris, C. (1998). Whiteness as property. In D. R. Roediger (Ed.), *Black on white: Black writers on what it means to be white* (pp. 103–118). New York: Schocken Books.

Roth, S. N. (2005). The mind of a child: Images of African Americans in early juvenile fiction. *Journal of the Early Republic*, 25, 79–109.

Tatum, B. D. (1997). *Why are all the black kids sitting together in the cafeteria?* New York: Basic Books.

Taylor, M. D. (1976). *Roll of thunder, hear my cry*. New York: Puffin Books Penguin Group.

———. (2001). *The land*. New York: SPEAK Penguin Group.

II

READER RESPONSE RESEARCH AND THEORY

6

Historical Fiction and Cultural Evocations in a Community-Based Literary Club

Susan Browne and Wanda M. Brooks

As early as 1922, Alice Dunbar Nelson identified African American litera-ture as a source of pride and purpose for African American children. Her words continue to resonate powerfully today: "Through all history, ancient, modern; each land, each nation, impresses most painstakingly upon the ris-ing generation the fact that it possesses a history and a literature, and that it must live up to the traditions of its history, and make that literature a part of its life" (Nelson, 1922, p. 59). Another voice that echoes Nelson's is that of Aunt Ester, a character in August Wilson's play *Gem of the Ocean* (2004). As Aunt Ester reveals the wisdom of her 287 years, it becomes clear that her longevity is not the result of her own desire but is attributed more to his-tory and necessity. Her power exists through story. As she conjures the memory of African slaves who did not complete the journey across the Mid-dle Passage, she transplants those who seek her healing to the "City of Bones," where the memory of those who dwell there transforms the spirit.

Like Wilson's Aunt Ester, Nelson reminds us that African American liter-ary traditions hold memory and offer an abundant reservoir that honors and maintains the past. Thereby, there is a strong connection between what Nelson wrote eighty-four years ago and Wilson's character Aunt Ester. Each of these women is pointing us to the historical context of African American literary traditions. Aunt Ester grounds our thinking in the purposefulness of oral traditions that were later to become written text, while Nelson reminds us that cultural consciousness is linked to literature that embodies the history of the culture. Each woman speaks to the need to hold to these traditions as we embrace the future.

An examination of African American children's literature must begin with the examination of African American literary traditions. The dominant themes present in adult African American literature such as fighting against oppression, the expression of pent-up emotions, self-reliance, and self-love have shaped definitions of African American children's and young adult literature. Since slavery, literature by blacks in America has largely included themes focusing on freedom and equality. The twentieth century brought social protest and voices calling for the rejection of racial distortions while sharing desires for full participation in America. The traditions found in slave narratives, works from the Harlem Renaissance, the black power movement, and the black arts movement have all contributed to the growing body of work broadly defined as culturally conscious African American children's literature.

Culturally conscious African American children's literature is written by African American authors and about African American characters. Its authors emphasize themes of freedom, ancestry, and identity. These writers recognize the political, racial, and social realities that shape the black experience in America; they illustrate through text that literature cannot stand apart from culture (Bishop, 1996). Harris (1997) calls these writers contemporary griots. The literature is set in African American homes or communities; it contains a variety of language patterns found among African Americans and also includes African American customs, rituals, and history. Through story, the literature continues oral traditions by using written language that entertains, educates, inspires, and socializes. Close readings of this literature can provide a vision of how its writers "portray the essence of a people who are a parallel culture community in America" (Hamilton, 1995) and how this essence exists in the body of work they have produced (Bishop, 2003). Culturally conscious literature for young readers challenges mainstream discourse. In this way, the literature is situated in a new literacies studies framework (Gee, 1996) that acknowledges culturally specific experiences. New literacies studies emerged out of beliefs and paradigms that recognize discourses as essentially a sort of identity kit or cultural DNA.

This chapter examines the culturally conscious themes found in *The Friendship* (1987) by Mildred Taylor and responses to the text by two groups of preadolescents participating in the Children of the Sun community-based literature discussion group. The children came from the immediate inner-city neighborhood and voluntarily attended weekly meetings at the Bushfire Theatre of Performing Arts in Philadelphia, Pennsylvania. Audio-taped literature discussions received full transcriptions. Conceptual categories were developed for verbal responses and dramatic interpretations, with the unit of analysis as conversational turns.

ABOUT THE TEXT

The Friendship, Taylor's 1987 historical fiction novella, is the fourth in a series of books focusing on the Logan family. Taylor's narratives come from family stories going back as far as slavery. Although born in the South, she did not grow up there. Family visits to Mississippi during her childhood and the memories shared by her father have been powerfully crafted to paint a picture of the segregated South and the impact of racial prejudice. In this Coretta Scott King Award–winning book, siblings Stacey, Cassie, Christopher John, and Little Man take readers through the pain and injustice of segregation in 1933 Mississippi. The novel begins with the Logan children walking home from school. They are stopped en route by Aunt Callie, a neighbor they refer to as aunt in deference to her age and long-standing presence in the community. Aunt Callie has a headache and asks the Logan children to get her some medicine from the Wallace store.

The first line of the novel is older brother Stacey Logan's warning: "Now don't y'all go touchin' nothin'"(p. 9). The children had been taught that storeowner John Wallace and his sons Thurston, Dewberry, and Kaleb did not "Treat our folks right and it was best to stay clear of them" (p. 10). A series of disconcerting events take place while the Logan children are in the store. In one instance, Little Man puts his hands on the glass counter as he looks around the store. Thurston throws Dewberry an ax and threatens to cut Little Man's hands off. The tension moves to another level when Tom Bee, an elderly man of the community, enters the store. He repeatedly calls the store's proprietor by his first name. The sons are angered by what they believe to be his presumption, and they urge their father to put him in his place. We learn that years before Tom Bee saved John Wallace's life, and it was promised that in return he could always refer to him by his first name. The story builds to the point of a disturbing gunshot blast that rips through Tom Bee's leg because he refuses to give John the title of "Mr." Although wounded, Tom Bee promises to call him John until the judgment day.

CULTURAL THEMES IN *THE FRIENDSHIP*

Themes found in *The Friendship* that are commonly explored in culturally conscious literature have to do with struggles for equality, the strength and resilience of African American people, and extraordinary events that create unlikely heroes (Harris, 1997), as well as interracial relationships. Additional themes linked specifically to *The Friendship* emerge through the characters Aunt Callie and Tom Bee. These themes pertain to community relationships that can be defined through expanded definitions of kinship and respect for elderly members of the community.

Several salient examples of both the interracial and community relationship themes begin with a warning. The warning to never go into the Wallace store is an attempt by the Logan parents to explicitly teach the children about boundaries based on race. Through teaching about racial prejudice and discriminatory behavior, they hope the children will be spared public indignities and other humiliating experiences. On this particular day, when Aunt Callie stops the children on their way home from school, they feel compelled to cross boundaries. "Aunt Callie Jackson, who wasn't really our aunt but whom everybody called that because she was so old, had hollered to us from her front porch and said she had the headache bad" (p. 11).

The children are reluctant to ignore their parents' admonishments about the Wallace store, yet they feel obliged to respond in deference to Aunt Callie's age and position in their local network. Kin terms in the black community are often extended to those who expand personal networks. A friend classified as a kin is given respect and responsibility. These fictive kin relationships are maintained by consensus between individuals and in some contexts can last a lifetime (Stack, 1974). In contrast to these relationships, Big Ma, the Logan children's grandmother, is often called aunty by white members of the community as an attempted measure of respect because she is in her sixties. However, Big Ma is not appreciative of the gesture. Her sentiments come as a result of the absence of authentic elements present in kinship relationships. Those sharing reciprocal obligations toward one another are actively linked participants in an individual's personal kindred (Stack, 1974).

We again see the children ignore what they have been taught about the Wallace store when they hang around waiting for Mr. Tom Bee despite feeling uncomfortable. This is clearly done in recognition of Tom Bee's age and as a measure of respect to him. In the store, even though the children are mindful of "staying in their place," they are unable to avoid torment and humiliation:

> Dewberry, a full-grown man, stared down at Little Man. Little Man, only six, looked up. "Now I'm gonna hafta clean that glass again," snapped Dewberry, "seeing you done put them dirty hands-a yours all over it!"
>
> "My hands ain't dirty," Little Man calmly informed him. He seemed happy that he could set Dewberry's mind to rest if that was all that was bothering him. Little Man pulled his hands from behind his back and inspected them. He turned his hands inward. He turned them outward. Then he held them up for Dewberry to see. "They clean!" he said. "They ain't dirty! They clean!"
>
> Dewberry came from around the corner. "Boy, you disputin' my word? Just look at ya! Skin's black as dirt. Could put seeds on ya and have 'em growin' in no time!"
>
> Thurston Wallace laughed and tossed his brother an ax from one of the shelves. "Best chop them hands off, Dew, they that filthy!" Little Man's eyes

widened at the sight of the ax. He slapped his hands behind himself again and backed away. (p. 14)

The insults to Little Man, the youngest Logan, about being dirty have a certain irony, because knowing Little Man means knowing he is a fastidious child. There is no doubt that he looked neat and clean that particular day. However, that did not prevent Dewberry Wallace from using the opportunity when Little Man placed his hands on the glass counter to verbally attack and threaten him.

Stacey tries to reassure Little Man and give him the affirmation he is looking for. He tells his baby brother that true, they can do plenty, but they cannot cut his hands off. "But-but Stacey, th-they s-said they was g-gonna c-cut off my hands. They done said they gonna do that c-cause they. . . they dirty!" (p. 20). Stacey continues to try to comfort Little Man by telling him that they were just joking. Little Man calms down, but after a few minutes it is clear that this is something weighing heavy on his mind. "He reached down and placed his hand flat to the dirt. He looked at his hand, looked at the dirt, then drew back again. Without a word, he folded his hands tightly together and held them very still in his lap" (p. 21).

Once again Stacey encourages his little brother to forget it. However, the humiliation powerful enough to cause self-doubt in a proud little boy is something none of them will forget. They have shared hurt derived out of the culture of oppression. Dewberry and his brothers have explicitly taught about the dangers of respecting and crossing boundaries of race when matters of community and interracial relationships are concerned. It is the kind of lesson that was inevitable in the segregated South that was characterized by racial division, yet the Logan children's parents had worked hard to protect them from it as well as prepare them for this reality. Humiliation as a powerful tool of the culture of oppression continues throughout the text. When Tom Bee attempts to charge four cans of sardines, Dewberry again serves as the collective voice of his white southern community when he tells Tom Bee that he already has too many charges and then proceeds to insult him: "You don't need no sardines. Ya stinkin' of fish as it is."

When Tom Bee addresses John Wallace by his first name in front of his sons and other store patrons, a furor rages in the Wallace boys.

Dewberry slammed his fist hard upon the counter. "Daddy! How come you let this old nigger disrespect ya this here way? Just lettin' him stand there and talk to ya like he was a white man! He need teachin', Daddy!" (p. 30)

John Wallace admonishes Tom Bee for calling him by his Christian name in front of others and tells him that it just is not right, "It ain't seemly, you here a nigger and me a white man" (p. 31).

The book's title, *The Friendship*, speaks directly to the themes of struggling for equality as well as the strength and resilience of African American people. As the text unfolds, we find out that Tom Bee's insistence on calling John Wallace by his first name has to do with what is right and just. When Tom Bee saved John Wallace's life in the swamp not once but twice, Wallace promised that he could always call him by his first name. Tom Bee is determined to hang on to the promise that Wallace made when he was a boy of fifteen. The issue of Tom Bee placing a title in front of John's name is clearly most significant when others can hear and question John's thinking. When a store patron, Mr. Sims, hears Tom Bee call John by his first name, he jumps up from the table.

> "John Wallace! You just gonna let this here old nigger talk t' ya this-a way? You jus' gon' let him do that?" Dewberry pulled away from the counter equally enraged.
> "Daddy! You don't shut this old nigger up, I'm gonna do it for you."
> Mr. Sims exploded and asked:
> "What kind-a white man are ya, John Wallace, ya don't shut his black mouth? What kind-a white man?" (p. 50)

Instituting and maintaining the culture of oppression requires a sense of superiority for John Wallace, his sons, and the patrons in the store. John Wallace feels a sense of indebtedness to those of his same race and no obligation to the man who saved his life and nurtured him back to health when he was a child. When John Wallace promised Tom Bee that he would never expect him to call him mister because he had been like a daddy to him, he was accurately describing their early relationship. Stack (1974) describes family as the smallest organized durable network of kin and non-kin who interact daily, providing domestic needs of children and ensuring their survival. Tom Bee acted as a parent to John Wallace during their time together; however, it is clear that this was not a durable relationship. In a brutal act of violence, John Wallace shoots Tom Bee in the leg for calling him by his first name. Tom Bee embodies struggle as a way of life, and he assumes the role of an unlikely hero when he promises to call John by his first name until the judgment day, even though his leg has been ripped apart.

RESPONDING TO THE THEME
OF STRUGGLES FOR EQUALITY

Cultural evocations by the study participants were those specific responses to the literature based on African American cultural knowledge, history, heritage, language, and values. When asked what it was like to live in segregated Mississippi in 1933, cultural evocations emerged that spoke to the textual theme of struggles for equality. There were layers of talk that included some critical analysis by group members. In two different discussion groups, children (Mercedes in Discussion Group One and Malik and Isaiah in Discussion Group Two) expressed an understanding of a segregated South that other group members then built on.

Discussion Group One

Derek: I could not believe that he shot him in the leg after he saved his life.

Brook: I know, right!

Derek: I wished he couldn't get away with that.

Mercedes: But that's the way it was in the 19 . . .

Susan: The 1930s.

The children had no difficulty identifying elements of this historical period that depicted a racialized history for African Americans. When Derek says that he wished John Wallace could not have gotten away with shooting Tom Bee, implicit is the understanding that this kind of behavior was sanctioned by larger structures in the South. Mercedes echoes Derek's understanding by saying that is how it was then.

Discussion Group Two

Susan: What was it like to live in the South during this period?

Isaiah: There was a lot of racism.

Susan: What does that mean to you, what Isaiah just said?

Tia: White people were treated good and black people weren't.

Malik: Black people weren't treated equally.

Isaiah: Even though slavery was over, they still treated black people bad and not equal and they would make mean remarks like, "I'll chop your hands off because they are dirty."

Jerome: They do that today too.

When Isaiah describes what it was like to live in the South during that period by saying "There was a lot of racism," cultural evocations by others in the group lead them to expand on the meaning of racism and an understanding of the time period. These cultural evocations by members of the group articulate the struggle for equality that goes back as far as slavery, within a culture of oppression fueled by racial prejudice. Tia, Malik, and Isaiah elaborate on societal disjunctions based on race. This cultural evocation fosters a descriptive analysis of complex human behavior. Isaiah says, "Even though slavery was over they still treated black people bad and not equal and they would make mean remarks like I'll chop your hands off because they are dirty." Jerome responds, "They do that today too." Jerome moves a step further by using the past as presented in the text to consider how people are treated based on their race today. He concludes that people continue to be treated unjustly and inhumanly as a result of racial identity.

Discussion Group Two

Tia: What stood out for me is when on page 24 it says: "But after a few minutes he did a strange thing. He reached down and placed his hand flat to the dirt."

Tia (continued): He didn't even like being dirty he liked to be clean.

Susan: What was that about?

Tia: Because he was mad because the man called him dirty.

Malik: He wanted to see if he put his hand in the dirt if it looked the same or not because of what Dewberry said about his skin was black as dirt.

Tia and Malik introduce issues of humiliation and self-doubt into the conversation by referring to when Little Man places his hands in the dirt to see if they are indeed black as dirt. Tia's talk is grounded in the meaning of the text. She points to the fact that we as readers know who Little Man is, yet where there is racial domination, the culture of oppression allows those seeking dominance the ability to define identity and position some as "others." Little Man, who is known to be fastidious and preoccupied with cleanliness, can be called dirty and painfully humiliated as a result of racism.

RESPONDING TO THE THEME OF STRENGTH AND RESILIENCE OF AFRICAN AMERICAN PEOPLE

Both Little Man and Tom Bee demonstrate strength and resilience throughout the story and serve as unlikely heroes. Here the groups respond to the presence of strong black characters in the text and the theme of strength and resilience as evidenced through Little Man's actions.

Discussion Group One

Erika: I like Little Man because he stood up for himself and his color.

Susan: What do you mean when you say he stood up for himself and his color?

Erika: He told that guy that his hands was not dirty . . .

Sunny (interrupting): He told Dewberry.

Brittany: I liked Little Man because he proved his hands was clean.

Susan: How did he do that?

Brittany: He showed them his hands. They could see that they was clean, but they still wanted to cut them off.

The discussion indicates that the group has engaged in "intensive reading" (Peterson and Eeds, 1990). They have extended themselves into the story world, and in this lived experience, they are able to read the words of the text and those messages that exist between the lines. When Brittany says that Little Man showed Dewberry and his brothers his hands and that they were able to see that they were clean, she demonstrates mindful and deliberate interpretation of the text. She is saying, "They could see that they were clean," yet to maintain an oppressive relationship they chose to make commentary on his skin color and suggest that black skin is equated with dirtiness.

RESPONDING TO THE THEMES OF INTERRACIAL AND COMMUNITY RELATIONSHIPS

At the point in the book when John shoots Tom Bee in the leg for continuing to call him by his first name, Brittany asks, "He shot him?" Similar questions in response to this section of the text have been asked in previous readings with other groups of children. Although the words have been read, there seems to be a need for verbal articulation. There is this feeling of disbelief that John would shoot an elderly man who saved his life and nursed him back to health. This type of response represents what Moller and Allen (2000) refer to as engaged resistance.

Discussion Group One

Lydia comments that she cannot understand why the book is called *The Friendship*. She shares a story about a television show that she has seen on the Disney channel called *The Color of Friendship*, which is about a friendship between characters of different races. In her intertextual connection (Sipe, 1996) between *The Friendship* and *The Color of Friendship*, she describes the clear issues around friendship in the television movie. She doesn't see the connection between the title and the events in the Mildred Taylor story.

Susan: Well why do you think Mildred Taylor titled this book *The Friendship*?

Janae: I think it's called *The Friendship* because . . . Mr. Tom Bee was kind of mad because John Wallace didn't keep his promises because Mr. Tom Bee was taking care of him, but he didn't keep his promise.

Jasmine: I think Mildred Taylor calls this book *The Friendship* because of the friendship John Wallace and Mr. Tom Bee had and because of the changes they had when they grew older. I think she wanted to talk about how you can have a friendship one day and then it could be a total disaster another day.

Brittany: He's going to shoot somebody just because they call him John.

Lydia: He should have respected Tom Bee. That is the one thing Tom Bee should have got after he got older. He could have just left him there without no shelter, no place to go, but he took care of him.

Mercedes: I think John felt embarrassed. He did not want his sons to know that he had a black friend that saved his life. It seemed like he was ashamed.

Nafeesa: He was embarrassed because his friends was prejudice. He probably didn't care if Mr. Tom called him John when nobody was around.

The power of talk in meaning-making becomes evident when Lydia begins to address her own question. Her intertextual connection enables a positioning outside of the dynamics of the narrative in order to take on new perspectives in relation to the story (Sipe, 1996). She articulates the relationship between the title of the book and the expectation that John Wallace should have been loyal to Tom Bee and respectful because of his age. The interracial relationship between John Wallace and Tom Bee further allows for the discussion of issues of fairness and justice. The group's active engagement with the text places them in the story world as subjects in a historical context rather than victims or objects (Leistyna, Woodrum, & Sherblom, 1996). As they name what is going on in the text, the power of the culture of oppression becomes explicit. Discussion serves as a mobilizing force able to shift power to the reader.

In response to *The Friendship*, Discussion Group Two develops several variations of a talk show with characters from the novel. On many occasions, group members have the opportunity and are encouraged to engage in some form of dramatic response because the location for the literature discussion groups is a theater. Dramatic interpretations contribute to literary understanding. In the exchange below, between Tom Bee (Malik) and John Wallace (Isaiah) facilitated by Cameron the host, there is a significant focus on the issue of respect. Taking on the role of the novel characters causes the group to rely heavily on interpretive processes that produce authentic intellectual activity and foster critical thinking.

Discussion Group Two

Cameron: Shooting someone over two letters, M and r . . .

Isaiah: (interrupting) It's called respect.

Cameron: Were you really influenced by the other white folks in the store or did you just snap?

Isaiah: I wasn't influenced by anybody.

Cameron: He just wanted chewing tobacco. He was your father. I'm thinking how silly this thing is between you two. Why did you change your mind?

Isaiah: Change my mind about what?

Cameron: Change your mind about him calling you Mr.: where did that come from?

Isaiah: What idea?

Cameron: The idea of white supremacy. Where did you pick that up?

Isaiah: I didn't pick it up, I knew it.

Cameron begins the discussion by asking Isaiah what he was thinking when he shot Tom Bee in the leg. Isaiah says, "About respect, that's what I was thinking about." Isaiah has reconfigured the language of the text. Here he has begun to demonstrate a deeper level of thinking; not only has he done some analysis of the events of the text, but he also uses some processes that require interpretation, synthesis, and evaluation. Cameron points out that Malik was the man who raised Isaiah, and thus Isaiah should respect him. Isaiah remains firm with the idea that Malik, a black man, should respect him, a white man, regardless of a previous father–son relationship. Cameron asks Isaiah if he was influenced by the presence of his sons and the other patrons in the store. Isaiah denies the influence of the onlookers as having an impact on his actions. When Cameron asks Isaiah where he picked up the idea of white supremacy, Isaiah responds, "I didn't pick it up, I knew it." Isaiah's response represents an organizing and construction of meaning about his character, John Wallace, and the construct of racism. Isaiah's remarks express the notion of racial superiority as not something that is picked up; it is something known. He spoke from a position of dominance in which racial superiority is embedded in a culture that seeks to oppress. Cameron and Isaiah have illustrated an awareness of concepts that moved beyond a mere superficial understanding. Their talk represents deep thematic understanding of interracial and community relationships in the segregated South that were shaped by a culture of oppression.

Using dramatic response, the members of the group demonstrate their knowledge and ability for talking about character. Powerful connections are made with Feldman's (1994) concept of text as a cultural organism. Dramatic interpretation further enlivens the cultural organism (text) and enables the forming and reforming of meaning using the humanly crafted tools of the reader. This process clearly enables possibilities for a deeper discovery.

CONCLUSION

The children's empathy for Little Man and Mr. Tom Bee demonstrated an awareness of history, lineage, and ancestral ties. Their cultural evocations were shaped by the cultural themes found in the text. The themes in Taylor's culturally conscious historical fiction novel enabled a situated examination of human subjects. Response acknowledged a larger history tied to segregation, racism, and individuals who fought against oppression and injustice in their own unique ways. In these discussions, both groups demonstrated the ability and willingness to discuss complex racial issues. The children approached race as a topic not to be avoided, but rather to focus on honestly. There were multiple opportunities for the children to think and talk about nonmainstream values as issues of racism and discrimination made way for the examination of the their own beliefs and provided opportunities to recognize different perspectives (Strehle, 1999).

The Friendship invited conversations about fairness and justice and encouraged the children to ask why some people are positioned as "others." The textual themes demonstrated that "literature can assist in more effectively raising the consciousness level and degree of proactive response of and from members of society too long immersed in the vestiges, results, and realities of racism" (Zoppa, 1994, p. 184). The textual themes ascribed to a criteria of critical literacy developed by Leland and colleagues (1999): (1) difference was not made invisible; (2) our understanding of history was enriched by giving voice to those traditionally silenced; (3) dominant systems of meaning were explored; and (4) the text did not feel obligated to provide a happily ever after ending (p. 70). Critical response produced cultural and historical texts of the children's lives, allowing them to come to know their own experience through textual themes.

Typically race is an incidental aspect rather than the main focus of many books where a leading or otherwise significant character is black. In exploring issues of race in children's literature, Pinset (1997) sees little value in books that avoid racial identity. In this study, racial visibility allowed the children to feel present while reading. Comer (1989) writes that textbooks and curricula in most schools inadequately address our racial history. He goes on to say that "many Americans—black and white—would prefer to end past race based inequities and injustices and try to create a more just society without fully considering the effects of the past" (p. 356). Likewise, according to Brooks (2006), "The more we know about the ways students from different ethnic backgrounds respond to texts, the better informed our curricula and instruction can become. Teachers have at their disposal cultural knowledge and experiences to rely and build upon during instruction" (pp. 389–390). As conversations continue in the field of literacy on the efficacy of culturally sensitive practice and what it means to embrace and implement culturally conscious literature for African American students, this study offers empirical data on the culturally conscious themes found in *The Friendship* and the cultural evocations these themes produced.

In the interpretive community of the nonschool literature discussion group, talk embodied the unique inscription of the reader. The discussions moved into a new literacies discourse that acknowledged background, experience, and sense of self as a member of a cultural, racial, and ethnic group while examining the nature and method of history. The textual themes in *The Friendship* provided a powerfully culturally mapped domain for the literature discussion groups. The groups engaged in processes of living through history, heritage, and tradition during what became an explicit study of race and culture.

The cultural themes of struggles for equality, the strength and resilience of African American people, interracial relationships, and community relationships that demonstrate kinship and respect for the elderly served as memory. Inherent in the groups' discussions is the range of ways the community can serve as August Wilson's Aunt Ester. The Children of the Sun Literary Club at Bushfire Theatre of Performing Arts is a place where culturally conscious literature for children and adolescents can strengthen the collective memory. When literature provides opportunities to make connections between learning and life, learning then moves from the cognitive to the social arena of self-understanding (Strehle, 1999, p. 213). Our discussions grounded these understandings and provided a context for acknowledging Nelson's (1922) concept of the rising generation realizing that they have a literature and a history.

REFERENCES

Bishop, R. (1996). Letter. *New Advocate*, 9, vii–viii.

———. (2003). *Reframing the debate about cultural authenticity.* In D. Fox & K. Short (Eds.), *Stories matter: The complexity of authenticity in children's literature* (pp. 25–40). Urbana, IL: National Council of Teachers of English.

Brooks, W. (2006). Reading representations of themselves: Urban youth use culture and African American textual features to develop literary understanding. *Reading Research Quarterly*, 41 (3), pp. 372–392.

Comer, J. (1989). Racism and the education of young children. *Teachers College Record*, 90, 351–361.

Feldman, D. (1994). *Beyond universals in cognitive development* (2nd ed.). Norwood, NJ: Ablex.

Gee, J. P. (1996). *Social linguistics and literacies: Ideology in discourses* (2nd ed.). London: Falmer.

Hamilton, V. (1995). Laura Ingalls Wilder Award acceptance speech. *Horn Book*, 51 (2), 113–121.

Harris, V. (1997). *Using multicultural literature in the K–8 classroom*. Norwood, MA: Christopher Gordon.

Leistyna, P., Woodrum, A., & Sherblom, S. (1996). *Breaking free: The transformative power of critical pedagogy*. Cambridge, MA: Harvard Educational Review.

Leland, C., Harste, J., Ociepka, A., Lewison, M., & Vasquez, V. (1999). Exploring critical literacy: You can hear a pen drop. *Language Arts, 77*, 70–77.

Möller, K. J., & Allen, J. (2000). Connecting, resisting, and searching for safer places: Students respond to Mildred Taylor's *The Friendship. Journal of Literary Research, 32* (2), 145–186.

Nelson, A. D. (1922). Negro literature for Negro pupils. *Southern Workman, 51*, 59–63.

Peterson, R., & Eeds, M. (1990). *Grand conversations: Literature groups in action*. New York: Scholastic.

Pinset, P. (1997), *Children's Literature and the politics of equality*. New York: Teachers College Press.

Sipe, L. (1996). *The construction of literary understanding by first and second graders in response to picture book read alouds*. Ann Arbor: UMI Dissertation Services.

Stack, C. (1974). *All our kin*. New York: Basic Books.

Strehle, E. (1999). Social issues: Connecting children to their world. *Children's Literature in Education, 30*, 213–220.

Taylor, M. (1987). *The Friendship*. New York: Puffin Books.

Wilson, A. (2004). *Gem of the ocean*. New York: Samuel French.

Zoppa, L. (1994). Color and class: An exploration of responses in four African-American coming of age novels. In Karen Patricia Smith (Ed.), *African-American voices in young adult literature: Tradition, Transition, Transformation*. Lanham, MD: Scarecrow Press.

7

My Boys and My Books: Engaging African American Young Men in Emancipatory Reading

Kimberly N. Parker

Much has been said about boys' lack of engagement with reading and the drop in their reading interest as they progress through high school (Wilhelm & Smith, 2002). What is important, however, is that boys and girls who are otherwise disengaged in school and considered to have lower levels of traditional literacy as measurable by standardized tests often excel in out-of-school literacies. Mahiri (2004), for example, describes environments where students, and in this case, young men, read magazines and participate in spoken-word performances while incorporating higher-level thinking skills to articulate their sentiments about their interactions with texts. Many boys who practice out-of-school literacies find acceptance and validation that they often do not receive during the course of their schooling. Out-of-school book clubs are also places where young men can demonstrate an active engagement and interest in reading.

The summer reading program described here, which I created and ran with a group of four African American and Caribbean American young men who were entering their senior year in high school, had two overall goals: to determine some of their successful reading habits based on my past knowledge of their reading behaviors, and to continue their reading engagement over the summer. The capstone project required the participants to create a brochure about starting book clubs intended for distribution to other young black men that included titles the participants thought their peers would enjoy reading in their own book clubs. In my work with these young men, I experienced their own struggles to negotiate their identities as black males.

When I first met them as their ninth-grade English teacher, they did not identify themselves as readers. They told me they had not read a book in their lives and said they did not think I was the person to make them start reading. Over my four-year association with them, however, I have watched their self-identities broaden to incorporate their reading beliefs.

BACKGROUND OF THE STUDY

This program was envisioned as a pilot study intended to determine some of the reading practices and habits used by young black men that kept them engaged with reading over the period of a summer. Of interest were the factors that contributed to their desire to continue reading a text, and how influential peers were in influencing individual and group reading behaviors. The program used multicultural young adult literature because of its cultural relevance to the participants as well as their past familiarity with the author of the selected texts, and the book club atmosphere seemed the optimal environment to explore these interests.

The participants were students I taught previously as freshmen and sophomores at a charter school in a large metropolitan city in the Northeast. Two, Antoine and Terrance (pseudonyms are used throughout), were of African American descent, and two, Christophe and Jean, were of Haitian American descent. All had been classmates for three years, though one student, Christophe, did not finish the eleventh grade at the school after expulsion for fighting. He attended another public high school in the city.

When I began teaching these students and their classmates, they had few positive experiences with reading. They described memories of books teachers attempted to make them read and that they never finished. Additionally, a large number had not visited the public library or entered a book store on their own volition. During the two years I taught them, looping with them for their freshman and sophomore years, I worked diligently to create a classroom environment that promoted literacy and reading. I explicitly taught them comprehension strategies and then encouraged them to apply and master those strategies using culturally relevant children's and multicultural literature. By the end of two years, their standardized reading test scores had increased, all passed the state language arts test, and perhaps most importantly, all students would engage in lengthy conversations about books that extended outside our classroom.

One particular example of these extended classroom discussions occurred during their sophomore year around a discussion of *The Last Shot* by Darcy Frey (2004), a nonfiction book about the difficult world of professional basketball. I relied on literature circles in my classroom and knew my students actively read the books they were assigned in those groups, and that they discussed them in authentic ways. For example, they connected the texts to their lives and even defended characters and their actions. The boys in the class were obsessed with basketball: at any spare moment, they would race to shoot around on the makeshift hoop behind our building, but I also wanted them to realize the diminished odds for them to pursue a professional basketball career (which at least half of the boys said was in their future). Over a two-month period, five boys met after school to discuss the book. I was not always present, and the meetings ran without any formal agenda or a designated leader. The boys reported attending the book club to talk about basketball with their friends, and to enjoy the food I provided.

After I left the school, I maintained my contact with a number of the students and was saddened to hear their stories of waning engagement with reading throughout their junior year. The boys had worked well together, read the texts they were assigned, and were usually prepared for the class discussions. They had cultivated successful habits in the past, and the desire to document those habits compelled me to conduct the pilot study that is the focus for the rest of this account.

The pilot study required four boys to attend daily book club discussions from Monday through Thursday. They would read two books and, at the end of the session, would create a brochure targeted to their peers. In this brochure, the young men would detail how to create and run book clubs as well as suggest some engaging titles for the book clubs. The book club suggestions were left entirely up to the participants.

SUMMARY OF THE TEXTS USED AND RATIONALE

Two works by Walter Dean Myers, *Somewhere in the Darkness* (2003) and *Bad Boy: A Memoir* (2002), were set as anchor texts because of the participants' experience reading his work and for the larger ability of Myers to reposition and recreate images of African American masculinity for young men. He is not "boring," primarily because he captures the lives of his readers—particularly, in this case, African American and Caribbean American young men—in an intimate and authentic manner.

Myers tackles black patriarchy and attempts to reconstruct black masculinity by depicting the complexity of black masculinity throughout his extensive body of work. After conducting numerous writing workshops with incarcerated young African American men, Myers deliberately began writing books that would resonate with this audience and a wider one of African American young men. His characters negotiate patriarchal systems as they attempt to carve out their own identities within the larger societies in which they live. "Myers has not only discovered a solution to the moral quandary regarding what aspects of realism should be presented to young readers, but he has excelled—particularly in the area of illustrating, interrogating, and problematizing how black masculinity comes to be shaped and (under)developed by socio-environmental nuances of class and experience" (Lane, 1998, p. 129).

African American young men who read Myers's texts find numerous examples and instances of young men who attempt to prevent the destruction of their souls and emerge from a multitude of circumstances (that are not always dire) with their hearts and minds intact. As Harris points out, Myers is adept at giving voice to the lives of African American young men in a way that depicts the difficulty of navigating life in an urban area. During his own work with young black men, "Myers wanted to inform the world of these youngsters" (Harris, 1992, p. 85) and their myriad capabilities. Similarly, Sims (1982) says: "Myers's work, then, mirrors the focus . . . on some of the positive aspects of Afro-American experience—the good times, the idea that the love and the support of family, friends and community can 'prop you up on every leaning side,' as a suitor promised in Zora Neale Hurston's *Jonah's Gourd Vine*. It also emphasizes the individual strengths and the inner resources that enable us to cope and to survive" (p. 96).

Additionally, African American young men are validated in their emotions, their anger, their indecision, as they interact with characters in Myers's novels with similar characteristics and dilemmas. Myers's texts do not stop there, however; they encourage readers to interrogate the texts and the worlds within which characters and readers reside (Brozo, Walter, & Placker, 2002). Further, Myers's definitions of the complexity of black masculinity move the reader beyond a passive experience. "The lessons learned by the inhabitants of Myers's urban world strategically arm the young reader for adversity: Through the whole and partial triumphs, the young black reader stands as a testifying witness to and an ex officio participant in the struggle" (Lane, 1998, p. 130). This repositioning allows African American young men to substantiate their personal struggles and validate their self-worth. Myers notes, "You want to see a book with your experiences. When you don't see your experiences, you don't feel positive about who you are. I believe it's up to people like me to take the African American experience and humanize it" (Williams, 2005, pp. 39–40).

Somewhere in the Darkness follows Jimmy, a thirteen-year-old African American boy, as he reacquaints himself with his father, Crab, who has escaped from prison. Crab convinces Jimmy, who has been living with his grandmother, to leave New York and accompany him first to Cleveland, then to Chicago, then to the South as he searches for the one man Crab thinks can acquit him of the crime he is charged with committing. Jimmy distrusts his father, blaming him for abandoning him. As the journey continues, Crab, stricken with a degenerative kidney disease, struggles to know his son but repeatedly fails Jimmy. Ultimately, the two switch positions, with Jimmy becoming the parent and Crab the child in a resolution that leaves the reader to question Jimmy's future.

The memoir *Bad Boy* chronicles the author's coming of age in Harlem and the influences on his writing. Similar to Jimmy, Myers struggles with his father for recognition. Myers did not have an easy childhood, leaving the rest of his family to live with his father and an adopted mother in New York. School was difficult for him, but once Myers began writing, he found acceptance.

Myers's writing offers the possibility of emancipatory literacy because his texts enable readers to see themselves in what they read while encouraging them to expand their thinking and ideas about their worlds and their futures. Young black men do not have to be limited by society's portrayal of them; through Myers's work, young men can define themselves.

SUMMER PROGRAM

The four summer program participants, Antoine, Terrance, Christophe, and Jean, socialized with each other regularly in their classes and after school over the course of the regular school year. The nature of the school of 120 students encouraged small class size (around fifteen to eighteen students per class) and extended time to produce quality projects. Students often worked together in groups from the time they began school as freshmen through their senior year. Several leaders emerged in the group, and one, Antoine, encouraged other boys to participate in the summer program. Even though Cristophe no longer attended the school, the other participants still considered him a friend.

When the program began that summer, and in the weeks preceding the creation of the book club brochure that would include directions for starting a book club as well as some suggested titles, we met daily to read Walter Dean Myers's *Somewhere in the Darkness* and *Bad Boy*. Both books feature African American men as protagonists and offer myriad topics for discussion. All four boys read Myers while either in middle school or early in their high school careers, and they regarded him as a favorite author, which influenced selecting these texts for the program. I also wanted them to read a wider selection of Myers other than the titles they already knew. Numerous times during a discussion, one young man or another would comment about similarities he observed between the books we were reading and others by Myers. For example, Jean noted about *Somewhere*, "This book, when I read other books by Walter Dean Myers like after, like before the chapter ends there's something that really grabs you. This book I don't, I don't feel the same thing. But you, you want to continue readin' it, but not, not because . . . of the last thing he's [Myers] done. You want to see what's going to happen. All his other books . . . before the chapter ends it's something, something crazy happens." Jean exemplified the group opinion that while this novel was not immediately as familiar as other Myers novels, they were willing to read.

Reading Myers offered them the opportunity to reconnect to a familiar author despite a text that was not immediately familiar. Their experiences, coupled with the dynamics of reading with their friends, provided enough impetus for the young men to continue reading the novel. One young man, Antoine, commented that the primary reason he enjoyed participating in book clubs was the opportunity to "chill with my boys—but we eventually get around to talkin' about the book."

I ran the initial meetings, relying on adaptations made from Harvey Daniels's (2001) book about literature circles, but the participants were extremely familiar with the procedures of literature circles based on their prior experience and eventually ran the discussions themselves. My role shifted more to a participant as the meetings progressed and as I interacted with the text much more as a reader than a researcher. Initially, the students were confused about my role, as I was no longer their teacher and our meetings were much more loosely structured. At times, however, I had to assume more of a teacherly role, as the young men drifted far off topic without any attempt to return to the text we were reading. It was difficult to encourage authentic dialogue during times when the students had not completed the agreed-upon reading or wanted to talk about something of interest in their lives. The issue of completing the readings became an increasingly prevalent problem with two of the boys because they were working jobs that left them little time to read. Christophe read on the bus on his way to the program in the mornings, but he admitted that he was exhausted. When this happened, one of the other boys would attempt to catch him up on the reading and, as a result, would adjust the daily discussions to parts that Christophe had read.

The participants felt comfortable disagreeing with each other as well as interjecting personal anecdotes and connections to the text. There were heated exchanges about character motivations and author intentions, but generally they were supportive of each other and listened patiently while each one spoke, encouraged each other, and attempted to build understanding among each other when a portion of the text was difficult to comprehend. Sometimes, they waited until a group member finished his thought only to provide alternate viewpoints, but the atmosphere was never hostile. It was young men passionately making their claim to their opinions about what they read.

Much of the early discussions focused on judging Jimmy's masculinity. The young men compared Jimmy's daydreaming to another of their classmates. They were particularly concerned that Jimmy daydreamed about knights and unicorns.

> *Christophe*: Fourteen? Still thinking about that [unicorns]? I think that he just don't have a father figure in his life.
>
> *Kim*: Who, Jimmy?
>
> *Christophe*: Yeah.
>
> *Kim*: So what, does that mean?
>
> *Christophe*: So he just daydreams about things.
>
> *Jean*: I think that . . . some people . . . I would, I would say they smart, but they, they think differently from you.
>
> *Christophe*: Cause Jimmy talks about how like, if he had a father or like how he wanted to go to a ballgame, and spend time with him and like he never had that but now that his father came back, I think that it might come true for him.
>
> *Kim*: Jimmy thinks a lot, right?
>
> *Christophe*: Yeah, he thinks a lot. Like, like, don't it say he thinks enough for three people?
>
> *Jean*: For two or three people, yeah. That's what, I was thinking, 'cause, when I think of Jimmy, I, I see it like, the person I think of is probably like Beethoven or Albert Einstein, everyone smart, they're just . . . crazy. Every smart person is . . . not, not necessarily crazy, but they think different. It's just, there's things they think about that other people don't think about like, who thinks about unicorns? Like he thinks, I don't know, just about different, a lot of different things. I think that's kind of like me, too, not the unicorns, but I think about mad stuff.
>
> *Christophe*: I think even the teacher talks about you're so smart, why you failing your classes? That's what I'm thinking about. Why can't he be good? Why?

In this exchange, Christophe and Antoine begin debating Jimmy's reasons for his constant daydreaming, which soon veers into a larger discussion about compensation for the absence of his father. There is also hope that Jimmy will have a relationship with his father once Crab returns. They both acknowledge Jimmy's intelligence, and while Jean rationalizes that Jimmy thinks enough for three people, Christophe expresses frustration that Jimmy does not go to class and channel that intelligence, echoed by his lament, "Why can't he be good? Why?" Christophe is angered because he thinks Jimmy is wasting his educational opportunities, while Jean thinks that just because Jimmy thinks "differently" does not necessarily make him odd. Instead, Jean seems to admire Jimmy, and even draws comparisons between Jimmy, Beethoven, Einstein, and himself for the capacity to think about a variety of ideas. Jimmy's complexity of character enables these two young men to debate his intelligence and motivations for engaging with schooling and negotiating his relationship with his father.

PARTICIPANTS' READING SUGGESTIONS

Throughout the four-week study, I was primarily a participant-observer in the interactions with the young men. I audiotaped every session, which lasted, on average, one and a half hours, and I kept extensive field notes. I also interviewed each participant individually when the program began and two times throughout the program, asking them to describe their reading history (e.g., when they remember reading, books they enjoyed, etc.) as well as identify influential teachers who encouraged them to either read or helped them become better readers. The interviews were transcribed verbatim and then coded. The patterns that emerged indicated that the ability to choose what they read was important for the participants to read a book. Choice also determined if a book was considered "good" by the participants. If a book was assigned in class, it had much less probability of being considered worthy of reading outside of school than one the participants had some part in selecting.

Peer influence also emerged as a theme: the ability to select a text was trumped by the larger appeal of participating in an activity with their peers. They did not necessarily report to the daily meetings because they were interested in the fate of Crab or Jimmy; instead, they wanted to socialize, and eventually they "got around to" discussing the text. Another theme that emerged was the participants' continuous referral to other texts they had read. These texts were primarily ones they had read when they were freshmen or sophomores. These references may be attributable to the fact that during those two years, the participants were given the greatest opportunity to read widely and they were encouraged to constantly read, both in and out of class.

When it came time to finally begin drafting the reading brochure, the participants were required to individually generate at least five titles they would recommend to their peers, as well as a statement of why they selected the texts, and some directions about how to run a book club. After all lists were compiled, the participants discussed their individual lists in a large group. The subsequent titles the young men generated were primarily ones from memory, and ones read during their freshmen and sophomore years of high school; a few suggestions even came from their time in middle school. They did not consult outside sources for their suggestions but relied on their own positive associations with the texts. In some cases, the young

men provided more than the minimum number of titles and included selections read in class during their freshman and sophomore years as well as
in literature circles and independently. In addition, each participant was
asked to designate one book as his top pick, the one he would recommend
above all others to a young man of a similar age.

Overall, the suggestions were eclectic and diverse and indicated the
ability of books to have a lasting effect on readers. What is also apparent
is the unpredictability of a text to appeal to a reader. As Terrance explained about *The Odyssey*, "It's weird, but it's fun. You get to learn about
the Greeks, and if you can get through *The Odyssey*, you can get through
any book. People should read it right now, in the ninth grade, because the
way I see it, when you start high school, you're not really ready. Reading
[*The Odyssey*] pushes you up, like, three, four, five notches for your reading and understanding."

Jean's Suggested List

"First, they're not too hard. They're easy to get through. When I read, I
tend to quit if it's difficult. There's always something to grab your attention.
In all these books, you'll be surprised by the ending—they all have a little
twist." Jean, Summer 2005

Sharon Draper, *Tears of a Tiger; Forged by Fire; Darkness before Dawn*
Walter Dean Myers, *Scorpions*
S. E. Hinton, *The Outsiders*
Russell Banks, *Rule of the Bone*
William Golding, *Lord of the Flies*

Top Pick: *Tears of a Tiger*

Terrance's Suggested List

"All these are books that stick with you. I don't remember any of the
books I've read except for these." Terrance, Summer 2005

Walter Dean Myers, *Hoops; Somewhere in the Darkness*
Jack London, *The Call of the Wild*
Harper Lee, *To Kill a Mockingbird*
Alex Haley, *The Autobiography of Malcolm X*
Robert Lipsyte, *The Contender*

Top Pick: *The Call of the Wild*

Antoine's Suggested List

"These books will amaze you. The opposite of what you think will happen, happens." Antoine, Summer 2005

Darcy Frey, *The Last Shot: City Streets, Basketball Dreams*
Sharon Draper, *Tears of a Tiger*
S. E. Hinton, *That Was Then, This Is Now*
Homer, *The Odyssey*
Walter Dean Myers, *Scorpions*

Top Pick: *The Last Shot: City Streets, Basketball Dreams*

Christophe's Suggested List

"There's a lesson to be learned in all these books. They might seem boring at first, but just keep reading—they'll get interesting." Christophe, Summer 2005

Lois Duncan, *Killing Mr. Griffin; I Know What You Did Last Summer*
Sharon Draper, *Tears of a Tiger*
Chinua Achebe, *Things Fall Apart*
R. L. Stine, *The Babysitter I; The Babysitter II*
Samson Davis et al., *The Pact: Three Young Men Make a Promise and Fulfill a Dream*
Earnest Gaines, *A Lesson before Dying*

Top Pick: *Things Fall Apart*

READING DEVELOPMENT

The participants' choices reflect their reading development: they selected books that they actually read (either in school or independently), that were familiar to them, and that appealed to a variety of interests. For example, Christophe went through an extended period during his sophomore year in which he selected only horror fiction to read; he continues to read this genre when he has an option. It was not surprising that *Tears of a Tiger* (1996) or the other novels comprising Sharon Draper's Hazelwood trilogy—*Darkness before Dawn* (2002) and *Forged by Fire* (1998)—appeared on multiple lists. Antoine was the first to read the books when he was a freshman, and he handed off the books to his peers, sparking a widespread interest in the books and creating a nearly insatiable demand. By the time Antoine and his peers entered their junior year, all the boys in the class had read at least *Tears of a Tiger*, either independently or as a book club selection in the fall of their sophomore year.

Draper's trilogy chronicles the lives of African American teenagers, a number of whom are basketball players, as they negotiate high school. *Tears of a Tiger*, an American Library Association Quick Pick for Reluctant Readers, unfolds quickly around the death of a star basketball player after a drunken driving accident. Draper uses a multigenre format—journal entries, newspaper accounts, dialogue—to explore various characters' reactions to the accident. The chapters are short and the slim book does not take as much time to read as the later books in the trilogy. *Tears of a Tiger* is an inviting entrée into the world of young adult fiction, but it also encourages students to think critically about issues of racial oppression and its effects on adolescent identity development (Franzak, 2003). Similarly, Sipe and Daley (2005) found that "culturally relevant stories often provided children with the opportunity to tell stories of their own" (p. 233), a finding observed when Terrance and the other young men read *Tears of a Tiger* and other books and subsequently discussed them with me or their peers.

When I gave Antoine the book as a freshman, he was an aliterate reader: he could read, but he elected not to. This decision was affected also by dyslexia that made reading tedious. Antoine read the first few pages of the novel in the classroom during an assigned sustained silent reading period. At its conclusion, he asked if he could take the book home. The next day, he burst into class; the book was finished, and he demanded we discuss the books we were reading because he wanted to talk about *Tears of a Tiger*. Within several days, three more boys were clamoring for a turn to read *Tears* and Antoine moved on to the other books in the series. From that point, Antoine changed his attitude toward reading. He began completing assigned readings and checking out books from the classroom library. His classmates also trusted his recommendations about what they should read next. With the right book, Antoine emerged not only as a social leader, but a literary leader, and his confidence improved proportionally. His transformation into a literary leader was so important to him that, two years later, he wrote his college application essay about being given *Tears of a Tiger* and my relentlessness to have him read as finally motivating him enough to try, and eventually become a competent reader.

Walter Dean Myers's appearance on more than one list is also not a surprise. All the young men had read at least one Myers book in middle school, either *Scorpions* (1990), *Monster* (1999), or *Slam!* (1998), and spoke positively of those experiences. For one young man, Jean, reading *Somewhere in the Darkness* allowed him to test out his own hypotheses of Myers's moves as a writer. For example, Jean argued that Myers makes Jimmy daydream about unicorns and other flights of fantasy because "I think that Walter Dean Myers is tryin' to show that he's [Jimmy] smart, like he thinks differently so, you know how most teenage boys think about cars . . . but he says that he's thinking differently." For others, reading *Somewhere* had an air of familiarity, given that they had read other Myers books. This confidence affected their responses to the text:

> *Antoine*: It's like, I don't know. I can't say a vault because . . . yeah, I think he is like a vault.
>
> *Jean*: Who?
>
> *Antoine*: A secret vault.
>
> *Jean*: You say Crab?
>
> *Antoine*: Crab.
>
> *Kim*: He's like what?
>
> *Antoine*: A secret vault. . . . Like where you keep personal things and stuff like that. . . . And then like when you break it open, you know, like you got this, this bench that it's something that you want, but when you open it, it's something totally different that you, you didn't expect it to be.
>
> *Jean*: He usually does that, too, Walter Dean Myers. I mean he, he'll make you build up things, he'll make you think one way about a character and then you'll find out the person is completely different.
>
> *Kim*: Cause that happened in what other books?
>
> *Jean*: *Slam!*
>
> *Kim*: Oh. What did he do in *Slam!*?
>
> *Jean*: Same thing. Like that kid, he was supposed to be a good kid.

I tried to have Jean continue talking about *Slam!* but he wanted to move on to another topic of conversation with Antoine. I was left to wonder if Jean would have made an accurate comparison of the characterization of the moves Myers made across the two books. (When I reread the transcript, I wished I had probed more.)

CHOICE VERSUS ASSIGNED READING

Numerous books on the participants' lists were ones they selected either independently or as book club selections. Jean read *The Lord of the Flies* (Golding, 1959) as a sophomore and again as a junior. Terrance read *The Contender* (Lipsyte, 1987) in a freshman reading class, *To Kill a Mockingbird* (Lee, 1988) as a freshman and sophomore, and *The Autobiography of Malcolm X* (Haley, 1987) as a book club selection as a sophomore. Antoine read *The Odyssey* (Homer, 1990) as a freshman and *That Was Then, This Is Now* (Hinton, 1998) in a sophomore book club. Christophe read *A Lesson before Dying* (Gaines, 1997) and *Things Fall Apart* (Achebe, 1994) as a sophomore and *The Pact* (Davis, Jenkins, & Hunt, 2003) as a summer reading assignment. For the most part, there were few assigned reading texts they would recommend, but they did recommend ones that they often selected during the related-themes literature circles that followed the in-class assigned reading. With the exception of Jean's *Lord of the Flies*, which he started as a sophomore but did not finish until later as a junior, none of the selections was from the junior year they completed prior to starting the summer pilot study.

The selections the young men made seem based much more on individual interests rather than cultural interests. When they were allowed to select texts for their literature circles, and they were books the young men connected to (either through personal connections or relating it to another book they read), those titles seemed much more likely to appear on their suggested reading lists. In addition, with the exception of *Mockingbird*, all the protagonists of their suggestions are males. These main characters share the primary qualities of courage, of triumphing against difficult odds, and of perseverance. Such characteristics cross racial and ethnic boundaries, as the protagonists are African, African American, and European American and from different social classes. What seems to matter most in the selections of these titles, as the young men say in their rationales, is that they hold the reader's interest for a prolonged period and that the plot is unpredictable.

GENRE SELECTION

Most of the selections are fiction, with the exception of *The Last Shot, The Autobiography of Malcolm X,* and *The Pact.* Antoine suggested the epic poem *The Odyssey* and explained that he thought it appropriate for book clubs because of its difficulty: "If someone reading it can get through this book, then they can get through anything." Antoine continued his explanation by recalling the in-class reading of the poem as a freshman, in which I used read-alouds, drama, and writing activities to increase their connection to and comprehension of the text.

CONCLUSION

This summer reading program illustrated the ability of young black men to engage with a multicultural text in a way that allowed mapping their development as readers. After two years in high school, they identified themselves as readers, only to regress less than a year later because they could not select the books they read nor did they consider reading an important activity in their lives.

Several factors affected their reading regression. Their junior year teacher, for example, did not spend as much classroom time talking about books and allowing students to spend prolonged periods of class time reading. He expected the students to read independently, outside of school. The students, however, had many more responsibilities: they worked as much as they could in after-school and weekend jobs, and without someone to continually encourage them to read and provide books for them to read, reading became less of a priority for them. When I occasionally mailed them books I thought they would enjoy, they reported reading them, but their trips to local bookstores were things of the past. I underestimated my role as their teacher because I thought that, after mastering the skills and practices needed to qualify as "competent, engaged readers," they would continue reading independently. Unfortunately, less than a year later, they resembled the same reluctant readers they were as freshmen. One conclusion is that the choice of texts does not matter as much as someone who encourages them to read, provides them with texts that have strong male protagonists and engaging plots, and gives them time to read those texts and discuss them with a group of their peers.

By the end of the program, the young men had fallen back into their earlier familiar reading patterns: they reported to the meeting room early and read until we started discussing the book, marked their books with post-it notes, and enjoyed the easy camaraderie that made the discussions easy to facilitate. As seniors, however, they still are not reading, regardless if the text is assigned. Their senior year has brought other challenges: SAT tests, portfolios, and college applications. In their words, there is simply "no time" for reading. They are apologetic when they speak to me, but they no longer promise that they will read books I send to them. "You know how it is, Kim," they say.

Future implications call for the need to learn more concrete strategies that provide time for young men to read books that resonate with their lives that they can also discuss with their peers. Such strategies need to reconsider what happens in the classroom and the role of the teacher in encouraging young black men's reading participation and development of successful reading habits and practices that can be continued from one year to the next, from one teacher to the next. If the learning they want to do and interactions they wish to have occur outside of school, classrooms increasingly become places of alienation.

The young men in this study created a brochure for their peers in hopes of involving them in informal book clubs. The brochures, still in the production phase, will eventually be distributed in the city's public libraries and high schools. This effort, and my past interactions with them, indicate these young men are not the uninvolved, tuned-out students often portrayed by media and educational researchers alike. Instead, these young men, along with their books, provide a salient hope: when given the choice and the chance—as well as a person who values reading and helping them become competent readers and who maintains the importance of reading—they will take the time to read in ways that are empowering and emancipatory.

REFERENCES

Achebe, C. (1994). *Things fall apart*. New York: Anchor.

Brozo, W., Walter, P., & Placker, T. (2002). "I know the difference between a tv man and a real man": A critical exploration of violence and masculinity through literature in junior high school in the 'hood. *Journal of Adolescent Literacy*, 45 (6), 530–538.

Daniels, H. (2001). *Literature circles: Voice and choice in book clubs and reading groups*. Portland, ME: Stenhouse.

Davis, S., Jenkins, G., & Hunt, R. (2003). *The pact: Three young men make a promise and fulfill a dream*. New York: Riverhead.

Draper, S. (1996) *Tears of a tiger*. New York: Simon Pulse.

———. (1998). *Forged by fire*. New York: Simon Pulse.

———. (2002). *Darkness before dawn*. New York: Simon Pulse.

Franzak, J. (2003). Hopelessness and healing: Racial identity in young adult literature. *New Advocate*, 16 (1), 43–56.

Frey, D. (2004). *The last shot: City streets, basketball dreams*. New York: Mariner.

Gaines, E. (1997). *A lesson before dying*. New York: Vintage.

Golding, W. (1959). *Lord of the flies*. New York: Perigree.

Haley, A. (1987). *The autobiography of Malcolm X*. New York: Ballantine.

Harris, V. J. (1992). Contemporary griots: African-American writers of children's literature. In V. J. Harris (Ed.), *Teaching multicultural literature in grades K–8* (pp. 55–108). Norwood, MA: Christopher Gordon.

Hinton, S. E. (1998). *That was then, this is now*. New York: Puffin.

Homer. (1990). *The odyssey*. New York: Random House.

Lane, R. D. (1998). "Keepin' it real": Walter Dean Myers and the promise of African-American children's literature. *African American Review*, 32 (1), 125–138.

Lee, H. (1988). *To kill a mockingbird*. New York: Warner.

Lipsyte, R. (1987). *The contender*. New York: HarperTrophy.

Mahiri, J. (2004). *What they don't learn in school: Literacy in the lives of urban youth*. New York: Peter Lang.

Myers, W. D. (1990). *Scorpions*. New York: HarperTrophy.

———. (1998). *Slam!* New York: Scholastic.

———. (1999). *Monster*. New York: Amistad.

———. (2002). *Bad boy: A memoir*. New York: Amistad.

———. (2003). *Somewhere in the darkness*. New York: Scholastic.

Sims, R. (1982). *Shadow and substance: Afro-American experience in contemporary children's fiction*. Urbana, IL: National Council of Teachers of English.

Sipe, L., & Daley, P. (2005). Story-reading, story-making, story-telling: Urban African American kindergarteners respond to culturally relevant picture books. In D. Henderson & J. May (Eds.), *Exploring culturally diverse literature for children and adolescents: Learning to listen in new ways* (pp. 229–242). Boston: Allyn & Bacon.

Wilhelm, J., & Smith, M. (2002). *"Reading don't fix no chevys": Literacy in the lives of young men*. Portsmouth, NH: Heinemann.

Williams, G. L. (2005, November/December). At their level: Seasoned children's author is at it again. *Black Issues Book Review*, 39–40.

8

Reader Responses to African American Children's Literature: A Sociolinguistic Perspective

Nina L. Nilsson

One of the challenges teachers face is finding effective ways to promote the literacy development of children whose language variety differs from the mainstream standard dialect taught in most schools. Guided by Rosenblatt's (1976, 1978) transactional theory of reader response, which takes the perspective that meaning evolves out of a transaction between the reader and the text based on the reader's life and literary experiences, researchers are increasingly conducting studies to address this challenge. Some of their research examines the processes in which readers engage while constructing meaning of culturally relevant literature (Brooks, 2001, 2005; Copenhaver, 1999a, 1999b; Gordon, 2000; Hefflin, 1997; Howrey, 2005; Lee, 1995, 2001; Miller, 2003; A. E. Rickford, 1996; A. M. Rickford, 1999; J. R. Rickford, 1999; Smith, 1995). In particular, investigators seek to learn how culturally influenced features in African American literature help shape reader responses, as well as how students' own cultural knowledge, such as prior linguistic knowledge, influences their reading and writing. By providing increased understandings and insights, researchers hope their findings will inform educational practice so that children's linguistic "funds of knowledge" (Lee, 2001; Moll, 1995) may be viewed as a bridge to learning rather than a liability to be overcome. This chapter presents a synthesis of the research on reader responses to African American children's literature so that this hope may become reality.

THE ACHIEVEMENT GAP

Many children struggle in their journey to become literate. Of particular concern, according to the National Assessment of Educational Progress (NAEP), 87 and 88 percent of fourth- and eighth-grade, African American public school students in the United States are reading below the proficiency level (Perie, Grigg, & Donahue, 2005). Furthermore, the gap in reading achievement of blacks and whites has changed little over the past decade. Although, as Harris (1997) asserts, "we are in the midst of a renaissance and an aesthetic revolution in children's literature depicting Blacks" (p. 21), it appears we are in the Dark Ages in terms of instructional practices that will help African American children who have been struggling as readers to succeed. According to the NAEP, African American students continue to score significantly more poorly on measures of reading achievement than their white peers.

AFRICAN AMERICAN VERNACULAR ENGLISH (AAVE)

African American Vernacular English, also known as Black English, African American English, and Ebonics, among other terms, is the language variety spoken by most African Americans who reside in inner cities (Labov & Baker, 2001), and it is more likely to be spoken by members of the African American working class than the African American middle class. Of note, AAVE is the most common native-English vernacular spoken in the United States (Wolfram, Adger, & Christian, 1999). Although some assert that AAVE is grammatically consistent across diverse, urban locations (Labov & Baker, n.d.), others suggest such claims may be overly simplistic (Taylor, 1989). The argument focuses, in part, on the fact that not all African Americans speak AAVE, and even within the same AAVE speech community, dialect features are not exhibited alike by all speakers. For the purpose of this discussion, *dialect* refers to a language variety that is characterized by distinctive grammatical patterns, vocabulary, and pronunciations, as well as ways in which language is used (Wolfram et al., 1999).

AAVE and Reading Achievement

A number of factors have been proposed to explain the gap in reading achievement, including factors related to society (e.g., poverty and racism), differing family socialization practices and language/literacy norms, and school practices and curricular materials that favor mainstream students in terms of content relevance and language style (Berrick, 1995; Brooks, 2001; Heath, 1982, 1983). With respect to linguistic-related variables, some attribute reading interference to the structural differences of AAVE compared with the mainstream Standard English (SE) dialect reflected often in school texts and classroom discourse (Labov, 1972; Steffensen, Reynolds, McClure, & Guthrie, 1982; Wolfram et al., 1999). In addition to structural differences across language varieties, investigators propose that contrasts in language use in the home versus school contexts may be a major source of reading interference (Copenhaver, 1999a, 1999b; Heath, 1982, 1983; Michaels, 1981, 1986). Of note, in terms of relative differences, Gee (n.d.) suggests, by linguistic norms (Labov, 1972), differences in language structures are minor in comparison to variations in language use.

The Structure of AAVE and School Literacy Learning

Despite the commonly shared perspective that all language varieties are complete and equally complex linguistic systems (Wolfram et al., 1999), a number of sociolinguists and scholars debate whether structural differences across language varieties (e.g., AAVE vs. SE) interfere with reading comprehension, particularly when the differences are not taken into account in the school literacy program (Goodman & Goodman, 2000; Labov, 1972; Labov & Baker, 2001; J. R. Rickford, 1997; Steffensen et al., 1982). Because the extent of the use of AAVE dialect features has a correlation with reading achievement (Labov, Cohen, Robins, & Lewis, 1968), and since 80 to 98 percent of all African Americans speak AAVE (Dillard, 1972; Smitherman, 1986), potential structural interference is an area of concern. Although experts in the field largely agree that most pronunciation differences associated with AAVE in comparison with SE generally do not cause major interference with comprehension of extended text written in SE (Wolfram et al., 1999), there is some evidence to suggest that reduction of verb endings may lead to a distorted sense of the time structure of text, particularly if the reader does not observe critical adverbial phrases in the surrounding discourse (e.g., *last month, before, afterwards*) (Labov, 1972; Wolfram et al., 1999; Steffensen et al., 1982). In particular, reduction of endings on verbs that are tense/aspect markers (Sidnell, n.d.), a feature of AAVE, may create the interference. Additionally, researchers have found that AAVE speakers who left off *s* endings on present-tense verbs more frequently lost track of whether the subject of the sentence was singular or plural, compared with SE speakers (Steffensen et al., 1982). These instances of dialect interference became more prominent when students read texts extending beyond a comfortable reading level.

Language-Use Patterns Associated with AAVE and School Literacy Learning

Some researchers suggest that differing patterns of language use may be another potential source of interference in the literacy development of

African American children, particularly if children use language in ways that their mainstream teachers misinterpret or do not understand (Copenhaver, 1999a, 1999b; Howrey, 2005; Lee, 2001; Miller, 2003; A. E. Rickford, 1996; Sipe, 2002). Across studies with African American children at the preschool level on up, researchers have found evidence of language-use practices that vary from the patterns used by their mainstream peers or other African American children from homes where the participation norms aligned more closely with those emphasized at school. However, in some of the studies, when teachers acknowledged the discourse differences, accommodated for them in the classroom context, and designed instruction in ways that built on students' linguistic strengths, positive literacy-related outcomes resulted (Copenhaver, 1999a, 1999b; Howrey, 2005; Miller, 2003).

FOCUS OF THE RESEARCH SYNTHESIS

This research synthesis examines the ways in which African American children who speak AAVE use their linguistic knowledge to construct meaning as they respond to African American literature they listen to or read. In particular, it considers the ways in which children use language to ask and answer questions and respond to read-alouds and independent readings, as well as ways in which they use their knowledge of AAVE and culturally related features of text (e.g., AAVE dialogue or narration, slang, signifying, word play, rhythm, rhyme) to help construct the meaning of text they listen to or read. It is hoped that this synthesis of the research will allow researchers and classroom teachers to gain new insights into possible sources of conflict in the reading development of children who speak AAVE. It is also hoped that the information will allow researchers and teachers to discover new avenues to explore, as well as new ways to address the issues.

Definition of African American Literature

For the purpose of this research synthesis, African American literature refers to books written by and about African Americans. In general, to be included in this research synthesis, studies had to involve African American children, within the grade-level range of K–12, listening to or reading and responding to books that fit this definition. Also, the research concerns had to intersect with the sociolinguistic concerns of this research synthesis. In some cases, children from other cultural groups were in the researchers' classroom contexts. Also, because most of the research investigations examined the children's responses to literature during the course of the regular school day, in some cases researchers examined children's responses to literature that was not African American but that was part of the curriculum.

However, the primary focus here is on those parts of the studies that involved African American children responding to African American children's literature.

There is one exception. The results of one study conducted by Howrey (2005), which included some books written about African American characters or themes, are shared with respect to literature discussion discourse patterns, although the books did not meet all the criteria for African American literature set out for this synthesis because they were not written by African American authors. Since there was limited research on literature discourse patterns that went beyond question-and-answer patterns, this information seems valuable to share. However, the results should be viewed with caution, as children's discourse patterns may vary with different literature types. This is an area in which further study is needed.

Otherwise, across studies, the African American literature books read varied by genre and included trade books in the form of chapter or picture books, folktales, historical fiction, contemporary realistic fiction, fantasy, poetry, biography, and mystery.

Search Strategies for Locating Studies

In order to locate studies on reader response with African American participants and African American literature, computer searches were conducted in the ERIC system and Proquest database for studies published from 1995 to 2006, using the descriptors *African American, Black, reader response, children's literature,* and *adolescent literature.* In addition, the reference sections of the articles retrieved were consulted, which provided additional studies on the topic. In all, ten studies published from 1995 to 2003 were retrieved (Brooks, 2001, 2005; Copenhaver, 1999a; Gordon, 2000; Hefflin, 1997; Howrey, 2005; Lee, 1995, 2001; Miller, 2003; A. E. Rickford, 1996; A. M. Rickford, 1999; Smith, 1995). While this number may seem limited, it is important to note that as recently as the mid 1990s, less than 5 percent of all books published were classified as African American literature (as cited in Brooks, 2001; Cooperative Children's Book Center, 2006).

The published studies appeared in journal articles (Lee, 1995, 2001; Smith, 1995), doctoral dissertations (Brooks, 2001; Copenhaver, 1999a; Gordon, 2000; Hefflin, 1997; Howrey, 2005; Miller, 2003; A. E. Rickford, 1996), a paper presented at a professional meeting published as an ERIC document (Copenhaver, 1999b), and in some cases in book format or within an edited volume (Brooks, 2005; A. M. Rickford, 1999), in part or in full, as well. As a prerequisite, each study involved participants in reading or listening to literature selections in hard-copy form, as opposed to exclusive reading of the selections in some other nontraditional format (e.g., films, audio recordings, videos, e-books).

Evaluating the Studies

Each study retrieved was coded according to ten variables of interest, in-cluding purpose of the study and research questions, the type of literature books read, the grade-levels and cultural groups of the participants and teacher/researcher, prior linguistic knowledge used, data collection and analysis methods, and results. Afterward, all of the data were compiled cu-mulatively into a single chart. This process helped to facilitate making cross-study comparisons and assisted with detecting patterns in the data.

Participants and Classroom Contexts

Across studies, there were as few as three participants (Smith, 1995) and as many as the number of students in six high school classes (four experi-mental and two control groups) (Lee, 1995). Participants ranged from kindergarten level through high school age and included students at nearly every grade level in between. All but one study (Copenhaver, 1999a, 1999b) was conducted with participants from primarily low-income areas, with the added note that details about one of the research contexts were not known (Smith, 1995). Although information about participants' reading abilities was not provided for two of the primary grade level studies (Copenhaver, 1999a, 1999b; Miller, 2003) and the measures reported across studies var-ied (e.g., reading level, percentile rank score), the students' overall reading abilities were low, with three exceptions (Gordon, 2000; Hefflin, 1997; Howrey, 2005). With regard to those exceptions, the four fifth-grade male participants in Gordon's (2000) study ranged in reading level from 3.2 to 6.2; the six third-grade students in Hefflin's (1997) study consisted of an equal distribution of students with good, average, and poor reading abili-ties; and of Howrey's (2005) twelve participants, the ten third-graders were described as average readers, and the two second-graders were considered above average.

Research Questions

Across studies, the research questions concerned what types of responses emerged (e.g., verbal, nonverbal, written, aesthetic vs. efferent, conventional vs. unconventional, the kinds of connections made with personal experi-ences as expressed in writing and drawings) during various literacy-related activities (e.g., discussions directed by questioning vs. discussions that were more conversational in nature, journal writing, read-alouds, independent silent readings), in some cases guided by prompts (e.g., culturally related vs. culturally unrelated) or directed by questions of different types (e.g., open ended vs. content specific, contextualized vs. decontextualized), using different kinds of texts (e.g., simple vs. complex, culturally relevant vs. texts un-related to culture, books of varied genres), and using books that contained a variety of culturally influenced text features (e.g., AAVE, signification, slang, rhythm). Some of the research also examined ways in which children's responses demonstrated their text understandings in terms of recall or interpretations. Also, Hefflin (1997) was interested in exploring how African American literature influences the quality of students' writing.

In some cases, the responses of African American children were com-pared with the responses of children belonging to other cultural groups or with a subgroup of African American students within the same classroom context. Most research contexts were situated within the classroom during the regular school day. However, in Gordon's (2000) study, the four fifth-graders met with the researcher after school. For the most part, read-alouds occurred within whole-class and small-group settings.

Also of note, the teachers or teacher-researchers across studies varied with respect to their approaches to reader response activities. Taking a more lib-eral approach, some allowed students to take greater control of discussions and written responses; in other research contexts, more direction was pro-vided. Taking a more structured approach, Hefflin (1997) used a question framework to guide discussions of African American literature read. In some classroom contexts, the teacher used a balanced approach that in-cluded a combination of open-ended and more directed response opportu-nities. For example, in Brooks's (2001) study, the teacher allowed the mid-dle school students to choose their own topics for journal response entries half of the time and assigned prompts the other half.

Responding to Delpit's (1988) charge for teachers to make explicit their expectations in order to empower students potentially at risk due to cultural and language backgrounds that may differ from those privileged at school, some researchers implemented instructional interventions in conjunction with reader response activities (Hefflin, 1997; Lee, 1995). For example, Lee (1995) supplemented literature discussions with instruction on the use of comprehension strategies. Specifically, Lee used African American literature with AAVE embedded in the narration, and drew on the African American students' linguistic knowledge of signifying, a form of discourse in the African American community that uses irony, double entendre, satire, and metaphor, as a scaffold for teaching skills in literary interpretation.

RESULTS

The purpose of this research synthesis is twofold. First, it examines the rel-evant research in order to draw conclusions with respect to ways in which children use their knowledge of discourse practices related to literacy learning. Second, it examines studies in order to draw conclusions about ways in which children use their knowledge of AAVE and culturally related features of text to help with their interpretations of African American literature. A discussion of the results in each of these two broad areas follows.

Knowledge of Discourse Practices Related to Literacy Learning

As a result of socialization practices in their homes and communities, children come to school already possessing a great deal of discourse knowledge related to literacy-related activities, such as how to ask and answer questions and participate in discussions (Copenhaver, 1999a, 1999b; Howrey, 2005; Lee, 2001; Miller, 2003; A. E. Rickford, 1996). By becoming aware of children's linguistic prior knowledge in these areas, teachers become better prepared to design instruction to effectively meet their needs. A synthesis of the research regarding children's knowledge in both of these areas follows.

Question-and-answer discourse practices. In their short-term, mixed-methods, and naturalistic investigations, Rickford (1996) and Copenhaver (1999a, 1999b) examine African Americans' discourse practices associated with questions and answers, and they compare those patterns within and across cultural groups living in their respective geographic areas. Specifically, Rickford evaluates the responses of sixth- and seventh-grade students to various question types. Rickford's sample includes a mix of students from diverse minority groups from low-income families living in the western part of the United States, most of whom are African American. On the other hand, Copenhaver compares the response patterns of different subgroups of African American children and white children in a K–2, multiage classroom in the Southeast. Rickford and Copenhaver note complex similarities and differences within and across cultural groups attending classes within schools in their respective low- and mixed-income communities.

Consistent question-type preferences across minority groups. First, Rickford (1996) observes that, despite their contrasting cultural backgrounds, the middle school African American, Hispanic, Tongan, Samoan, and Fijian participants in her study are all significantly more successful answering contextual, experience-based types of questions, which she categorizes as "higher-order" types of questions, than they are answering decontextualized, text-based types, classified as "lower-order" questions. In this classroom community, there are few differences in the question types preferred across cultural groups. However, it should be noted that the students in Rickford's study who belong to different cultural groups are all members of minority groups; none of the students are mainstream. This important distinction may explain, at least in part, why the results contrast with Heath's

(1982, 1983) earlier long-term ethnographic study of the questioning styles of African American and European American working-class families living within just a few miles of each other in the Piedmont Carolinas. In that study, Heath observes that the question type preferred by each cultural group differs: the African Americans tend to ask and effectively answer analogy-type questions (e.g., "What's that like?"), whereas in the European American families, "known-answer" questions (e.g., "What is the name of this animal?") are more common.

Just as students experienced greater success with answering "higher-order" questions, Rickford (1996) reports that the overall mean score for responses to the questions is better for longer rather than shorter stories, and for females as opposed to males. Of note, all questions were based primarily on African American folktales and contemporary narratives, genres Rickford chose based on the children's expressed interests as indicated on a preliminary survey administered. Thus, it appears likely the favored question-related discourse styles of the participants in Rickford's study may be explained by a multitude of factors, such as cultural factors, including minority group status, as well as gender issues, student interest, or possibly other variables unrelated to reading ability.

Varied response patterns within and across cultural groups. Similar to the findings of Heath (1982, 1983), Copenhaver (1999a, 1999b) found differences in the response patterns of some of the African American children and white students who attended class together. Of note, as an important class distinction, in contrast to the working-class African American and European American participants of Heath's study, all of the African American children in Copenhaver's investigation receive free or reduced-cost lunch and live in low-income neighborhoods; and all of the white children live in middle- or upper-middle-class neighborhoods. Additionally, there are some important differences between Copenhaver's findings and the results of Heath's earlier research. Copenhaver observes that discourse practices do not fall strictly along the lines of social class or racial group. While participation patterns of the white students during whole-class read-alouds align well with the teacher's expectations, those of the African American children are somewhat more complex.

Unlike some of their African American peers, the K–2 children in one African American subgroup that Copenhaver (1999a, 1999b) refers to as "marginalized" tend to call out during the whole-class read-alouds, rather than sitting quietly and raising their hands, waiting to be called on before speaking. As Copenhaver observes, they often end up being reprimanded by their European American teacher and moved to the back of the classroom. As Copenhaver observes, for the children in this subgroup, home norms do not match school norms.

In contrast, other African American children in class exhibit somewhat different discourse patterns (Copenhaver, 1999a). For example, one high-achieving, African American boy exhibits behaviors similar to the white students during read-alouds. He works well with African American or white children and moves easily between groups. During a home visit and interview with his mother, the researcher learns that the discourse norms of home and school are quite similar. Due to work schedules, one parent is always at home, and each parent restricts the boy's circle of playmates outside of school to other members of the family who exhibit the discourse patterns the parents support, which are similar to those expected at school.

In contrast, in the case of another high-achieving African American student, Copenhaver (1999a) observes that although this African American girl performs more like the white students than her African American peers on standardized achievement tests, her discourse patterns during read-alouds conflict with the expectations of the teacher. As a pattern, the teacher asks mostly efferent or informational question types, a pattern that becomes even more prominent as time runs short during read-alouds and literature discussions, and although the girl demonstrates in other ways that she is listening during the read-alouds and knows the answers, it is evident she has not yet figured out the implicit rules regarding how to successfully respond to these types of questions.

In general, except for the high-achieving, African American boy noted earlier, the white students are much more successful in answering efferent question types (Copenhaver, 1999a). Thus, having the content knowledge but lacking critical discourse knowledge limits the girl's success in the classroom. Also, perhaps related to the negative responses of the teacher to the girl when she calls out or wanders around the room and appears as if not paying attention, the other white children regard her negatively and exclude the girl from their social network, even though the girl is more like the white students academically than most of her African American peers. As a result, it appears that the girl does not fit into any cultural group in the classroom.

A home visit and interview with her parent reveals differences between the discourse patterns advocated by her parents and the discourse patterns of those with whom the girl spends most of her time out of school while both parents work (Copenhaver, 1999a). Thus, even when social group and academic achievement levels are informally controlled, due to important differences in the home and school environment, it is evident that participation patterns within a cultural group can be complex and varied.

Accommodating response patterns. At Copenhaver's (1999a, 1999b) suggestion, when the teacher changes the structure of the read-aloud experience and pauses after reading each page, allowing for students to respond naturally throughout the read-aloud rather than waiting until the end, the number of speaking turns for the "marginalized" students doubles and the children's stance becomes more aesthetic (i.e., characterized by shared "associations, ideas, attitudes, sensations, or feelings" experienced while reading) (Rosenblatt, 1991, p. 445) rather than "efferent" (i.e., concerned with text-based information) (Rosenblatt, 1976, 1978). Copenhaver (1999a, 1999b) also notes some of the "marginalized" children respond personally and explicitly to sensitive issues of race during read-alouds of culturally relevant selections. By restructuring the situation to accommodate the response patterns with which the "marginalized" children are most familiar, the read-aloud experience becomes more positive for everyone.

Consistent with these findings, in a kindergarten classroom situated in a low-income urban community in the East, teacher-researcher Miller (2003) observes that her African American students offer more profound responses if she stops periodically during the read-aloud to allow children to interject their personal views rather than waiting until the end. Although not African American, Miller provides information that indicates she has gained knowledge in how to address children's needs during book discussions as a result of growing up in an African American community. Also, Copenhaver (1999a) notes work in small-group settings has a similar effect of creating more response opportunities and eliciting more aesthetic responses from the African American students.

Of note, although most of the books used in Sipe's (1997) study of storybook read-alouds with a culturally mixed group of first- and second-graders does not meet the criteria of African American children's literature, Sipe observes that as much as two-thirds of the talk occurs during the story readings rather than before or afterward. Sipe additionally notes that, since certain types of responses (e.g., performative responses, predictions, talking back to the story) are likely to occur only during the course of the read-aloud, by making room for them while the storybook reading is ongoing, the teacher encourages responses that are not only greater in number, but also richer in type.

Corroborating the positive results that Copenhaver (1999a) observes when the teacher changes the read-aloud format to align with the discourse practices familiar to the "marginalized" African American children (Copenhaver, 1999a, 1999b), when the teachers in Heath's (1982, 1983) earlier study adapt their questioning styles so that the questions asked resemble the types with which the African American children are most familiar, the students participate more in class, display greater interest, and share more of their personal experiences.

Teaching alternate question-and-answer practices. A. E. Rickford (1996) suggests that the children she works with who show greater skill answering contextualized questions should receive instruction on how to answer all question types. This recommendation is supported by the conclusions of

Heath's earlier study (1982, 1983). Based on her findings, Heath surmises that the teacher's questioning style is more like that of the European American children in her study, and the mismatch in the question-answer patterns familiar to the African American children versus the teachers is most likely responsible, at least in part, for the African American children's poor academic performance. At her recommendation, the teachers in Heath's earlier study expose the African American students to conventional, known-answer types of questions on audiotapes and invite the children to answer these questions on the audio recordings, thus exposing them to mainstream discourse patterns, as well as accommodating those with which they are more familiar.

Thus, it appears a complex array of factors, including factors related to gender, literary genre, interest, cultural group, and possibly whether the group is mainstream or a minority group, may play a role in the question-and-answer discourse practices of students. Additionally, it is evident that patterns in discourse practices can vary widely within, as well as across, social groups, regardless of race or family income levels. These factors individually or in combination with one another may explain why discourse practices sometimes differ across widely separated geographic regions or even within the same local community (Copenhaver, 1999a, 1999b; A. E. Rickford, 1996).

Based on these studies (Copenhaver, 1999a, 1999b; A. E. Rickford, 1996) and corroborated by Heath's (1982, 1983) earlier research, it appears that if the question-and-answer discourse practices of students are not aligned with the expectations of the teachers at school, then academic performance and literacy development of students in class may suffer. On a positive note, if teachers adapt their instruction to accommodate the communicative patterns of their students, positive literacy-related learning outcomes can result.

Literature Discussion Discourse Patterns

In addition to question-and-answer discourse patterns, researchers have also investigated the discourse patterns of literature discussions. Some of the results of their studies suggest that, in certain contexts, students respond more aesthetically when questions are curtailed, and instead, responses to literature are shared in a conversation-like format, particularly when nonverbal as well as verbal behaviors are considered as possible forms of aesthetic response (Howrey, 2005). Similar to variations in question-and-answer discourse patterns, with regard to discussion groups, researchers have found variations in the patterns of verbal and nonverbal discourse practices of students who speak AAVE, who range from primary grade through high school levels, and who vary from below average to above average in overall level of academic ability (Copenhaver, 1999a, 1999b; Lee, 2001). Also, across studies, results suggest the verbal and nonverbal communication patterns of students at times are misinterpreted by teachers, particularly teachers who are not African American.

Assuming an aesthetic stance when discussion becomes conversational. Howrey's (2005) study suggests children's discourse practices may vary depending on the manner in which book discussions are structured. In her investigation of the read-aloud conversations of African American second- and third-graders attending an urban school located in a low-income community in the Midwest, Howrey observes that the children, who are average or above average in academic ability, exhibit a more aesthetic stance when teacher-directed questions are restricted and the discussion becomes more conversational in nature, particularly when the children self-initiate contributions. Extending the definition of a reader response to include nonverbal as well as verbal indicators of student involvement and enjoyment, Howrey considers the following behaviors to be indicative of an aesthetic stance: laughter, gasps of disbelief, expressions of surprise (e.g., "Oooo!") at story events, expressions of disappointment (e.g., "Ohhhh!") at the end of a read-aloud session, singing or humming music related to the story plot, and actions such as moving forward, sitting on knees to see better, or continuing to raise hands as the read-aloud time ends.

It should be noted that the children in Howrey's (2005) study attend a school that follows the prescribed Success for All (SFA) model, using texts that are from the basal or supplemental level books that come with the basal. Although the texts do not fit the criteria of this research synthesis to be considered African American literature, the information is included because it provides insights into the children's discourse knowledge with respect to discussion. However, it is possible that conclusions drawn based on this study may not apply to contexts in which children read African American literature and should be viewed with caution.

As Heath (1982, 1983) suggests based on her study, perhaps infrequent questioning practices in the students' home contexts, or socialization practices that familiarize the children with different question types, explain the more aesthetic literary responses which the children in Howrey's (2005) research context display when the discussion becomes more conversational. Although students sometimes provide aesthetic responses to teacher questions, more often, they tend to shift gears and produce more "efferent" types of responses (Howrey, 2005). In particular, Howrey (2005) observes that when the teacher interjects questions related to grammar, punctuation, pronunciation, or spelling into the literature discussion, the children's stance shifts sharply to an efferent one. Also, when questions of any sort are asked, the students' responses and story understanding appear to be negatively affected if the children are required to raise their hands before responding.

Performing the discourse of AAVE during literature discussion. In a study of students' literature discussion discourse patterns that involves an older age group, Lee (2001) conducts a discourse analysis of one day of instruction in an English language arts class in a poor, urban high school. As part of her data collection, Lee captures on videotape the verbal and nonverbal behaviors of the low-achieving African American freshmen, all of whom speak AAVE, as they discuss the culturally relevant novel *Rattlebone* (Claire, 1994). Through her close analysis of the instruction, as one goal of the study, Lee aims to make explicit the ways in which she, as teacher and researcher, uses the students' cultural knowledge and culturally relevant text to scaffold the students' responses to literature, initially, until students learn useful strategies to employ later on when they will be ready to transition to literature for which they have less social knowledge.

Making reference to the multiparty, overlapping, loud talk exhibited by the students on the videotape and other videotapes similar to it, Lee (2001) observes that in her work with African American adolescents, she has found these behaviors to be fairly typical indicators of engagement. However, she also notes the misinterpretations of other teachers, particularly teachers who are not African American, who view the videotapes of similar interactions of students in her class and regard the behaviors as off task and unruly.

Consistent with the position of noted linguists and scholars (Labov, 1972; Wolfram et al., 1999), Lee (2001) asserts, in addition to the pronunciation and grammatical features of AAVE, as with all language variations, AAVE is carried out in a distinctive manner of performance. For example, Lee reports that during book discussions, students signify on one another, using double entendre and other forms of figurative language, emphasize meanings using various forms of body language, and exhibit a dramatic display of rhythm and prosody (i.e., the ability to read text orally using appropriate pitch, stress, and juncture) (Richards, 2000) in their talk. In order to prevent misinterpretations, Lee posits that it is critically important for teachers, whatever their cultural backgrounds, to become familiarized with the discourse patterns of their students.

Validating Lee's (2001) observations and highlighting the importance of her recommendation for teachers, the earlier research of Michaels (1981) on the unique sharing styles of African American and European American children during "show-and-tell" time in a first-grade classroom is important to mention, in that it illustrates further how misinterpretations can occur if teachers don't understand their students' discourse patterns. In her study, Michaels finds the "unconventional" sharing style of the African American children is more difficult for the European American teacher to interpret and understand than it is for the African American instructional aide in the classroom. The aide in the classroom is able to ask appropriate questions that facilitate the children's expansion of the narrative and overall organization of the ideas. In contrast to the European American middle-class children who exhibit a topic-centered style characterized by focusing on one topic and presenting the content in sequential order followed by a resolution, the poor and middle-class African American children use a sharing style that Michaels terms "topic associating." Accordingly, the African American students verbally share a series of episodes that relate to a theme; however, the connections among the episodes are not made explicit. Michaels observes that the European American teachers, whose discourse practices are more like those of the European American children, consider the African American children's "unconventional" sharing style to be incoherent and deficient. However, as psychologist, educational anthropologist, and applied linguist Cazden (1988) has suggested, although different from the "topic-centered" style of the European American children, the logic in the topic-associating narrative is equally valid.

In another classroom context, however, researcher Howrey (2005) notes the positive manner in which students' European American teacher responds to the second- and third-grade African American children in her classroom who exhibit a topic-associating, sharing style in their oral responses to literature. In this context, the classroom teacher finds a link between what the children are saying and the events in the story, and makes this connection explicit.

Thus, this first part of the results section has examined the prior linguistic knowledge of children who speak AAVE with respect to their knowledge of discourse practices (i.e., question-and-answer discourse practices and discussion discourse patterns) related to literacy learning. In a number of the studies cited, the linguistic knowledge of the children who spoke AAVE is misunderstood and devalued by some of the children's teachers, who in some instances are not African American, and these misunderstandings have the potential to impact negatively on the students' literacy learning. However, in a number of contexts, when the patterns in the children's discourse practices that vary from the standard variety taught in school are acknowledged and accommodated, improvements in the learning environment occur. It is worth noting that some of the researchers suggest the importance of additionally providing children with instruction on the discourse practices expected at school (Lee, 2001; A. E. Rickford, 1996), a position supported by others in the past (Delpit, 1988; Heath, 1982, 1983).

Knowledge of AAVE and Culturally Influenced Features of Text

In addition to discourse knowledge related to questioning and literature discussions, many African American children come to school with a rich knowledge of AAVE. The studies examined for this portion of the research synthesis suggest ways in which children from the primary grades through high school use that knowledge to enhance recall and deepen literary interpretations when they encounter AAVE-related components embedded in text. Some AAVE-related components embedded in texts across studies consist of distinctive grammatical patterns that vary from those of SE, including vocabulary, slang and idiomatic expressions, rhetorical styles, such as call-and-response, and signifying (Brooks, 2001; Gordon, 2000; Lee, 1995, 2001; Miller, 2003; Smith, 1995).

Responding to variations in characters' dialogue and deriving important story meanings. Across studies, students ranging in age use their familiarity with various aspects of AAVE as a recognizable tool to analyze literature (Brooks, 2001; Lee, 1995; Miller, 2003). For example, even as young as five or six years of age, the kindergarten children in Miller's study respond with contrasting body language to the differing language styles of the main characters in *Flossie and the Fox* (McKissack, 1986). Miller suggests the author's interesting use of language not only draws the children into the story, but more importantly, it provides critical clues to the story's meaning, which the children sense and express in various ways. When Flossie speaks in her informal language style influenced by a southern drawl, the children sway back and forth and bob their heads rhythmically. During those portions when the sly "stuffy" trickster, the fox, speaks in more formal SE, the children sit up tall, taking on a rigid posture. In response to "catchy" phrases or varied dialects they hear during the read-aloud, the children jump in and mimic the words, sometimes chorally.

Carrying over literary responses to new writing and reading contexts. Miller (2003) observes later on that the children repeat the dialogue when writing and illustrating in their journals. Additionally, she notices their stories and illustrations reflect more of the story details. Also, their attention to the language plays a role in observed "storybook reading" during free reading time later on in the day when children seek out the books shared during the read-alouds and repeat the catchy phrases and dialogue while perusing them. Storybook reading is recognized as an emergent reading behavior that young children exhibit as they move along the continuum to becoming conventional readers (Valencia & Sulzby, 1991).

Using signifying to gain insights into characters and their interrelationships. In Brooks's (2001) study with middle school students, students use their knowledge of rhetorical styles associated with AAVE to detect complex subtleties in relationships between characters. For example, from growing up in African American families and communities, the eighth-graders are able to draw on their prior knowledge of "signifying" in its various forms to detect the playfulness in the dialogue between the characters, Jamal and his younger sister, Sassy, in *Scorpions* (Myers, 1988), as well as the affectionate nature of their relationship. Based on the good-natured but frequent verbal battles between the brother and sister, the students in Brooks's study also recognize the younger sister's challenges to the authority of her older brother.

Using slang to make inferences about characters. Drawing on prior linguistic knowledge, one student in Brooks's (2001) study is able to infer from a character's language variation that the character probably lives in "the projects." Tapping into linguistic knowledge from multiple interpretive communities at times, students are able to translate meanings for much of the slang terminology in character dialogue. Also, they are able to use distinctive linguistic markers to detect character loyalties and alignment. For example, the gang members in *Scorpions* (Myers, 1988) use slang more frequently than the other characters and in a manner that could be difficult to understand outside of the context of the novel, perhaps serving as a sort of self-defense against mainstream society, as Brooks suggests.

Drawing parallels between signifying and literary devices in complex fiction. Teacher-researcher Lee (1995) draws from her high school students' prior knowledge of signifying as a strategic tool for interpreting complex fictional works that use AAVE as a dominant mode of narration. Her immediate goal is to make explicit the ways in which students' knowledge of signifying and its use of metaphor, satire, irony, and shifts in point of view are applicable to the role of these literary devices in complex literary works. Lee makes clear her long-term mission is to build students' repertoire of strategies to a point where they can independently apply the strategies to other fictional works, not necessarily culturally relevant. Based on quantitative analyses of pre/post measures of reading achievement for experimental groups that use signifying as a scaffolding tool versus no-treatment groups, Lee notes significant differences between groups. The experimental groups have significantly greater gains in reading achievement than the control groups. Additionally, based on a qualitative analysis of instructional discourse, the experimental groups show notable change in student participation, deeper interpretations of complex inferential questions about texts, and greater independence of the teacher compared with the control groups.

Analyzing the linguistic components of literature to prepare for teachable moments. It should be noted that the studies of Gordon (2000), Brooks (2001), and Lee (1995), involving participants ranging from fifth grade through high school, illustrate the potential benefits of conducting content analyses of literature selections prior to introducing them to students. By recognizing in advance the AAVE-related linguistic components embedded in literature, the teachers or teacher-researchers within each classroom context studied are able to deliver instruction that draws on students' prior linguistic knowledge. For example, by creating culturally focused response prompts tailored to each book read, Gordon (2000) is able to direct students' attention to important literary devices, such as authors' interesting use of language. Response prompts of this sort provide opportunities for students to draw on their prior knowledge as they respond. As Sipe (1997) learns from his own research on storybook read-alouds with first- and second-graders, in order to anticipate "teachable moments" (p. 324), it is essential to think through the possibilities in advance.

Similarly, by becoming aware of the linguistic components of novels under consideration before introducing them to students, Brooks (2001) is able to locate three novels that not only build on but also expand students' prior linguistic and cultural knowledge. For example, the three novels selected, *Scorpions* (Myers, 1988), *The House of Dies Drear* (Hamilton, 1968), and *Roll of Thunder, Hear My Cry* (Taylor, 1976), represent three different genres (historical fiction, mystery, and realistic fiction) and vary in settings by time (1930s, 1960s, and 1980s) and place (a middle-class, rural community in Ohio; a poor, inner-city area of New York; a southern farming community in Mississippi). Within each novel, the dialogue reflects the diverse settings. Through the introduction of this text set, Brooks allows students to encounter a range of language variations used by African Americans across generations and diverse geographic locations (e.g., AAVE with slang expressions popular during the 1980s, AAVE infused with southern dialect, and SE), among other variations.

Based on the results of these studies, it is evident that children of all grade levels who speak AAVE bring with them into the classroom tremendous linguistic resources useful for constructing meaning from the literature they listen to and read. Now the challenge remains for teachers and researchers to find ways to tap into them.

RECOMMENDATIONS FOR FURTHER RESEARCH AND EDUCATIONAL PRACTICE

Based on this synthesis of the research on reader responses to African American children's literature, there are several recommendations of potential interest to researchers and classroom teachers. The recommendations suggest ways to help improve the literacy-related communicative interactions of teachers and students, as well as ways to promote children's construction of meaning as they listen to, read, and respond to African American literature.

Examine Nontraditional Literary Response Types

Across studies, researchers have observed African American children's verbal and nonverbal responses, sometimes of a nontraditional nature, to read-alouds and independent readings. Less conventional responses include body movements and repetitions of interesting words, dialogue, or catchy phrases (Gordon, 2000; Miller, 2003; Smith, 1995). Additionally, Smith

(1995) describes the call-and-response behaviors of a student who interjects utterances such as "Hmmm" and "Well" during readings of African American literature, "as if at an African American church service" (Smith, p. 572). Gordon describes the "silent confirmation agreements" of the four male African American fifth-graders in her study who make eye contact with one another and exchange smiles, nods of agreement, or shrugs as they listen to an African American literature selection read aloud, which she interprets as signals confirming the interconnectedness of the group.

These response types and other "unconventional" responses like them that are potentially culturally linked need to be studied in terms of their possible value for enhancing literature understandings and interpretations. It is important to understand their value so that these behaviors are not misconstrued as misbehaviors. It is possible we may need to expand our notions of reader responses, as well as find effective ways to elicit them.

Also, some of the research conducted in this area does not use African American literature, as defined in this essay (Howrey, 2005; Sipe, 2002). It would be valuable to expand this research to contexts that use quality literature selections written by and about African Americans, since literature of this sort has much to offer.

Use Culturally Influenced Text Features to Enhance Text Understandings

Given the potential educational value of "speakerly" texts of African American fiction, Gates's (1988) term for literature that includes character dialogue reflecting AAVE and other authentic speech forms of the African American community (e.g., proverbs, signifying used artistically as a literary device), African American literature selections which provide rich, linguistic resources for scaffolding the literary responses of students who speak AAVE need to be woven into the curriculum, and exploited for all they have to offer. Literature of this type holds great potential for providing children with opportunities to draw on their prior linguistic knowledge as they work to construct meaning of literature they read. As Lee (1995) has suggested, speakerly texts provide students with the scaffolding they need while developing strategies that will allow them to tackle other types of texts later on, independently. Also, as evident in Brooks's (2001) research, text sets that portray the diversity within a culture offer opportunities for children to expand their cultural understandings.

Offer Variety in Literary Genres and Reader Response Opportunities

It should be noted that reader responses vary by the personality of the reader (e.g., vocal students tend to elicit more vocal responses during shared readings) (Smith, 1995), but also according to the type of text (e.g., more challenging texts appear to elicit indicators of greater engagement; poetry readings elicit poetry writings) (Rickford, 1996; Smith, 1995), the specific reader response task (e.g., spontaneous laughter and repeating humorous words or phrases, as well as "silent behavior agreements" or confirmations, occur during read-alouds but rarely during silent readings) (Gordon, 2000), the type of questions asked during discussions (e.g., open-ended questions elicit more aesthetic responses and content-specific questions are designed, at times, to elicit processes of meaning making, such as summarizing or predicting) (Brooks, 2001), and prompts or no prompts during journal writing (e.g., when no prompts are provided, new categories of response emerge, such as comments about humorous and interesting language) (Gordon, 2000). Based on these findings, teachers are advised to offer variety in terms of text genres and reader response tasks in order to maximize response opportunities and evoke richer response types.

Expand Teacher Training Programs

A number of the studies evaluated for this synthesis (Copenhaver, 1999a, 1999b; Howrey, 2005; Lee, 2001; Miller, 2003; A. E. Rickford, 1996), as well as prior research conducted (Heath, 1982, 1983; Michaels, 1981, 1986), pointedly illustrate how teachers' discourse practices can become barriers to literacy learning for many African American children. Given the mismatch in the race, social class, and language background of teachers and students in most classrooms in the United States and the projection that this discrepancy is likely to continue and grow (Gomez, 1993), research is needed to find ways to effectively train pre-service teachers as to how to address the needs of children who are members of cultural groups different from their own.

Although changes in attitudes and practices have been found to evolve slowly (Ahlquist, 1991), there have been some promising results with pre-service programs requiring community service work (Beyer, 1991), pairings of student-teachers and children of differing cultural backgrounds to promote friendship-building and mentoring along with opportunities to reflect on the experiences in supervised seminars (Larke, Wiseman, & Bradley, 1990), and field experiences, particularly ones in which mainstream student-teachers are placed for extended time periods in cultures in which they are in the minority (Cooper, Beare, & Thorman, 1990). More research on effective practices in this area is needed.

Embrace Children's Linguistic Knowledge

The research reviewed for this synthesis suggests most of the barriers to literacy learning in the contexts examined are not due to children's dialect differences, but rather to the school's failure to acknowledge and appreciate the language varieties children bring with them from their homes and communities. Teachers are advised to find ways to build on the linguistic strengths of their students who speak AAVE, while also teaching them an alternate code and discourse practices to use in school and other settings when appropriate.

REFERENCES

Ahlquist, R. (1991). Position and imposition: Power relations in a multicultural foundations class. *Journal of Negro Education, 60*, 158–169.

Berrick, J. D. (1995). *Portraits of women and children on welfare: Faces of poverty.* New York: Oxford University Press.

Beyer, L. E. (1991). Teacher education, reflective inquiry, and moral action. In B. R. Tabachnick & K. M. Zeichner (Eds.), *Inquiry-oriented practices in teacher education* (pp. 113–129). New York: Falmer Press.

Brooks, W. M. (2001). *Reading, literature, and culture: A case study of middle school students' responses to African American fiction for children.* Doctoral dissertation, University of Pennsylvania. *Dissertation Abstracts International, 62,* 1776.

———. (2005). Reading linguistic features: Middle school students' response to the African American literary tradition. In B. Hammond, M. E. R. Hoover, and I. P. McPhail (Eds.), *Teaching African American learners to read: Perspectives and practices* (pp. 253–263). Newark, DE: International Reading Association.

Cazden, C. B. (1988). *Classroom discourse: The language of teaching and learning.* Portsmouth, NH: Heinemann.

Claire, M. (1994). *Rattlebone.* New York: Penguin Books.

Cooper, A., Beare, P., & Thorman, J. (1990). Preparing teachers for diversity: A comparison of student teaching experiences in Minnesota and South Texas. *Action in Teacher Education, 12,* 1–4.

Cooperative Children's Book Center. (2006). *Annual Statistics.* University of Wisconsin at Madison. Retrieved 9/18/07 from www.education.wisc.edu/ccbc/books/pcstats.htm.

Copenhaver, J. F. (1999a). *Children's responses to read-alouds and group-shared writing in a multi-ethnic, multi-age primary grade classroom.* Doctoral dissertation, University of Florida. *Dissertation Abstracts International, 60,* 339.

———. (1999b, October). *The intersections of response and ethnicity: Elementary school students respond to multicultural children's literature.* Paper presented at the meeting of the South Central Modern Language Association, Memphis, TN.

Delpit, L. (1988). The silenced dialogue: Power and pedagogy in educating other people's children. *Harvard Educational Review, 58,* 280–298.

Dillard, J. L. (1972). *Black English: Its history and usage in the United States.* New York: Random House.

Gates, H. L. (1988). *The signifying monkey: A theory of Afro-American literary criticism.* New York: Oxford University Press.

Gee, J. P. (n.d). What is literacy? *Journal of Education*, 171, 18. www.ed.psu.edu/ Englishpds/Articles/CriticalLiteracy/What%20is%20Literacy.htm.

Gomez, M. L. (1993). Prospective teachers' perspectives on teaching diverse children: A review with implications for teacher education and practice. *Journal of Negro Education*, 62, 459–474.

Goodman, Y., & Goodman, D. (2000). "I hate 'postrophes": Issues of dialect and reading proficiency. In J. Peyton, P. Griffin, W. Wolfram, & R. Fasold (Eds.), *Language in action: New studies of language in society* (pp. 408–435). Cresskill, NJ: Hampton.

Gordon, J. J. (2000). *A case study of four male African American fifth graders' responses to African American children's literature using culturally focused response prompts.* Doctoral dissertation, Kansas State University. *Dissertation Abstracts International*, 61, 4290.

Hamilton, V. (1968). *The house of Dies Drear*. New York: Simon & Schuster.

Harris, V. J. (1997). Children's literature depicting Blacks. In V. J. Harris (Ed.), *Using multi-ethnic literature in the K–8 classroom* (pp. 21–58). Norwood, MA: Christopher Gordon.

Heath, S. B. (1982). Questioning at home and at school: A comparative study. In G. Spindler (Ed.), *Doing the ethnography of schooling: Educational anthropology in action* (pp. 102–131). New York: Holt, Rinehart & Winston.

———. (1983). *Ways with words: Language, life, and work in communities and classrooms.* Cambridge, UK: Cambridge University Press.

Hefflin, B. R. (1997). *African American children's literature and its connections to enriching learning.* Doctoral dissertation, University of Pittsburgh. *Dissertation Abstracts International*, 58, 2209.

Howrey, S. T. (2005). *Reader-response theory and culturally relevant read-alouds with low-income African-American children.* Doctoral dissertation, Georgia State University. *Dissertation Abstracts International*, 66, 2518.

Labov, W. (1972). *Language in the inner city.* Philadelphia: University of Pennsylvania Press.

Labov, W., & Baker, B. (n.d.). Linguistic component: African American literacy and culture project. www.ling.upenn.edu/~wlabov/FinalReport.html.

———. (2001). *Testing the effectiveness of an individualized reading program for African-American, Euro-American, and Latino inner city children.* Paper presented at the meeting of Principal Investigators of IERI Projects.

Labov, W., Cohen, P., Robins, C., & Lewis, J. (1968). *A study of the non-standard English of Negro and Puerto Rican Speakers in New York City.* Cooperative Research Report 3288, Vols. 1 and 2. Philadelphia: U.S. Regional Survey, Linguistics Laboratory, University of Pennsylvania.

Larke, P. J., Wiseman, D., & Bradley, C. (1990). The minority mentorship project: Changing attitudes of preservice teachers for diverse classrooms. *Action in Teacher Education*, 12, 5–12.

Lee, C. D. (1995). A culturally based cognitive apprenticeship: Teaching African American high school students skills in literary interpretation. *Reading Research Quarterly*, 30, 608–630.

———. (2001). Is October Brown Chinese? A cultural modeling activity system for underachieving students. *American Educational Research Journal*, 38, 97–141.

McKissack, P. (1986). *Flossie and the fox.* New York: Dial.

Michaels, S. (1981). Sharing time: Children's narrative styles and differential access to literacy. *Language in Society,* 10, 423–442.

———. (1986). Narrative presentations: An oral preparation for literacy. In J. Cook-Gumperz (Ed.), *The social construction of literacy* (pp. 94–116). Cambridge: Cambridge University Press.

Miller, T. D. (2003). *Literature discussion groups respond to culturally relevant children's literature in the kindergarten classroom.* Doctoral dissertation, University of Pennsylvania. *Dissertation Abstracts International,* 64, 834.

Moll, L. C. (1995). Bilingual classroom studies and community analysis: Some recent trends. In O. Garcia & C. Baker (Eds.), *Policy and practice in bilingual education: A reader extending the foundations.* Bilingual education and bilingualism 2 series (pp. 273–280). Bristol, PA: Multilingual Matters.

Myers, W. (1988). *Scorpions.* New York: Scholastic.

Perie, M., Grigg, W., & Donahue, P. (2005). *The nation's report card: Reading 2005* (NCES 2006-451). U.S. Department of Education, National Center for Education Statistics. Washington, DC: U.S. Government Printing Office.

Richards, M. (2000). Be a good detective: Solve the case of oral reading fluency. *Reading Teacher,* 53, 534–539.

Rickford, A. E. (1996). *Cognition, comprehension, and critical evaluation in a multicultural classroom: A study in literary analysis and appreciation.* Doctoral dissertation, Stanford University. *Dissertation Abstracts International,* 57, 3399.

Rickford, A. M. (1999). *I can fly: Teaching narratives and reading comprehension to African Americans and other ethnic minority students.* Lanham, MD: University Press of America.

Rickford, J. R. (1997, January 22). Letter to Senator Specter, chairman, U.S. Senate Subcommittee on Labor, Health, and Human Services and Education. www.stanford.edu/~rickford/ebonics/SpecterLetter.html.

———. (1999). Language diversity and academic achievement in the education of African American students: An overview of the issues. In C. Adger, D. Christian, & O. Taylor (Eds.), *Making the connection: Language and academic achievement among African American students* (pp. 1–30). Washington, DC: Center for Applied Linguistics.

Rosenblatt, L. M. (1976). *Literature as exploration.* New York: Modern Language Association.

———. (1978). *The reader, the text, the poem: The transactional theory of the literary work.* Carbondale: Southern Illinois University Press.

———. (1991). Literature–S.O.S.! *Language Arts,* 68, 444–448.

Sidnell, J. (n.d.). African American Vernacular English (Ebonics). www.une.edu.au/langnet/aave.htm.

Sipe, L. R. (1997). *The construction of literary understanding by first and second graders in response to picture storybook readalouds.* Doctoral dissertation, Ohio State University. *Dissertation Abstracts International,* 57, 4268.

———. (2002). Talking back and taking over: Young children's expressive engagement during storybook read-alouds. *Reading Teacher,* 55, 476–483.

Smith, E. B. (1995). Anchored in our literature: Students responding to African American literature. *Language Arts,* 72, 571–574.

Smitherman, G. (1986). *Talking and testifying: The language of Black America.* Detroit: Wayne State University Press.

Steffensen, M. S., Reynolds, R. E., McClure, E., & Guthrie, L. F. (1982). Black English vernacular and reading comprehension: A close study of third, sixth, and ninth graders. *Journal of Reading Behavior, 14,* 285–298.

Taylor, H. U. (1989). *Standard English, Black English, and bidialectalism: A controversy.* New York: Peter Lang.

Taylor, M. (1976). *Roll of thunder, hear my cry.* New York: Puffin Books.

Valencia, S. W., & Sulzby, E. (1991). Assessment of emergent literacy: Storybook reading. *Reading Teacher, 44,* 498–500.

Wolfram, W., Adger, C. T., & Christian, D. (1999). *Dialects in schools and communities.* Mahway, NJ: Lawrence Erlbaum.

9

Reading Our Richly Diverse World: Conceptualizing a Response Development Zone

Karla J. Möller

As a European American literacy educator and children's literature researcher interested in equity and diversity, I have focused for some time on the complexities of response to literature in our richly diverse world. Committed to the continuing struggle for justice in literacy education, I am guided by Edelsky's (1994) call for "literacy for democracy" (p. 254) for all students. One part of this journey for me has been to articulate the connections between my research and teaching in children's response to literature and my personal grounding in an emancipatory multicultural approach to teaching and learning—and to demonstrate these understandings in my practice through my advocacy for incorporating issue-rich, culturally diverse, socially conscious literature in public school elementary classrooms.

Over the past decade of my work with schools, my focus on diversity and dialogue in teaching with literature has led to a range of challenging questions—some internal and some posed by others: Is it realistic to believe that teachers and students can engage in group discussions of literature, especially works of multicultural literature containing social justice themes, in ways that help participants examine and expand on their responses without devaluing participants' initial reactions? Can educators help to create spaces in which they and their students feel safe addressing injustices and fears in productive and healing ways while also maintaining a focus on the literature and on content comprehension? Can participants in literature discussions support each other's learning about self and the world, prompting each other to expand on initial responses, to look at other avenues of response, to connect aspects of their lives to books and group dialogue, and to engage in critical reflection of social issues? My experience tells me yes— but how does this happen and what does it look like?

What I propose in this chapter is a theoretical construct applicable to reading and responding to multicultural books. This construct—a *response development zone* (RDZ)—encompasses the potential each reader has for creating and extending responses to literature within sociopolitical and historical as well as local contexts. Together, groups of readers create collective RDZs that offer expanded opportunities to develop multilayered understandings in response to literature.

The explication of this theoretical argument draws on dialogue from a literature circle discussion of *The Friendship* (Taylor, 1987) in which I was a teacher, participant, and researcher (Möller & Allen, 2000). This book is a highly praised example of culturally conscious African American literature (defined by Sims, 1982; discussed by Brooks, 2006) by the award-winning author Mildred D. Taylor—an African American writer and scholar who has based her novels on her family's history in the United States. The main characters offer intelligent, honorable, honest depictions of African American children growing up during the 1930s in the South. The transcript data shared here are the result of teaching that led to the development of my theoretical understandings of response to literature within a dialogue-oriented, critical multicultural approach. This in turn led to the development of the RDZ construct.

In our discussion group, four fifth-grade girls and I read and responded to Taylor's *The Friendship* within shifting individual and collective response development zones. The girls—Nicole, Jasmine, Tamika (all three African American), and Carmen (white with Hispanic heritage)—had previously experienced difficulty in student-led literature circle discussions. I was the teacher—in a participant observer teacher-researcher role—for our small-group discussions, which met outside the regular classroom for seven days over a period of two weeks. How I positioned myself and was positioned as a teacher, learner, researcher, and participant shifted during our discussions, but a primary responsibility lay in encouraging student dialogue about book content and personal response while guiding the girls to develop strategies that would help them engage in meaningful student-led book discussion groups in the classroom.[1]

A RESPONSE DEVELOPMENT ZONE IN A NUTSHELL

A response development zone is a construct I created to describe my theoretical framework for examining response to culturally diverse literature, especially to those texts that offer opportunities for students to engage in discussions of issues of social justice. The RDZ offers educators a way to conceptualize response to literature as a zone for personal revelation, for textual and contextual consideration, and for consideration of how all readers—students and teachers—are shaped by the world they inhabit and by what they read and how they in turn shape that reading and that world. A shifting and multifaceted learning space for response to literature, an RDZ includes aspects of learning related to individual conceptual development, communicative competence, peer interactions, reading comprehension, and other factors. Our responses to literature (and to each other and our world) are mediated by signs (e.g., language) and by the tools (e.g., dialogue) we have been taught to use to make meaning from those signs. By engaging in dialogue about meaning-making processes in response to issue-rich literature, readers create their thoughts verbally, giving them form. This provides a chance for all readers to respond and to reflect on how they use assumptions—for example, about race, class, and gender—to make meaning with text. They engage in the critical literacy practices of articulating their thinking, responding to others, and questioning self, other, literature, and their world.

In their RDZs, teachers and students share interpretations of literature (or any incarnation of "text" broadly defined), adding layers to their evocations of text, self, and the world and gaining access to multiple perspectives from which they can form and expand on their acquisition of concepts. This interaction offers each member of the discussion an opportunity to expand his or her understanding of concepts in a social space—intermental conceptual development (i.e., shared between minds)—as a precursor to developing more complex or multilayered understandings of complex concepts on an intramental plane (i.e., personal thought processes). Knowledge, perceptions, and understandings that are socially shared and created can impact each of the group members in ways that allow a transformation into new, individual, but socially connected knowledge. This process is applicable to acquisition of difficult concepts such as *equity, diversity, racism,* and *injustice* as well as understanding the incredible variety of contextualized human responses to actual situations involving racism or injustice.

This work will introduce components of the RDZ theoretical construct step by step, drawing frequently on examples from the literature discussions mentioned earlier. The RDZ theory is laid out in sections on the key components, focusing in turn on the interrelated components. The discussion begins with the theory's grounding in Vygotsky's notion of learning within a zone of proximal development. Following sections focus on dialogue, critical literacy, reader response, and concept development as key aspects of the RDZ construct. The focus then shifts to teaching within the RDZ. One question relevant throughout is as follows: In what ways can connecting these theories and learning tools support the reading of multicultural literature from a stance that allows for multifaceted and multilayered responses while creating opportunities for sustained dialogue on issues of social justice and equity that underlie emancipatory purposes of multicultural education?

THE ZPD AS A BASIS FOR CONCEPTUALIZING A RESPONSE DEVELOPMENT ZONE

Vygotsky's (1934/1986, 1978) zone of proximal development (ZPD) was drawn on in formulating the theoretical construct of individual and collective RDZs. Perhaps Vygotsky's most well-known construct, the ZPD incorporates essential aspects of his theory of learning and development, including the role of mediation by signs, the social nature of learning, and the connection between inter- and intramental planes of knowledge. The ZPD has been defined as the distance between what an individual can accomplish independently and what can be achieved with guidance of or in collaboration with an adult or a more capable peer, and it has been interpreted in many ways (e.g., Ashton 1996; Bruner, 1975; Lave & Wenger, 1991; Moll, 1990a; Moll & Whitmore, 1993). While some uses of this oft-cited construct focus on the supposedly more capable leading the supposedly less capable (Tudge, 1990), my research focuses on expanding and redefining education's views of "more capable" through an expanded interpretation of struggling and of capability as contextually rather than individually situated (Möller, 2001, 2002, 2004/2005). The power of the ZPD, embedded in Vygotsky's broader theory of the social nature of learning, is not in creating a more capable/less capable dichotomy, but in its ability to enlighten aspects of learning that people encounter as they construct meaning from a myriad of external and internal stimuli in multiple situations.

According to Wertsch (1985), the ZPD was introduced to address "assessment of children's intellectual abilities and evaluation of instructional practices" (p. 67). Vygotsky (1934/1986, 1978) wanted to assess not just fossilized abilities, but the potential for further development existing at any point in time. He felt this could be measured more accurately on the social, interpsychological plane. Vygotsky focused not only on signs (e.g., words, symbols) as mediators of thought and activity, but on the mediation of signs themselves within the social activity of learning. Rather than a banking education (Freire, 1970/1987) model in which skills are transferred from the more to the less competent, Vygotsky advocated wholeness and a move away from reductionism. Learning and development were embedded in social activity. This focus provides support for incorporating cultural and social practices into teaching and learning.

Moll (1990b) framed learning within one's zone of proximal development as the "collaborative use of mediational means to create, obtain, and communicate meaning" (p. 13). Collective zones of proximal development (Moll, 1990b) and "zones of possibilities" (Moll & Greenberg, 1990, p. 327) are spaces in which students' social, cultural, and familial funds of knowledge are valued and interconnected with schooled knowledge in a contextualized fashion. By bringing these ways of knowing into classrooms, an exchange of funds of knowledge between home and school is created that allows the complementary systems of knowledge to operate as "extended zones of proximal development" (Moll & Greenberg, 1990, p. 344). Educators must trust and assist students, creating supportive learning environments that provide tools and resources that encourage displays of competence, and providing space for exploratory talk, dialogue, and other social mediations that help children take control of learning and connect it to their lives. This reciprocal process—in which social life aids understanding of a transformed curriculum, and class activities enhance awareness of social realities—creates spaces in which all participants have opportunities to function as more capable at some point in the learning process.

Though necessary assistance by the teacher or more capable peers is often spoken of in conjunction with a scaffolding metaphor (Bruner, 1975), Dyson (1990) suggests instead a weaving metaphor that is less linear and less focused on conventional internalization of skills. Her metaphor is a nonconformist connecting of opportunities for learning and for demonstrating knowledge that asks teachers to weave children's interests, resources, intentions, and abilities from other learning spaces into new activities. Together, Dyson's (1990) weaving metaphor and Moll's and Greenberg's (1990) discussion of social and cultural learning related to funds of knowledge create not only a context for guidance within both students' and teachers' ZPDs that is interactive rather than unidirectional, but also a context for expanded views of capability.

Our ZPDs are fluid spaces. They are continually shifting to account for new learning contexts as well as change due to maturation and development. The focus is not to analyze a static system, but to examine the role played by social mediation in creating space for change and for the facilitation and creation of new learning. Using another construction metaphor, Moll (1990b) states: "The Vygotskian theoretical structure is a habitable building. But, as with any important building, it may need renovations and improvements, without altering significantly its classical structure" (p. 3). The question for many educators is, in what ways is the theory useful for understanding and providing spaces for learning in schools? For the argument made here, the usefulness is in the combination of individual and collective zones (Moll & Whitmore, 1993), both of which focus on social and cultural aspects of contextualized learning and create spaces for teachers and students to shift between guiding and being guided.

AN EXAMPLE OF SHIFTING POSITIONS OF CAPABILITY

Mildred D. Taylor is an award-winning African American author with a Newbery Medal as well as multiple Coretta Scott King Awards and many other literary honors to her credit. Her socially conscious historical fiction depicts with honesty the brutality of a racist society while also sharing the strength of people working against great odds toward a better world. In *The Friendship* (1987), Taylor realistically depicts an event that takes place at the local white-owned general store in the course of one afternoon as an elderly African American man and four African American children experience and witness racist violence. What follows is an example of collaborative meaning-making in *The Friendship* discussion.

All of the girls in the discussion group had been having problems with comprehension. They had been asking questions, orally and in writing, about the book's title and the notion of friendship between two men—one black (Tom Bee, a community elder) and one white (John Wallace, storeowner)—who did not "seem like friends" (Jasmine). After several days, the girls had not come to any conclusions that settled their curiosity and confusion. Tamika realized the men had been friends in the past: "Tom Bee says, 'He [Wallace] promised me a long time ago that I could call him by his first name.'" I took the opportunity to help them organize the information and responses they had collected and created: "Jasmine noticed in her paper, when I read her responses, that she doesn't notice they're friends now. What, what's going on?" (Karla).

Carmen: He [Tom Bee] called him John.

Karla: So what happened?

Nicole: I don't know.

Karla: Why were they friends and they are not friends now? Why did he tell him he could call him John, and now he's shooting him with a gun?

Carmen: Because Mr. Tom Bee had saved John a long time ago like twice.

Nicole: He saved him a long time ago.

Carmen: Saved his life.

After the group established why the men had been friends, I asked the same question the girls had been asking: "Why aren't they friends now?"

Carmen: Probably his friends that he's got now.

Nicole: Probably ashamed about his name.

Karla: Why did that make him mad?

Nicole: 'Cause he called him by his first name!

Tamika: They, uh, 'cause white folks at that time used to make bl, sure black folks called them by they name, Mr.—

Nicole: And he got mad.

Tamika: And Mrs. and stuff, but they got to, they get to call black folks by, um, they first name, like they call um, Bi', um—

Carmen: Big Mama.

Tamika: Yeah, Big Mama, and she say "Don't call me Big—

Carmen: Auntie.

Tamika: Yeah, Aunt, Big Auntie, or something and that and she say, "Don't call me Big Auntie, or something, she say, 'cause I ain't your auntie."

Karla: Why did they do that?

Tamika: Because she was living, they really agreeing they say that to her 'cause she been around so long. But I don't, they, white folks thought they were bad back then, and they ain't had to tell folks like—

Carmen: I believe that . . . the friends [Wallace] gots now . . . told him when he left Mr. Tom Bee, when he found some friends, that's what I think about it.

Karla: I didn't get that. Say that one more time now.

Carmen: That, um, Mr. Tom Bee was saving his [life]. When . . . John Wallace was better, . . . he went somewhere. I believe he had made some friends and there was, he told them about this old man, this old, this old Mr. Tom Bee and, um, they were, and he said that he was black and they were talking about how mean they'd be . . . That's what I think.

The reasons for the change in Tom Bee's and John Wallace's friendship are not made explicit in the book, and this caused problems for these readers who were having difficulty with inferential comprehension. The questions I posed in this exchange were all questions that the girls had asked in their writing or in previous discussions without coming to any closure, and they were designed to encourage the girls to expand on their ideas. Rather than leave their insights unconnected, I prompted them to build on what they said in looking for their answers while validating their responses, connections, and questions. In this context, Carmen created important inferential understanding about John Wallace's betrayal of Tom Bee. Tamika and Jasmine made textual connections which Tamika and Carmen extended to historical connections about expected rules of address between blacks and whites in the 1930s and about the resistance of many African Americans to the inequities they faced.

The girls built on this new understanding later in the same session and in the next as they continued to discuss the text from multiple stances, at times taking a more textual approach, at other times focusing more closely on their authorial reading or narrative stances, and at still others, moving further from the text to the intensely personal tragedies and fears the text brought to their minds. As these shifts occurred, my position also shifted. I was participant, teacher, and researcher; at times a more capable and at others a less knowledgeable member of the group. The girls also moved in and out of positions as the more capable peer. This next excerpt shows, for example, how Tamika and Nicole functioned as more capable peers, helping Jasmine with important textual comprehension.

Jasmine: I got a question about those children.

Tamika: They're not his [Tom Bee's] kids.

Nicole: They the lady's, their momma's. Somebody else's that ain't in the store.

Karla: She's not there?

Tamika: Yeah, they do got a dad. Why she always talking something about "Pa said"?

Nicole: You know that she, they ain't in the store.

Tamika: Pa said, "We don't do this."

Jasmine: I don't think they belong to anybody. I think they in an orphanage or something. I think they live in a box or something.

Tamika: Well, what they said right here: "Pa said, we don't do this."

Nicole: Yeah, [what] about when, they, she said, "Mama said not to go to the store for that . . . aunt."

Jasmine: Well, I don't remember about that.

The children in the text were part of a close-knit biological family and a cohesive cultural community, and knowing this was important. This sense of belonging, love, and joint responsibility for self and for others is a key element in all of Mildred Taylor's works. In later discussions, the extent to which Tom Bee cared for these children, who were not his biologically, helped the girls understand and connect with his actions. It also helped them question both the characters and the author herself, especially when another community member whom the children called Aunt Callie put them in harm's way by sending them to the store they had been warned by their parents to avoid. Weaving in and out of the capable peer role, with each other's help, all five of us learned a new kind of talk.

THE POWER OF DIALOGUE WITHIN
THE RESPONSE DEVELOPMENT ZONE

Dialogue plays a central role in the RDZ theoretical construct. In teacher education there has been much discussion about the use of dialogue in classrooms to unlock learning potential and create opportunities for students to grow. Not all have been in agreement as to the potential for teachers to lead this dialogue or for dialogue to occur in ways that are supportive of all students (Ellsworth, 1989). Having experienced the powerful potential for learning through shared reading and responding to literature in a small-group setting through my earlier teaching and research, my exposure to potential negative effects of unsupportive peer interactions (Allen, Möller, & Stroup, 2003) forced me to reflect on the theoretical and practical grounding required for dialogue to have positive power.

While schools are not the answer to society's ills, often having been part of the problem itself (Adams, 1995; Anderson, 1988; Apple, 1990), they are also the places where children and teachers have a chance to learn from and grow with each other. If literature teachers—regardless of their or their students' ethnic and racial backgrounds—do not find ways to engage children in discussions about their transactions, themselves, and the world, they lose a valuable chance to provide access to multiple viewpoints that can enhance understanding of social issues. Feelings of fear or guilt, confusion or anger about racist or sexist tendencies in society or in oneself may simply go underground if there is no safe space for children to address them. Rather than leaving these issues unexamined, teachers and students can immerse themselves in literature that celebrates diversity and opens pathways to new perspectives. If teachers fail to initiate dialogue with students, both adults and children lose opportunities to create learning spaces in which they can collectively conceptualize, for example, the history of issues relating to diversity as it connects to literature, to life, and to societies today.

Vygotsky (1934/1986) saw the word as "a direct expression of the historical nature of human consciousness" (p. 256). Humans do not simply verbalize thought directly into language: "Thought undergoes many changes as it turns into speech. It does not merely find expression in speech; it finds its reality and form" (p. 219). People give their thoughts form in speech, while the speech itself simultaneously provides more food for their thoughts. This cycle, in the form of dialogue with others, continually recreates one's consciousness and conceptual reality of the world. Thought and word are connected in a "living process," a symbiotic relationship (p. 255).

Bakhtin (1986) also emphasized dialogue, expanding it to refer to connecting words and ideas not only between people in the present, but also across time and within individuals. He wrote about the connectedness of each utterance to all that has gone before. Speech and thought are always dialogical, even within an individual. Life is by its very nature dialogic. Utterances, the basic units of language meaning in Bakhtinian terms, are inhabited by the voices of others. The words we use in the present are never solely ours, but are tied to the voices and the contexts in which they previously have been uttered. According to Bakhtin (1981), "Our ideological development is just such an intense struggle within us for hegemony among various available and ideological points of view, approaches, directions and values. The semantic structure of an internally persuasive discourse is not *finite*, it is *open*; in each of the new contexts that dialogize it, this discourse is able to reveal even newer *ways to mean*" (p. 346).

It helps to think about the multiple meanings and historical legacy of terms such as *racism* or *multicultural education*. Since an utterance can be understood only if its relationship to other utterances is understood, no words stand outside of time or context. Instead they are alive in "an intense interaction and struggle between one's own and another's word, a process in which they oppose or dialogically interanimate each other" (Bakhtin, 1981, p. 354). Human consciousness has at its very roots dialogue, within an individual and in interaction with others.

Vygotsky's and Bakhtin's ideas about human consciousness as expressed through the social use of language, though not exactly the same, both show how people are intimately connected through language. People's words, utterances, and thoughts are tied to their sociocultural ideologies (Bakhtin, 1986), but through dialogue and mediation they may acquire new language tools to expand their thinking, leading them to action for change (Freire, 1970/1987). A Vygotskian (1934/1986) interpretation extends this notion: "Thought is not merely expressed in words; it comes into existence through them" (p. 218).

It becomes clear that people's thoughts on what they read are part of a dialogic process—even if verbalized as inner speech for oneself using language that is connected to others only through usage across time and space. Through the transformation of thought into words, the thought is itself transformed. Thus, there is potential for a person's thinking to be fundamentally changed—perhaps expanded in its understanding of the complexity of many aspects of life—through response to literature within a social atmosphere.

But how can we as teachers create spaces for dialogue that engages us and our students in discussions of multicultural literature in multidimensional ways? One option is Freirean dialogue (Freire, 1970/1987; Freire & Macedo, 1996). Such dialogue includes conversation centered on the sharing of individual experiences, but it moves beyond the personal psychological to a focus on reflection and action for political, social, and individual change. It blurs the dichotomous boundaries often ascribed to Rosenblatt's (1995) efferent/aesthetic distinction, creating a reading and response zone in which personal, social, reflective, aesthetic, critical, and action-oriented responses can interact and overlap. Dialogue is by no means a cure-all for the problems of the world, nor does it always feel safe (Ellsworth, 1989). However, as Freire (1970/1987) stresses, "Only dialogue, which requires critical thinking, is also capable of generating critical thinking. Without dialogue there is no communication, and without communication there can be no true education" (p. 81). Delpit (1995) agrees, calling for educators to find ways to include all learners in a process of creating emancipatory knowledge through dialogue, honestly shared and heard.

AN EXAMPLE OF THE POWER OF DIALOGUE

An example of dialogue in response to *The Friendship* (Taylor, 1987) may help to clarify these points. In the book, one event in the white-owned general store marks a turning point in the lives of the elderly African American Tom Bee and the four African American children from the Logan family (a family that populates several of Taylor's books). During the five discussion days, the four girls shared feelings of connection, isolation, and fear as they developed an ever deeper awareness of the racist implications the author included in this book set in rural Mississippi in the 1930s.

Tamika, Jasmine, Carmen, and Nicole revealed personal reactions to the story and the characters, and they added layers of meaning and understanding as they discussed and relied on each other, on me, and on the story text for support. On the first day, Tamika described feeling connected to the characters. She could see herself in Stacey, the older brother, "because I take up for my little brother and don't like when people fuss at him." When she read out loud about the threats and abuse of the white people in the store (e.g., calling the six-year-old "dirty" and threatening to chop his "dirty" hands off after he touched the display case), Tamika embellished without pausing: "I think these people who was at the store, um, just 'cause they ain't like their family, I don't think they have a right to be mean to that little six-year-old boy." Recording possible discussion topics in writing before group, Tamika exhibited empathy and a clear conception of fairness: "Why did they do that boy like that? He did not have to fuss at him." She later added, "I felt sorry for the little boy." The injustice the characters suffered was felt by Tamika personally:

Um, when that, um, man was fussing at that little boy, the brother he looked over there and tried to see who it was . . . his brother ran over there to him

and . . . and his brother was behind him like this and he put his hands behind his back and, um, they just wanted to get that headache medicine and
get out of the store. And he didn't want his brother like to get fussed at. I
don't think he, I think that hurt his feelings, too.

Asked why she thought the man was fussing at the boy, Tamika explained:

It's just because he had his hand on the, um, the glass and he say he had dirty
hands and that little boy say, "No I'm clean. My hand's not dirty" And . . . the
man he hadn't had to get all over him, . . . he could'a said it in a nice way. He
ain't had to said it in no mean, like, um, "Your hands, your skin is black as
dirt." He hadn't said that. He could'a said, um, um, "Could you go wash your
hands?" or something. I don't know.

Despite the intensity of her personal and emotional connection to the
character, Tamika remained outside the novel's sociohistorical context and
accepted the racist remarks as truth. Through dialogic interaction that engaged fully with Tamika's response, however, the reason for the men's abu-
sive behavior came to light as the girls discovered together, with capable
peer and teacher input, that the men were white and that "back then they
didn't, didn't like black people" (Carmen). I prompted them to think back
on Tamika's question by asking, "Why do you think the man said that like
that?" After discussing whether the storeowner's sons were white or black,
deciding they "might be white, I don't know" (Tamika), Nicole referred
back to Little Man, the six-year-old, and to textual clues. She emphasized
the child's strength and stamina:

Nicole: He took up for him. He took up for hisself, too—the little boy in the
story.

Karla: Oh, yeah, tell me about that Nicole.

Nicole: Um, . . . you know, most . . . six-year-olds like'll cry or run somewhere,
. . . but he just stand there and said, "My hands ain't clean" and so—

Tamika: He said, "My hands *is* clean"

Nicole: I mean, yeah, "My hands is clean."

Two days later the girls returned to their confusion over the men's intentions when Nicole, Tamika, and Jasmine joined Carmen in her assessment
that racism was behind the men's actions.

As shown here (and through additional data excerpts throughout the following sections), the girls used dialogue to expand on immediate reactions
and confusions as they read, using personal, social, and group knowledge
as they made intertextual connections to films depicting racist violence and
intercontextual connections to historical events that highlighted aspects of

their evocations. They moved from the text as they made personal and societal extratextual connections to their life experiences and to the fear their discussion aroused. These responses were important parts of their evocations as individuals and as a group. Any of these response modes in isolation would have decreased the richness of their transactions.

TAKING A CRITICAL LITERACY PERSPECTIVE WITHIN A RESPONSE DEVELOPMENT ZONE

A critical literacy perspective is a third component essential to the RDZ construct—connecting the need for dialogue and for a zone in which learning develops with capable peers. From a critical theory perspective, people are to some extent products of the social and economic institutions within which they have matured (Apple, 1990; Shannon, 1995). This is especially relevant for children coming of age in what Omi and Winant (1994) describe as a mood of "social meanness" in U.S. society (p. 113) that is both an "explicit revitalization of the racist ideologies of the past" (p. 114) and a rearticulation of race and racism that "often makes use of racial themes as a framework by which to comprehend major problems" (p. 115). Taxel (1997) was alarmed at students' willingness "to publicly articulate racist and sexist sentiments" (p. 419). In such a climate, it becomes easy to see how debates over multiculturalism are waged with "a ferocity, a self-righteousness, and a mean-spiritedness" (p. 418) in attempts to reaffirm a Eurocentric, male-dominated focus.

A critical literacy education provides teachers and students with tools (e.g., dialogue) they can use to reconstruct certain racist, sexist, or classist assumptions that many may accept as givens. The essence of a critical approach is that questions are the most effective tools for change and weapons against ignorance and injustice (Shannon, 1995). It is through questioning that people begin to see how past and present inequalities are sustained and how future ones are created. Contradictions are more easily revealed, and doors are opened for hope. Recall Delpit's (1995) call for engaging all learners in the creation of emancipatory knowledge through dialogue, honestly shared and heard. One way for this dialogue to begin is in response to thought-provoking, issue-rich literature.

One argument for critical literacy and dialogue is that intellectual and emotional growth is encouraged through the sharing of ideas (Freire & Macedo, 1996; Greene, 1996). The key is for the sharing to be done in ways that do not impose, keeping in mind that silence and the withholding of alternative viewpoints can be exceptionally powerful forms of manipulation and imposition (Freire 1970/1987; Weiler, 1988). Children need to be taught new ways to respond to literature and to discuss in a group. They must be "provided with the tools for weighing the various images of life" that books present to them (Rosenblatt, 1995, p. 251).

Critical literacy theorists have been accused of politicizing schooling and knowledge acquisition. Arguing forcefully that education is not neutral, Apple (1990) counters that "until we take seriously the extent to which education is caught up in the real world of shifting and unequal power relations, we will be living in a world divorced from reality" (p. viii). Williams's (1989) concept of a "selective tradition" delineates how, from any larger knowledge base, "certain meanings and practices are selected for emphasis and certain other meanings and practices are neglected or excluded" (p. 58). Power and privilege are played out in what and how educators teach as well as in what and whose knowledge counts as valuable. These pieces of history and knowledge are then transmitted as the only acceptable reality. Shannon (1995) writes:

> Perhaps the injustices in our lives continue unabated because too many Americans have constructed identities that accept the impositions of racial, gender, and social class biases, competitiveness, and war as facts of life without stopping to ask why things are the way they are, who benefits from these conditions, and how we can make them more equitable. Critical literacy education, then, is not a politicized imposition that young and old must accept. Rather, it is a tool they can use to deconstruct the walls that separate the few who can build mansions from the many who can build only dreams. (pp. 123–124)

This quote is a reminder that knowledge and the curiosity to pursue it are powerful tools. Simply not using them because one does not know how, is not aware of their existence, or is afraid of getting hurt in the process of reconstructing new realities does not alter the inequities one faces. As Glenn-Paul (1997) states: "In my mind, some of these criticisms are a result of society's discomfort with acknowledging difference and discussing issues of race, class, and gender" (p. 274). Morrison (1992) argues: "a criticism that needs to insist that literature is not only 'universal' but also 'race-free' risks lobotomizing that literature and diminishes both the art and the artist" (p. 274). These theorists challenge views that there is a natural way to read or that pleasure is separate from and preferable to honest inquiry.

Reading is a learned behavior. Children learn about reading from observing and interacting with older children and adults (see, e.g., Purcell-Gates, 1995; Smith, 1988). From an early age, they are an audience for the texts that are chosen for them in various ways by adults, either through what is purchased or borrowed, what is available and accessible in the home, and what is written, published, or carried in bookstores. In addition, when children are read to, their attention is focused on the text and the interaction by the reader's implicit and explicit expectations. Naively assuming that learning to read is a natural or neutral process does not negate the influence of sociocultural factors. Simply refusing to attend to particular signs in books and in the world does not minimize their import (Glenn-Paul, 1997; Hade, 1997).

I am not encouraging a text-based view of response that focuses on singular meaning or hidden messages that a reader must correctly ferret out. Nor would I suggest that educators, in adopting a critical literacy perspective, should attempt to force children to adopt particular ideological stances. Instead, I emphasize an interpretative reader-based approach. Reading is about "interpreting certain signs with which we have a relationship that includes experience, culture, and value" (Hade, 1997, p. 240). Race, class, and gender are, in society as it is currently constructed in the United States, "signs to be interpreted" (p. 241). Refusing to make this explicit does not erase these signs from an individual or collective consciousness. Only by opening these constructs up to dialogue can people create opportunities to wrestle with their complexities.

TAKING A CRITICAL LITERACY
APPROACH IN A LITERATURE DISCUSSION

In the midst of an intense and frightening discussion of the Ku Klux Klan, white racism, and questions about why such hatred existed, Tamika excitedly proclaimed: "I got something to say," adding when the others did not yield the floor, "I gotta go next" and "Mine ain't no story."

Tamika: It's about Barbie dolls!

Nicole: Go.

Jasmine: Barbie dolls. [Jasmine laughs. All are smiling.]

Tamika: OK, when you know you look at a [catalog] . . . and Barbie dolls, white folks' Barbie dolls, they be on the big side. They're big, be on the front.

Nicole: And the little black dolls—

Tamika: And black dolls be in a little box on the side. And I don't like that.

Karla: I noticed that, too.

Nicole: Um-hm.

Karla: I also noticed that the black Barbie dolls look just like the white Barbie dolls, just with darker skin, but everything's exactly the same. It looked like the same person.

Jasmine: Yeah, only in a small box.

Tamika: And, I don't know.

Nicole: Yeah, but they have them in a little box, like, they have a big ol' box for the white ones, with the corners on it.

In an example of critical literacy, Tamika had connected our discussion of racism in a book, a film, and present-day life to racism in relation to the marketing of Barbie dolls. She verbalized her irritation at how the black Barbies were displayed less noticeably in catalogs (smaller, inset boxes). Nicole anticipated where Tamika was going with her comments and extended the observations of the catalog displays to the actual cartons for the dolls (smaller, less elaborate boxes). Jasmine also joined in. The girls connected toy marketing decisions to their experiences as girls of color. They used language as a tool both to share their experiences and to resist the metaphoric "packaging" of people of color that sends a racist message that they are of lesser value. This short but powerful data excerpt connects clearly the power of dialogue, of space for response development, and of the value of critical literacy perspectives to expand our thinking.

Discussing literature from a critical literacy perspective is a distinct speech genre, and as Bakhtin (1986) wrote, the more people have control over and are comfortable with a variety of genres, the more flexibility and freedom they have at getting their meaning across and the more precisely they do so as well. It is not just a new way of speaking; it is also a pathway to new ways of thinking. A critical literacy education can provide a language of critique. A literary response framework that recognizes the power of a response development zone—or collective RDZs created through group interaction—can create a space for the use of that language to explore and question text and author, self and society. After creating an environment in which meaning is expressed, responded to, and valued—be it oral, written, drawn, or gestured—"the teacher [or another student] then seeks to create a situation in which the student becomes aware of possible alternative interpretations and responses and is led to examine further both his own reactions and the text itself" (Rosenblatt, 1995, p. 214).

GENRES OF RESPONSE TO LITERATURE: ADDING THE NEXT LAYER TO THE RDZ

Connecting zones of proximal development, dialogue, and critical literacy perspectives with reader response theories is a short step. As a female high school student quoted in Miller (1998) states: "I think hate starts with not listening to people. I never think of myself as hating, but sometimes I'm too concerned with myself to really listen to other people" (p. 22). This statement accentuates the extent to which listening involves hearing the other voices in dialogue, in literature discussions, and in books. Reading involves listening to authors and characters (Rabinowitz & Smith, 1998) and to one's own inner speech or thoughts for oneself (Vygotsky, 1934/1986). If readers limit the voices to which they will listen, they limit the intensity of their response to literature, to themselves, to their fellow humans, and to their world.

In the field of reader response, debates have arisen over the question of what should be privileged: the personal and the emotional, the textual or the contextual, authorial readings or a resistance to that authority. Because of these tensions, reader response theory is clearly "not a unified critical position" (Thompkins, 1980, p. ix). Beach (1993) differentiated between textual, experiential, social, psychological, and cultural perspectives. Cai (1997) discussed uniactional, interactional, and transactional response theories, describing a range from reader-focused to text-focused views and from views of readers and texts as distinct bodies in interaction to views of them as united within a transactional evocation.

HOW IS READER RESPONSE CONCEPTUALIZED WITHIN AN RDZ?

The RDZ theoretical construct envisions a blurring of boundaries in reader response. When examining children's responses to books, it becomes clear that too narrow a focus on any one response mode can limit a reader's response repertoire. When connecting response to multicultural literature, texts that are many times resisted on a variety of levels, it is helpful to envision a coming together of reader, author, text, and context in such a way that responses constructed from a number of vantage points are encouraged, shared, and built upon from a nonhierarchical standpoint. Authorial readings, personal emotions and memories, and textual, intertextual, and extratextual interpretations can be woven into a framework that encourages as much diversity in response as in literature itself.

The purpose is neither to ignore experiential or psychological aspects of response nor to wallow in egocentric evocations. Neither is the goal to find the author's meaning any more than to ignore the creative power behind the words on the page. Similarly, initial response is not a terminal product of a transaction, but a starting point that can be enriched by individual reflection and by the perspectives of others. Response is a careful process of evocation and reflection. It includes an attempt to see through the eyes of authors and characters in very different lived situations from the reader's own, as well as an examination of one's own line of vision. There is a balance to be reached across texts and over time. Situating response within a response development zone framework can help to create that balance.

Such spaces are ongoing learning zones in which reactions and responses can develop in complexity and become more multilayered understandings of self, other, and world.

A literature response group is a coming together of socially, historically, and culturally influenced individuals with varying development zones for reading comprehension, "response-ability" (Rubin, 1990, p. 5), discussion skills, knowledge of self and society, and other factors. Together, these individuals also have a collective response zone for talking about books. Each reader becomes an active participant in the construction of meaning by drawing on both textual and contextual information as well as her or his own prior knowledge and experiences, with the teacher and peers mediating learning in an environment that encourages shared knowledge and social interaction. Here Vygotsky's (1978) notions of learning as a social act are especially relevant: "learning awakens a variety of internal developmental processes that are able to operate only when the child is interacting with people in his environment and in cooperation with his peers" (p. 90).

Across the space of texts and time, the teacher's position is multifaceted—a thoughtful blend of teaching and openness to learning with children, of facilitating and participating, of providing support and of taking personal risks. As the responsible adult, the teacher becomes most critical when individual or group transactions move the students' discussions beyond their experiential or personal comfort zones. When story themes affect a child's sense of self or safety, again the teacher has a responsibility to provide realistic emotional and educational support.

Viewing response as existing within shifting, multifaceted RDZs—zones in which readers share personal and sociocultural revelations as well as textual and contextual responses in an effort to expand their consideration of how all readers are shaped by the world they inhabit and by what they read and how they in turn shape that reading and that world—supports the "need to examine how we read and how we teach children to read" and helps children "examine how an author uses race (or class or gender) to mean" (Hade, 1997, p. 243). Rosenblatt (1995) states: "Both from the view of literary criticism and from the point of view of preparation for actual living, [a reader] should be stimulated to evaluate the ethical and social implications of the images of life encountered through literature" (p. 251). Readers infuse the signs on the page with life, creating meaning by bringing knowledge and experiences to the words and by attending to certain signs and not others. Teachers and students can expand on these choices in ways that neither detract from a meaningful transaction nor dictate a correct response, but that deepen knowledge and enhance the reading. Readers can build on initial reactions by discussing responses, by expanding their understanding of the role of context in shaping meaning (both text world context and transactional setting), and by developing a willingness to share even potentially disturbing reactions and to respond thoughtfully to those of others.

Much that is written on response to literature and the benefits of talk in the classroom draws on Vygotsky's theories (e.g., Daniels, 1994; Galda, 1988; Gambrell & Almasi, 1996; McMahon, Raphael, Goatley, & Pardo, 1997; Villaume, Worden, Williams, Hopkins, & Rosenblatt, 1994). Less discussed is how his ideas connect with teaching from a critical multicultural perspective, especially regarding frank discussions in schools about persistent racism in society and systemic inequities that pervade many institutions, including education (Möller, 2001). Other response researchers combine a focus on aesthetic and critical literacy but do so outside of an explicit Vygtoskian framework. McGinley and colleagues (1997) suggest that students need opportunities to engage in literacy activities that relate to their lives and also to realize "that stories can be a means of personal and social exploration and reflection—an imaginative vehicle for questioning, shaping, responding, and participating in the world" (p. 43). Samway and Whang (1996) describe an attempt to foster classroom discussions that might "counter the prevailing mood in the nation, one of hostility toward others who do not share one's race, language, culture, or social standing" (p. 100). Their diverse class frequently discussed prejudice and racism. During one book discussion, a student admitted, "I think I might have been a little bit racist before coming to Hawthorne" (p. 115). The literature discussions had enabled him to grow toward a better understanding of others, of himself, and of the concept of racism in his world. Beach (1997) agrees that literature can have "life transforming functions" but cautions that "an awareness of how one's own ideological stance shapes the meaning of one's experience with literature" (p. 83) is an essential component.

Response extends beyond the social context and into how that context has shaped each person's views. Enciso (1997) writes of the need to recognize not only the "social, political, and cultural context in which literature is produced but also the complex, intertextual, identity, and power relations that are parts of the reader's interpretation of the literature" (p. 22). She led a discussion of Spinelli's *Maniac Magee* (1990) with a group of "predominantly European American" fourth- and fifth-graders (Enciso, 1997, p. 27). In this setting, race was often overlooked or sidelined. An African American boy was effectively silenced when he upheld the humanity of Mars Bar, one of the black characters. Because of the dynamics and ideological focus of the group, racism was briefly acknowledged, but it either became a joking matter or was considered inconsequential and quickly dropped.

In commenting on Boyd's (1997) work with a cross-aged literacy program, Alvermann (1997) was interested in how participants "interpret[ed] texts on the basis of the meaning available to them in a given place and time"— meanings influenced by factors such as "one's values, beliefs, race, class, and

gender" (p. 182). In order to "direct their attention toward how the availability of different meanings for a text will influence how they interpret the
text" (p. 182), Alvermann wanted to explore how the children connected
current social issues or events with the historical scene they were reading.

Just as Delpit (1995) argued for a more critical approach to progressive
theories of education, so did Edelsky (1994) make it clear that many "progressive" theories and practices, including reader response and transactional theory, "can as easily support avoiding looking at white privilege, for
example, as they support looking at it" (p. 254). Educating "for democracy"
(p. 254) would entail retheorizing language education and addressing the
systemic nature of racial, social, and gender-related privilege and injustice.
Where some reader response theorists talk about "accepting children's plau-
sible interpretations of literature," Edelsky wants to hear "talk about the positions people are put in by texts, what premises we're positioned to accept,
and how we accept or resist those" (p. 255). In practice and theory, educators need to move from "being satisfied with personal responses to literature, with identifying what resonates with self and family" (p. 256) to starting with those and encouraging "a sustained look at the social issues that
are suggested by so many pieces of literature and that languish unexamined
in personal responses" (p. 256).

This requires awareness, stamina, and effort. It requires a desire to read and
a hope for a more just future. Maintaining it also requires an expanded notion of pleasurable, aesthetic responses to literature that includes transactions
and discussions that are not always safe or free of pain—for students or their
teachers, who must also enter into the individual and group transactions as
learners and be open to the same potential joys and discomforts, risks and
benefits of developing new knowledge and taking new perspectives.

DEMONSTRATING A MULTIFACETED
READER RESPONSE IN ACTION

When the group discussing *The Friendship* began connecting issues of racism
in the past to their present lives and experiences, Jasmine was the most
naive in her understanding of the Ku Klux Klan and its acts of hatred and
violence. This exchange occurred after a particularly intense discussion in
which Jasmine asked, "Who, who is Que Klux? Who, who, who is that people?" and her peers responded by describing Klan attire and some activities.

Jasmine: I heard, I heard it, I watched it on a movie called A Time to Kill. And
I saw these people that stuck a cross in these people's yard and burnt the cross
and then they did all this stuff. I, I didn't [silent; fearful expression].

Karla: That's one thing some Klan people do.

Jasmine: I know, but ain't know about them until now y'all told me. And, um, I'm afraid now they gonna come to my house.

Karla: They're not gonna come to your house, honey, no. The thing, Klan people don't just not like black people. They, some of them don't like women.

Nicole: Well, back then they did do it.

Karla: Some of them don't like Jewish people . . . Some . . . don't like Hispanics—

Nicole: Back then, they used to do! Come to people's houses!

Though Jasmine had seen a movie with related racial hatred and violence, she had not connected that knowledge to the Klan or to her present reality as a person of color. She shared a personal fear that the Klan would come to her home—a focused fear of concrete actions that Tamika and Nicole shared. Fearful myself that this was too much for the girls, my instinct to comfort Jasmine, to move her from the focus of Klan hatred, was as automatic as my knowledge that the dangers of racism are still all too real. Though Jasmine seemed soothed, Nicole challenged that shred of safety I attempted to hold out. After a few conversational turns, however, Nicole sought that same minimal comfort despite her personal experience that horrible things were possible:

Nicole: They cain't uh, they cain't, uh, do that stuff no more, like burn crosses in your yard, no more . . . They cain't do that no more. [pause] Can they?

Karla: It's against the law.

Jasmine: And you mean they, they—

Tamika: They can write on your windows, and they spray on your windows, like "We come to kill you."

Jasmine: You mean they, they're—

Tamika: I swear they did that. They showed that on the news.

Jasmine: You, mean, they are arresting them if they, um, they come to your house?

Tamika: They put tissue all in you yard and on your trees.

I substituted my previous false comfort for the fact that at least laws had changed. The girls felt more personally, however, that their safety could indeed be threatened. Nicole told her story:

Nicole: OK, like, it was like Halloween night, right. And like, my grandma and them, they stay . . . on the other road, . . . in her row of houses, and they stay right there. The Ku Klux Klan like behind them, on the other road. And it be

Halloween . . . we, um, me and my cousins and them, we were walking the streets, like, and then, all of the . . . you know them . . . ?

Karla: Army jeep things, uh-huh.

Nicole: You know, you know them things, you know.

Tamika: They started hollering out the windows, then.

Nicole: Yeah, and they were shooting birds and stuff, and then they throw some, they throw some tomatoes, and, at my grandma's house. They throw some tomatoes, some tissue all in her yard in everything. And we would go. We would hide around that little old car . . .

Tamika: [So] they wouldn't kill you?

Nicole: We was scared.

Karla: That was pretty scary. I'll bet that was scary.

Tamika: Who with you?

Nicole: Um-hm. [to Karla] Huh? [to Tamika]

Tamika: Who with you?

Nicole: My, my cousin. And, they put, and they put "Dead" in the middle of the street right there, with the spray paint.

After this exchange, Jasmine seemed especially afraid. I spoke with her during and after our group and suggested she talk with her parents. The next day, she shared that conversation:

Jasmine: Yesterday, . . . I had told my [dad], "Do you know who the Kru Klux Klan is?" And he said, "Yeah." And then I said "I do, too. I ain't know who they was at first." He said, "Who are they then?" And I said, "They these people that wear these pointy hats and [they] string them up." And he said, "Yeah." And I said, um, "Do they still come around here?" He said, "Yeah." And I said, "I thought they couldn't come here . . . any more?" He said, "They still come, though." I said, "I hope they don't come to my house." And then he said, . . . "Don't worry, . . . nobody, no Kru Klux Klan come to our house. They had to get through me first." And the puppies, which . . . going to be big by that time.

Karla: So your dad is talking about how there really is Klan still today.

Jasmine: Uh-huh. And my mama said that they was these bad people that go around everywhere trying to hurt people. And they have, carry spray paints and stuff. And my brother said he know who they are and he said he forgot who they were. And I told him and he said, "Oh, yeah, I remember." And I don't know if he knew really. I don't know.

Discussing this difficult topic gave the girls new insight into the characters in the book—for though the Klan is never mentioned in this text, it was clearly a factor for many African Americans in Mississippi in the 1930s. It also provided an outlet for the girls to discuss personal fears and encounters with present-day racist hatred. Expressing understanding and emotions from their vantage point as children of color, the girls went on to connect events from the real life of a friend and from the movie they had discussed (*A Time to Kill*) with the fears of characters in the historical text. Previously Jasmine had not made such a personal connection to the acts of violence the girls had discussed. The new connections intensified her transaction, creating both a more textually based interpretation of the characters' fears and a more intensely personal response based in part on her identity as a child of color. Jasmine stated she had begun comparing the story with her life, and Tamika developed an even deeper sympathetic connection to the characters: "I hate when they treat them boy like that. I felt sorry for Mr. Tom Bee. Now, I did, I feel real sorry now."

The girls connected to the characters' situations in ways I could not—in part because, as Tamika put it, "They [the Klan] ain't . . . gonna' get you 'cause you white." Though I guided the girls in their discussion at times, they were in many ways more capable peers for me—especially as they shared the extent to which the long arm of racism reached out of the historical book's narrative and touched their lives and fears in the present.

CONCEPT DEVELOPMENT: THE FINAL COMPONENT OF A RESPONSE DEVELOPMENT ZONE

Bruner (1986) describes a socially based "tool kit" that each person has, containing "concepts and ideas and theories that permit one to get to higher ground mentally." Key to this mental development is "consciousness armed with concepts and the language for forming and transforming them" (p. 73). Participation in an RDZ that attends to cultural life and social justice expands the range of interactions between peers and the responsibilities of a teacher as mediator, as mentor, and as learner. The dialogue that ensues requires that all learn to interpret the sign systems that mediate understandings of world, other, and self within a sociocultural context and to use the tools that highly developed communicative and cognitive functions of language provide. These signs and tools include written and oral language as well as visual (e.g., art) and kinesthetic signs (e.g., behavior). It is through these signs and tools that concepts are created and developed—concepts that allow us to organize our thinking and better understand our world.

HOW DOES CONCEPT DEVELOPMENT FIT IN THE RDZ?

Distinguishing between complexes, pseudo-concepts, and concepts, Vygotsky (1934/1986) stresses that people do not achieve full-blown conceptual development from one event to the next. Instead they use speech (including discussion and inner speech) as the primary mediating tool as they move from thinking in complexes, characterized by concrete connections and subjective impressions, to acquiring abstract conceptual understanding. Vygotsky argues that "it is not only possible to teach children to use concepts, but that such 'interference' may influence favorably the development of concepts that have been formed by the student" (p. 152).

Just as difficult math or science concepts such as irrational numbers or gravity can be acquired with assistance, so too can critical sociocultural conceptualizations of justice and equity be learned through interaction with adults and peers. In their RDZs, teachers and students share interpretations, adding layers to their evocations of text, self, and the world and gaining access to multiple perspectives from which they can form and expand on their acquisition of concepts. Through this social interaction, intermental conceptual development toward a more socially egalitarian approach can be transferred to a learner's intramental plane and be transformed into new individual but socially connected knowledge. This is applicable to acquisition of difficult concepts such as *equity, diversity, racism,* and *injustice* as well as understanding the incredible variety of contextualized human responses to actual situations involving racism or injustice (see the extended dialogue example below of how the children's interconnected dialogue supports their acquisition of deeper understanding of the concept of *resistance* as they discuss Tom Bee's context-specific method of resisting racism while protecting the children in his care).

When read from a critical literacy perspective, "Children's literature can be a powerful, positive force in the lives of children. . . . It can make them conscious that there is more than one way of being normal" (Nodelman, 1996, p. 114). The key is to "discuss these matters with children, and to share our . . . attitudes with them" (p. 86), because what each of us considers "harmful" or "painful and confusing" for children will differ somewhat, and "ignorance is always likely to do more harm than knowledge" (p. 86). Knowledge *can* be painful and confusing. Teachers and parents must take care that adult preconceptions do not shut off inquiry. However, just allowing children to read a book is not enough. It can be irresponsible even.

DIALOGUE EXEMPLIFYING CONCEPT DEVELOPMENT IN ACTION

An extended example from the literature circle underscores the points made in this section about concept development intertwined with earlier discussion of key RDZ components of dialogue, critical literacy, and reader response. In our group, we shared passages we found moving or interesting by reading them aloud and then describing why we chose them. We also took time between group discussions to write down our thoughts or questions. In one instance when I asked if anyone wished to share, Tamika, who often used this space to raise thought-provoking issues, volunteered, sharing the scene in which Tom Bee attempts to buy sardines and uses the store-owner's first name. We had had multiple discussions about why the characters at times seemed to acquiesce to the storeowners' violent threats and racist remarks. After reading about Tom Bee's range of context-specific responses to the awful treatment, the following discussion took place.

Tamika: Now, I got something to say about Mr. Tom Bee. They act like this man too old to know what he's talking about, and like when he went to the store and he said he need four cans of sardines, and that man said, "You don't need no four cans of sardines."

Nicole: He's already got some fish.

Tamika: And um, and now, um, "You has some fish in your hand." And they don't know . . . what he need. They think he, and, um, Cassie . . . said "Mr. Tom Bee must be really brave to go, um, calling, um, what that boy's name, Mr. Dewberry and them daddy, and . . . she was like peeping in the door and stuff. And I think its only, when he would have got hurt she would'a did something. Mr. Tom Bee, I think . . . they act like he too old and stuff. If she, I think if they . . . would'a beat him up or something, uh, all them three men, I think, Cassie, and she would'a probably went and got them other kids and probably would'a help, helped fight.

Carmen: And he [Tom Bee] asked them for some candy canes. And then he, they were talking about him, and said that, "You don't need no candy canes because you don't got no teeth to eat with."

The girls were silent. To provide guidance, I asked, "What'd y'all think about that?"

Tamika: They act like he don't know what he be talking about!

Jasmine: I think he mean.

Tamika: Who's mean?

Jasmine: Mr. Tom Bee.

Nicole: I don't.

Jasmine: Well, some, when I was reading this it sounded like he was kind of yelling at them sort of.

Carmen: *They* are yelling at *him* . . .

Jasmine: Well, um, what I just know is, Mr. Tom Bee's kind of mean and old. He was talking about some candy canes and it was sort of like, I forgot.

Tamika: Mr. Tom Bee, I don't think he mean.

Jasmine: I read that last night when I had came home.

Tamika: I think he, . . . care for folk. I think, he might be old. I don't think he mean. I think he care for people. I don't know why they treat him like that. And I thought they thought he was too old to know what he talking about.

Jasmine: They say he—

Tamika: They probably think he so old that they can rule him.

Jasmine: They said that he had a . . . mean look in his eye and [unintelligible word].

Karla: Do you remember where that was in your book? Can you find it?

Jasmine: I think so.

Karla: What about you, Nicole? What did you notice?

Nicole: That, . . . I feel that, um, well, he is kind of, he is nice though, to them, though, and stuff . . . They had no business. I don't know.

The girls continued to debate Tom Bee's supposed meanness and his age as reasons for the mistreatment. Though helping each other make meaning, they were still unsure as to why Tom Bee was treated so badly. Not basing the negativity as having to do with the Wallaces' intense racism and not yet fully appreciating the dangerous realities Tom Bee and the children were facing, Tamika was confused and frustrated at the unfairness of the situation and at Tom Bee's apparent refusal to stand up for himself. Before coming to group this day, Tamika had written two questions she wanted to discuss: "1. Why do Mr. Wallace think someone is going to respect him? 2. Why do Tom Bee let people rule him?" These questions addressed issues also raised by race theorists, such as why African Americans have so often been portrayed as having passively accepted their fate and not fought for their freedom and education despite all the knowledge to the contrary (Anderson, 1988; Obadele, 1995). As the next day's discussion developed, the girls for the first time voiced racism as behind the white men's treatment of Tom Bee and the children. Armed with a new interpretive framework for understanding the motives of the storeowner and his sons—an enhanced conceptual understanding of historical racism in the 1930s as exhibited by John Wallace and other white characters, and of resistance as demonstrated by the actions of Tom Bee—Tamika was ready to answer her own questions:

Tamika: I think Tom Bee didn't worry about nothing. I think he was like Mr. Martin Luther King . . . He don't worry about nothing nobody say. When they, when they said something to him, he ain't said nothing back, he just went on about his little business.

Nicole: Uh-huh.

Tamika: He called the father in there.

Nicole: And he told the, like, he—

Tamika: I was talking, Nicole.

Nicole: Like he told that little boy not, not to worry about nothing and stuff . . .

Carmen: He, I think he was just standing up for his rights. [Jasmine nods.] . . .

Tamika: I, I, think he act like Mr. Martin Luther King. He . . . said, he don't worry about nothing nobody say. And he tell them children not to worry about nothing nobody say. And he tell them what true and what not true. And, um, you know, Martin Luther King had four children, too, so he got little four peoples.

By connecting Tom Bee to Martin Luther King Jr., who was not mentioned in this text set in the 1930s, Tamika recognized the resistance inherent in Tom Bee's actions. Rather than continuing to view Tom Bee as someone who "lets people rule him," the girls commented on how he stood up to the storeowner, demanding his rights to purchase what he wished and to call the storeowner by his first name as he had been promised. Tom Bee also took care of children, protecting them from harm even as he put himself in danger by facing down the angry racist men. This story and the group's dialogue provided the girls with a new way to interpret language and behavior that had previously been confusing and that at times had led the girls to blame Tom Bee or the Logan children for the frightening events. They came to new realizations that many African Americans stood up for justice even in the face of threats of physical pain and death and that others resisted in less obvious ways, enduring ridicule and hardships in order to protect the community's children from the very real dangers of white racism.

Though not a guarantee that this will impact other experiences with literature and life, it is a critical step. Up to this point in our discussion, textual clues about the racism of the white storeowner and his sons had been overlooked and their hateful remarks accepted as fact. Ignoring the theme of racism contradicted many goals for including such a book in a multicultural curriculum. However, I had not pushed the issue until Tamika's self-chosen passage and written discussion questions provided an opportunity to lead with a questioning approach—not dictating the response, but providing space for a deeper understanding to be evoked through the social dialogue in the group.

ENGAGING TEACHERS AND STUDENTS IN RDZ'S: ISSUES OF TRUST AND SAFETY

The kind of interaction required to create a proactive RDZ needs to be taught. Children and teachers who are used to answering known-answer questions in raised-hand turns, whether in student-led or teacher-led groups, will need to learn new strategies to accommodate more spontaneous turn-taking and focused inclusion of all peers that moves past a more capable/less capable dichotomy (see Möller, 2004/2005, for an extended discussion of this aspect). Safety and trust are essential since the RDZ includes the sharing of and building on alternative and discrepant responses, a critical literacy focus, and dialogue that addresses such probing questions as "Why do we believe what we believe?" and "How much of what we believe is true?" (Miller, 1998, p. 17).

Multilayered responses to issues such as diversity, society, history, and injustice often extend the boundaries of what is considered acceptable instructional content for school, especially for elementary students. A sense of safety is required for children to share aspects of their lives that they feel make them different or vulnerable to teasing by their peers. In our discussions of *The Friendship*, Jasmine developed this sense of safety over time by having her evocations listened to and respected while also being encouraged by her peers and her teacher to expand on her reactions. Tamika at one point speculated as to why Jeremy, a white character who shyly attempts to bridge the barriers of racism and violence reinforced by his relatives, was so reticent.

Tamika: I think that Jeremy, he shy and he's the only white boy playing with black children.

Jasmine: That's how I feel when I go to church. I go to a white church.

Karla: You go to a white church?

Jasmine: Everybody white.

Karla: And you feel how?

Jasmine: I feel weird.

Karla: Why is that?

Nicole: You go to a white church?

Jasmine: Uh-huh [to Nicole]. I feel weird 'cause, uh, all these people are white and I'm black and I'm the only black, black person in—

Tamika: Your mom and dad.

Jasmine: I know.

Carmen: Have you ever made friends there?

Jasmine: Uh, yeah, everybody my friend there.

This was the first time the girls mentioned racial differences as a reason for Jeremy's reticence.

Jasmine turned the textual connection from the impersonal to the personal, sharing information she felt made her vulnerable: "I'm afraid people gonna pick on me so that's why I don't talk about church." After our responsive questioning and dialogue, however, Jasmine developed her revelation into an extended personal narrative. Nicole connected to Jasmine's narrative, expressing surprise: "I'm surprised 'cause we don't go to no white church. I ain't know that she was going." Nicole also shared her preferences: "I ain't never been to no white church and I've been in the black part, and I know if I go to white folks' church I won't like it. I probably would like that how they talk and their speech and stuff, but I don't know, 'cause I wouldn't like it 'cause I'm the only black person." This prompted an extended discussion about their churches that ended with a comparison of levels of racial integration. Carmen explained, "I go to a black church and I'm not the only one there who's white." Nicole responded, "I know. It be some white folks at some black churches." Tamika joined in, exclaiming, "I go to a all black-folks church . . . Not all black folks, but . . . it ain't nothing but about one set of white folks there. That all I see."

Exposing herself by introducing the topic of church attendance, Jasmine took a risk that led to dialogue. By discussing segregation in churches and reasons for their discomfort at attending churches in which they are in the minority, the girls developed new understanding of Jeremy's shyness and of their own need for strong cultural and community ties to their churches.

Just as children and adults do not naturally read (Shannon, 1995), it cannot be assumed they will naturally interact openly and productively in groups when discussing socially conscious literature. McMahon (1997) describes the book club program as a place where "No student personally attacks another" (p. 55) but frankly states that this does not happen without carefully planned instruction on how to converse productively in a group discussion about literature. She also emphasizes that the book club did not simply encourage "more student talk but a high quality of student discourse related to texts" (p. 91). Such dialogue is not an automatic result of opening classrooms up to discussion, as others have discovered (e.g., Allen et al., 2003; Lensmire, 1993; Villaume et al., 1994). Dialogue that relates life to text and text to life and that asks hard questions about economic equity and social injustice must often be consciously taught, woven into the fabric of the classroom, with instruction leading development through discussion.

Along with the position of teacher comes power that must be acknowledged openly and exhibited by the educator or other adult (Delpit, 1995; Shannon, 1995). This is inevitable and carries with it a great responsibility. However, one's authority need not rest on the control of predetermined knowledge. Work in an RDZ can be genuine and open despite differences in power if educators "are willing to admit that we and our students are all people, and that as people, we are incomplete and contradictory in both our beliefs and actions" (Shannon, 1995, p. 107). It can be meaningful if both teachers and students are willing or able to discuss injustices openly (Delpit, 1995) with each other's help and guidance, leading through a questioning approach. It can be honest if teachers and students take time to get to know one another and to trust each other enough to risk honesty.

In our group, it took time to create this trust. Before we started reading *The Friendship*, for example, Tamika expressed her distrust readily: "I believe ya'll are going to try to get us held back. I believe that's why we're getting to go out of this class." By the end of our discussions, however, it was Tamika who asked to share her final response writing first and who asked us to read another book together as a group—one from her favorite American Girls series. Tamika had brought her entire collection of Addy books, supplemented by volumes that were available in her classroom: "This is my favorite book, y'all. It's called Meet Addy . . . I goin' to tell y'all about it." Tamika read the back cover of *Meet Addy* (Porter, 1993), told us in her own words about the book, introduced us to all the characters, shared her negative personal feelings toward the "Master," and read the first page out loud with relish.

Advocating the use of dialogue, response, peer interaction, and critical literacy in the ways I have discussed leads back to my initial questions about how teachers and students explore beyond initial reactions, create spaces where they feel safe enough to engage in critical reflection of social issues, and engage in content-based literary discussions that do not revert to reliance on the teacher as the sole source of knowledge. Once it is recognized that both adults and children learn within their ever changing response development zones, the importance of the teacher's choices and actions becomes clear. Within the constraints of their zones, teachers function as more capable tutors, explicitly at times, but in other instances by creating opportunities in which all students can serve as more capable peers (Möller, 2002; Möller, 2004/2005).

As Delpit (1995) states, "One of the most difficult tasks we face as human beings is communicating meaning across our individual differences, a task confounded immeasurably when we attempt to communicate across social lines, racial lines, cultural lines, or lines of unequal power" (p. 66). Teachers who teach from a culturally relevant perspective (Ladson-Billings, 1994) can foster this communication of meaning by acknowledging both their own and students' responsibilities for learning and by believing their students to be capable of excellence. These teachers feel connected to their students and the community and "help students make connections between their local, national, racial, cultural, and global identities" (p. 25). They view knowledge as "continuously re-created, recycled, and shared by teachers and students alike" (p. 25) and maintain a critical perspective on the curricular content they teach. They do not expect children to enter their classrooms able to connect their knowledge and skills to new experiences, but see their responsibility as helping them to do exactly that.

Freire and Macedo (1996) emphasize two critical features of dialogue: the promotion and maintenance of "epistemological curiosity" (p. 206), a curiosity to engage in an examination of knowledge, and the use of talk that demonstrates critical engagement. Students become apprentices in a new body of knowledge. Throughout the process, the concept of funds of knowledge (Moll & Greenberg, 1990) provides essential balance. It is part of the space in which the student is the recognized expert and the teacher the apprentice. A clear example is when the girls collaboratively shared their personally connected knowledge of Ku Klux Klan with me.

CONCLUSION

True to my belief in critical literacy, a questioning stance, there are no easy or final answers. I have attempted to lay out a theoretical framework—supported by examples from the research literature and from my work with Carmen, Jasmine, Nicole, and Tamika—that may offer educators a way to conceptualize response to literature as a zone for personal revelation, for textual and contextual consideration, and for consideration of how all readers—students and teachers—are shaped by the world they inhabit and by what they read and how they in turn shape that reading and that world. While it would be naive to assume that reading and discussing quality literature such as Mildred Taylor's work is the cure for modern society's ills, reading and sharing such texts can open the lines of communication between and within groups, prompting all to address issues that may have been ignored. Through the exchange of ideas on an interpersonal plane, there is an increased opportunity for conceptual growth that brings with it hope for new understandings and new directions toward social justice.

Belief in the power of literature emphasizes the need for future classroom-based research that builds on the theoretical conceptualization of a response development zone and on the work of educators whose social justice orientations and their own continual self-reflection make them exemplary models of ways for teachers and students to open up spaces for collectively enhanced response to literature. For example, we must be willing to examine prejudice in our own classrooms (e.g., Michalove, 1999) and to raise issues that might cause pain, dissent, even anger, in the hopes of moving to new levels of dialogue on racial injustice (e.g., Diaz-Gemmati, 1995) or self- and group-reflection on class privilege (e.g., Blackburn, 1999). We need more work such as the study by Brooks (2006) of urban youths' use of cultural knowledge and African American text features in creating literary meaning in response to African American literature. Brooks describes in detail the power of shared cultural knowledge as a tool in the development of sophisticated group responses to literature.

Despite the potential this research reveals for powerful discussions and personal growth to come out of honest dialogue in classrooms, it also illustrates how much is left to be done. The field of response to multicultural literature needs to know more about the kinds of conversations children have when they read and discuss books in which difficult social issues are both implicit and explicit. How do the children create both individual and collective response development zones, and how do they shift across time, experience, and context? Which aspects of the books do children reflect individually, and how are they helped by peers to extend this vision? How are they taught different ways of reading? In what ways does taking a reflective stance on social issues impact an aesthetic response to literature? What impact does this have on children's desire to read and learn? What do teachers do if or when students resist?

Another essential line of research would extend the response development zone to teaching, looking at the willingness and preparedness of educators to examine their own teaching and learning, to engage in the dialogue this essay encourages, and to risk being the less capable member of a discussion group. For example, how can teachers who are just beginning to look at racism in their own lives be aided in opening spaces in their classrooms for literature discussions on issues of equity and justices that may be outside their comfort zones? How can teachers who are ready to embark on such discussions move forward if they have little administrative support?

Though it would be foolhardy for anyone to claim to have achieved all these goals or the answers to these difficult questions, I am confident that through self-reflection and responsive practice educators can work with students within their individual and collective response development zones to encourage a variety of personally meaningful discussions focused on literature with social justice themes that will enhance their own and their students' awareness of critically important social issues and their interest in reading. I look forward to the possibilities these teachers embody.

NOTE

1. The research was part of a collaborative project on meeting the literacy needs of fifth-graders who were reading and writing significantly below grade level. All four girls were having difficulty with inferential comprehension and vocabulary, based on various assessment tools, the classroom teacher's professional observation, and the girls' own assessment. With the exception of Jasmine and Carmen, the girls rarely socialized with each other. Tamika and Nicole belonged to separate small circles of friends that were at times antagonistic toward each other and at other times

connected by common interests. Since it is not the purpose of this work to present the research study (see Möller & Allen, 2000), I provide contextualization as necessary with each illustrative excerpt.

REFERENCES

Adams, D. W. (1995). *Education for extinction: American Indians and the boarding school experience, 1875–1928.* Lawrence: University Press of Kansas.

Allen, J., Möller, K. J., & Stroup, D. (2003). "Is this some kind of soap opera?" A tale of two readers across four literature discussion contexts. *Reading, Writing Quarterly: Overcoming Learning Difficulties, 19,* 225–251.

Alvermann, D. E. (1997). Commentary. In S. I. McMahon & T. E. Raphael (Eds.), *The book club connection: Literacy learning and classroom talk* (pp. 182–183). New York: Teachers College Press.

Anderson, J. D. (1988). *The education of blacks in the South, 1860–1935.* Chapel Hill: University of North Carolina Press.

Apple, M. (1990). *Ideology and curriculum* (2nd ed.). New York: Routledge.

Ashton, P. (1996). The concept of activity. In L. Dixon-Kraus (Ed.), *Vygotsky in the classroom: Mediated literacy instruction and assessment* (pp. 111–124). White Plains, NY: Longman.

Bakhtin, M. (1981). *The dialogic imagination: Four essays by M. M. Bakhtin* (M. Holquist, Ed.; C. Emerson & M. Holquist, Trans.). Austin: University of Texas Press.

———. (1986). *Speech genres and other late essays* (V. W. McGee, Trans.). Austin: University of Texas Press.

Beach, R. (1993). *A teacher's introduction to reader-response theories.* Urbana, IL: National Council of Teachers of English.

———. (1997). Students' resistance to engagement with multicultural literature. In T. Rogers & A. Soter (Eds.), *Reading across cultures: Teaching literature in a diverse society* (pp. 69–94). New York: Teachers College Press.

Blackburn, M. (1999). Studying privilege in a middle school gifted class. In J. Allen (Ed.), *Class actions: Literacy education for a democratic society.* New York: Teachers College Press.

Boyd, F. (1997). The cross-aged literacy program: Preparing struggling adolescents for book club discussions. In S. I. McMahon & T. E. Raphael (Eds.), *The book club connection: Literacy learning and classroom talk* (pp. 162–181). New York: Teachers College Press.

Brooks, W. (2006). Reading representations of themselves: Urban youth use culture and African American textual features to develop literary understandings. *Reading Research Quarterly, 41,* 372–392.

Bruner, J. (1975). The ontogenesis of speech acts. *Journal of Child Language, 2,* 1–40.

———. (1986). *Actual minds, possible worlds* (pp. 70–78). Cambridge, MA: Harvard University Press.

Cai, M. (1997). Reader-response theory and the politics of multicultural literature. In T. Rogers & A. Soter (Eds.), *Reading across cultures: Teaching literature in a diverse society* (pp. 109–212). New York: Teachers College Press.

Daniels, H. (1994). *Literature circles: Voice and choice in the student-centered classroom.* York, ME: Stenhouse.

Delpit, L. (1995). *Other people's children: Cultural conflict in the classroom.* New York: New Press.

Diaz-Gemmati, G. (1995). . . . *And justice for all* (Occasional Paper No. 41). Berkeley: University of California, National Center for the Study of Writing.

Dyson, A. H. (1990). Weaving possibilities: Rethinking metaphors for early literacy development. *Reading Teacher, 44,* 202–213.

Edelsky, C. (1994). Education for democracy. *Language Arts, 71,* 252–257.

Ellsworth, E. (1989). Why doesn't this feel empowering? Working through the repressive myths of critical pedagogy. *Harvard Educational Review, 59,* 297–324.

Enciso, P. E. (1997). Negotiating the meaning of difference: Talking back to multicultural literature. In T. Rogers & A. Soter (Eds.), *Reading across cultures: Teaching literature in a diverse society* (pp. 13–41). New York: Teachers College Press.

Freire, P. (1987). *Pedagogy of the oppressed.* New York: Continuum. (Original work published 1970.)

Freire, P., & Macedo, D. (1996). A dialogue: Culture, language, and race. In P. Leistyna, A. Woodrum, & S. A. Sherblom (Eds.), *Breaking free: The transformative power of critical pedagogy* (pp. 199–228). Cambridge, MA: Harvard Educational Review.

Galda, L. (1988). Readers, texts, and contexts: A response-based view of literature in the classroom. *New Advocate, 1,* 92–102.

Gambrell, L. B., & Almasi, J. F. (Eds.). (1996). *Lively discussions! Fostering engaged reading.* Newark, DE: International Reading Association.

Glenn-Paul, D. (1997). Toward developing a multicultural perspective. In V. J. Harris (Ed.), *Using multiethnic literature in the K–8 classroom* (pp. 257–276). Norwood, MA: Christopher Gordon.

Greene, M. (1996). In search of a critical pedagogy. In P. Leistyna, A. Woodrum, & S. A. Sherblom (Eds.), *Breaking free: The transformative power of critical pedagogy* (pp. 13–30). Cambridge, MA: Harvard Educational Review.

Hade, D. D. (1997). Reading multiculturally. In V. J. Harris (Ed.), *Using multiethnic literature in the K–8 classroom* (pp. 233–256). Norwood, MA: Christopher Gordon.

Ladson-Billings, G. (1994). *The dreamkeepers: Successful teachers of African American children.* San Francisco: Jossey-Bass.

Lave, J., & Wenger, E. (1991). *Situated learning: Legitimate peripheral participation.* New York: Cambridge University Press.

Lensmire, T. (1993). Following the child, socioanalysis, and threats to community: Teacher response to children's texts. *Curriculum Inquiry, 23,* 265–299.

McGinley, W., Kamberelis, G., Mahoney, T., Madigan, D., Rybicki, V., & Oliver, J. (1997). Re-visioning reading and teaching literature through the lens of narrative theory. In T. Rogers & A. O. Soter (Eds.), *Reading across cultures: Teaching literature in a diverse society* (pp. 42–68). New York: Teachers College Press.

McMahon, S. I. (1997). Reading in the book club program. In S. I. McMahon & T. E. Raphael (Eds.), *The book club connection: Literacy learning and classroom talk* (pp. 47–68). New York: Teachers College Press.

McMahon, S. I., Raphael, T. E., Goatley, V. J., & Pardo, L. S. (Eds.). (1997). *The book club connection: Literacy learning and classroom talk.* New York: Teachers College Press.

Michalove, B. (1999). Examining prejudice in history and in ourselves. In J. Allen (Ed.), *Class actions: Literacy education for a democratic society.* New York: Teachers College Press.

Miller, S. M. (1998). Entering into multicultural conversations in literature-history classes. *Arizona English Bulletin,* 40, 10–24.

Moll, L. C. (Ed.). (1990a). *Vygotsky in education: Instructional implications and applications of sociohistorical psychology.* Cambridge: Cambridge University Press.

———. (1990b). Introduction. In L. C. Moll (Ed.), *Vygotsky in education: Instructional implications and applications of sociohistorical psychology* (pp. 1–27). Cambridge: Cambridge University Press.

Moll, L. C., & Greenberg, J. B. (1990). Creating zones of possibilities: Combining social contexts for instruction. In L. C. Moll (Ed.), *Vygotsky in education: Instructional implications and applications of sociohistorical psychology* (pp. 206–222). Cambridge: Cambridge University Press.

Moll, L. C., & Whitmore, K. F. (1993). Vygotsky in classroom practice: Moving from individual transmission to social transaction. In E. A. Forman, N. Minick, & C. A. Stone (Eds.), *Contexts for learning: Sociocultural dynamics in children's development* (pp. 19–42). New York: Oxford University Press.

Möller, K. J. (2001). *Reading socially in a multicultural world: Fourth graders' group discussions of literature with social justice themes.* Unpublished doctoral dissertation, University of Georgia, Athens.

———. (2002). Providing support for dialogue in literature discussions about social justice. *Language Arts,* 79, 467–477.

———. (2004/2005). Creating zones of possibility for struggling readers: A study of one fourth grader's shifting roles in literature discussion. *Journal of Literacy Research,* 36, 419–460.

Möller, K. J., & Allen, J. (2000). Connecting, resisting, and searching for safer places: Students respond to Mildred Taylor's The Friendship. *Journal of Literacy Research,* 32, 145–186.

Morrison, T. (1992). *Playing in the dark: Whiteness and the literary imagination.* New York: Vintage Books.

Nodelman, P. (1996). *The pleasures of children's literature* (2nd ed.). White Plains, NY: Longman.

Obadele, I. A. (1995). Multiculturalism: War in America continues. In S. Jackson & J. Solis (Eds.), *Beyond comfort zones in multiculturalism: Confronting the politics of privilege* (pp. 37–51). Westport, CT: Bergin & Garvey.

Omi, M., & Winant, H. (1994). *Racial formation in the United States from the 1960's to the 1990's* (2nd ed.). New York: Routledge.

Porter, C. R. (1993). *Meet Addy: An American girl.* Middleton, WI: Pleasant.

Purcell-Gates, V. (1995). *Other people's worlds.* Cambridge, MA: Harvard University Press.

Rabinowitz, P., & Smith, M. (1998). *Authorizing readers: Resistance and respect in the teaching of literature.* New York: Teachers College Press.

Rosenblatt, L. (1995). *Literature as exploration* (5th ed.). New York: Modern Language Association of America.

Rubin, D. L. (1990). Introduction: Ways of talking about talking and learning. In S. Hynds & D. L. Rubin (Eds.), *Perspectives on talk and learning* (pp. 1–17). Urbana, IL: National Council of Teachers of English.

Samway, K. D., & Whang, G. (1996). *Literature study circles in a multicultural classroom.* York, ME: Stenhouse.

Shannon, P. (1995). *Text, lies, and videotape: Stories about life, literacy, and learning.* Portsmouth, NH: Heinemann.

Sims, R. (1982). *Shadow and substance.* Urbana, IL: National Council of Teachers of English.

Smith, F. (1988). *Joining the literacy club.* Portsmouth, NH: Heinemann.

Spinelli, J. (1990). *Maniac Magee.* New York: Harper Trophy.

Taxel, J. (1997). Multicultural literature and the politics of reaction. *Teachers College Record, 98,* 419–448.

Taylor, M. D. (1987). *The friendship.* New York: Dial Books for Young Readers.

Thompkins, J. (Ed.). (1980). *Reader-response criticism: From formalism to poststructuralism.* Baltimore, MD: Johns Hopkins University Press.

Tudge, J. (1990). Vygotsky, the zone of proximal development, and peer collaboration: Implications for classroom practice. In L. C. Moll (Ed.), *Vygotsky in education: Instructional implications and applications of sociohistorical psychology* (pp. 155–172). Cambridge: Cambridge University Press.

Villaume, S. K., Worden, T., Williams, S., Hopkins, L., & Rosenblatt, C. (1994). Five teachers in search of a discussion. *Reading Teacher, 47,* 480–487.

Vygotsky, L. (1978). *Mind in society.* Cambridge, MA: Harvard University Press.

———. (1986). *Thought and language* (A. Kozulin, Trans.). Cambridge, MA: MIT Press. (Original work published 1934.)

Weiler, K. (1988). *Women teaching for change: Gender, class, and power.* Westport, CT: Greenwood.

Wertsch, J. V. (1985). *Vygotsky and the social formation of the mind.* Cambridge, MA: Harvard University Press.

Williams, R. (1989). Hegemony and the selective tradition. In S. de Castell, A. Luke, & C. Luke (Eds.), *Language authority and criticism: Readings on the school textbook* (pp. 56–60). London: Falmer Press.

III

PEDAGOGICAL ISSUES

10

African American Children's Literature in Rural Schools

Patricia E. Bandré

Each year, students in the rural public school where I taught received books through the Reading Is Fundamental (RIF) Program. On RIF distribution days, my class walked especially slowly down the hallway in the morning, hoping to catch a glimpse of the books laid out in the library awaiting their perusal. They craned their necks trying to read titles and recognize familiar book covers, and upon entering the classroom they would immediately begin asking when it would be their turn to go to the library and select a book. Our library media specialist worked hard to purchase quality children's books with the funds allotted. She tried to make sure that a wide variety of genres, award-winning titles, and books by their favorite authors were available.

One RIF distribution day, I stopped by the library and noticed that copies of *Bigmama's* (1991) by Donald Crews and *Mississippi Bridge* (1990) by Mildred D. Taylor were lying on the table among other books that had not been chosen. Recognizing both of these award-winning African American authors, I queried the library media specialist as to why she thought these books had not been selected. "Those books have been here since the last RIF distribution," she said. "They're good books, but I can't get any of the kids to take them. I think it's because they have African American characters on the covers."

Most of the books made available during RIF distributions were pieces of contemporary realistic fiction and fantasy, and these genres were the most frequently chosen. Some informational books and works of historical fiction were available for selection as well; however, regardless of the genre, books with images of people of color on the cover tended to be left behind. Students appeared to disregard books that contained protagonists who were not of Anglo-European descent.

The population of the school was fairly homogeneous, as was the community in which it was located. Most of the students were Caucasian, Christian, and from families with an agricultural background. Homogeneity in regard to race and socioeconomic status tends to be the norm in rural areas (Lowery & Pace, 2001). Rural schools also tend to be small, often serve as the focal point of the community, and employ a large number of citizens from the surrounding area (Ayalon, 1995; Dinsmore & Hess, 1999). Physical and social isolation from the resources and diversity found in suburban and urban areas is a reality for many rural citizens (Altieri, 1997).

While it is true that students in rural areas may be presented with images of sociocultural diversity through the media during time spent at school or at home, it is not enough to provide an accurate or complete picture of any cultural group (Kruse, 2001). When used appropriately in the classroom, carefully selected children's books can help expand and enrich the cultural knowledge of rural students. Rudine Sims Bishop (1990), a respected scholar in the field of African American children's literature, observes that children "need books that will help them understand the multicultural nature of the world that they live in, and their place as a member of just one group, as well as their connections to other humans. In this country where racism is still one of the unresolved social problems, books may be one of the few places where children who are socially isolated and insulated from the larger world may meet people unlike themselves" (p. xi). If students do not elect to independently read books written by and about people of color, then it becomes imperative that teachers regularly read them aloud in the classroom.

This chapter outlines a study conducted to explore what types of books teachers select for read-alouds in rural schools and the factors that influence their decisions. The number of books written by and about African Americans will be highlighted, and the implications of those choices will be discussed as well.

METHODOLOGY

In order to discover what books were being selected for use as read-alouds in rural K–6 public school classrooms and the rationale behind their selection, a mixed methods approach was used. The first phase of the study was conducted in the spring so that the data collected had the potential to be representative of the literature that the teachers had selected for read-alouds over the course of the school year. This phase was quantitative in nature and involved the use of a cross-sectional survey in order to gather information from a random sample of the population through a mail questionnaire (Fraenkel & Wallen, 2000).

At the time of the study, the teachers selected for participation taught in kindergarten through grade six classrooms in districts designated to be rural by the Ohio Department of Education. This rural classification is based on a number of factors, some of which include workforce occupations, average income, median income, amount of college education, population density, and the amount of agriculture and industry. Rural districts in Ohio tend to be located in the Appalachian areas of the state or just outside these areas (Ohio Department of Education, n.d.). Of the 611 state school districts, 235 were classified as rural at the time of the study. Each district's superintendent was contacted by letter and asked to participate. The letter asked the superintendents to return a participation form as well as a list of their K–6 teachers with building assignments. A total of 61 (26 percent) districts responded positively and forwarded the requested information.

Using a random number table, 25 percent of the teachers in grades K–3 (primary) and 4–6 (intermediate) from each of the lists provided by the participating school district superintendents were sent questionnaires. A total of 535 cover letters and questionnaires were mailed. Complete, eligible questionnaires were returned by 48 percent (151) of the 314 primary-grade teachers, and 42 percent (93) of the 221 intermediate-grade teachers. Overall, this was a 45 percent rate of return, which is considered average for a mail survey (Chiu & Brennan, 1990).

Enclosed with the questionnaire was a separate document that outlined the second phase of the study. This phase used interviews and an on-site visit in order to gather descriptive data regarding the teachers' selection and use of children's literature (Bogdan & Biklen, 1992). Those who wished to participate were asked to complete the document and return it along with the completed questionnaire. A total of 112 teachers volunteered for this phase of the study. Responses were divided into primary and intermediate grade level groups and numbered chronologically. Using a random number table, six teachers were selected from each grade level group, resulting in a total of 12 second-phase participants. It was felt that this number would provide a rich pool of data and serve to confirm or disprove survey data as well as provide additional insight.

Data for this phase of the study were collected during four consecutive weeks in October, approximately five weeks into the start of a new school year. This time period was chosen in order to allow teachers the opportunity to establish classroom routines, yet avoid the busy holiday schedules and extended recesses that normally occur in November and December. The months of January and February were excluded due to the occurrence of Martin Luther King Day and Black History Month, events that typically influence the amount of children's literature written by and about African Americans that is read aloud in elementary school classrooms. Standardized testing, spring recesses, and end-of-the-year activities were thought to possibly restrict the number of read-alouds conducted in the spring. Therefore, it was felt that data collected in early fall was least likely to be limited to topical and/or seasonal selection or restricted by time factors.

Two of the questions the study sought to answer are (1) what books are teachers choosing for classroom read-alouds, and (2) what criteria are used in order to determine what books are selected? Teachers completing the questionnaire were asked to list the title and author of a book they were currently reading aloud to their students and comment on what factors were most important and least important when selecting that book as a read-aloud. Eight prompts were provided from which to choose, and teachers were asked to mark their top three prompts for each designation. The prompts were (1) favorite book of past students, (2) book is a personal favorite, (3) award-winning book, (4) topic/theme matches or supports curricular standards, (5) author/illustrator recognized for doing quality work, (6) book was recommended in a professional publication, (7) book was recommended by a colleague, and (8) book presents a multicultural perspective. These prompts were used due to their similarity with those found in the literature. In addition, space was provided in which the respondents could list other most and least important factors. Respondents were also asked to list two additional titles that were read aloud during that school year.

Teachers participating in the second phase of the study recorded the title and author of all the books chosen for classroom use during four consecutive weeks, and an on-site interview was conducted upon the completion of data collection. At this time, a discussion of the survey completed the previous spring, the list of books read during the fall, and the rationale behind the selection of those books was held.

FINDINGS

Overall, survey respondents listed a total of 452 different read-aloud titles and noted that personal favorites, favorites of past students, and books that matched or supported curricular standards were preferred for read-alouds. Most frequently cited as least influential factors were that a book had been recommended in a professional publication, had won an award, or contained multicultural perspectives.

Books written by Eric Carle were most frequently listed as read-alouds by the primary-grade teachers. His titles were listed a total of 26 times. E. B. White, Roald Dahl, Beverly Cleary, Barbara Park, and Jan Brett were the other authors whose books were listed on questionnaires 10 or more times. The single most frequently listed primary-grade read-aloud title was *Char-*

lotte's Web (White, 1952). It appeared on 14 different questionnaires. Intermediate-grade teachers reported reading books by Louis Sachar more frequently than those written by any other author. Titles by Gary Paulsen and Roald Dahl also topped the intermediate-grade read-aloud list. Paulsen's Newbery Honor winner *Hatchet* (1987) was the single most listed intermediate-grade read-aloud title and appeared on 7 different questionnaires. Tables 1 and 2 illustrate these data.

Each of these authors is Caucasian and most of their books listed on returned questionnaires include characters who are predominantly white and middle class. A few of the titles listed by these authors are fantasy stories or traditional tales that contain anthropomorphized animals as main characters. Although the settings and themes are somewhat varied, the views and opinions presented by the characters in these stories, for the most part, reflect those of the cultural majority. The race of the characters, rather than their socioeconomic status or any other attribute, tends to be a deciding factor.

The lack of importance given to the inclusion of varied perspectives is reflected in the number of multicultural titles chosen, and specifically in the number written by and about African Americans. Although there is no general consensus as to how multicultural children's literature is defined, for the purposes of this chapter a broad definition was used first to categorize selected titles, then narrowed to reveal how many are written by and about African Americans. Multicultural books include those that are "from non-western countries outside of the United States," books that describe "relations

Table 10.1. Authors Whose Books Were Listed as Read-Alouds Ten or More Times by Primary-Grade Survey Respondents

Author	Number of Different Titles Listed by Survey Respondents	Total Number of Books Listed by Survey Respondents
Carle, Eric	8	26
White, E. B.	3	17
Cleary, Beverly	7	14
Dahl, Roald	5	14
Park, Barbara	8	13
Brett, Jan	5	10

Table 10.2. Authors Whose Books Were Listed as Read-Alouds Ten or More Times by Intermediate-Grade Survey Respondents

Author	Number of Different Titles Listed by Survey Respondents	Total Number of Books Listed by Survey Respondents
Sachar, Louis	4	12
Dahl, Roald	8	11
Paulsen, Gary	4	11

Table 10.3. Multicultural Books Selected for Read-Alouds by Primary-Grade Survey Respondents

Author	Title	Number of Times Listed
Allen, Debbie	Brothers of the Knight	1
DiSalvo-Ryan, DyAnne	City Green	1
Dorros, Arthur	Abuela	1
Hong, Lily	Two of Everything	1
Jordan, Delores	Salt in His Shoes	1
McKissack, Patricia C.	George Washington Carver	1
Muth, John J.	Stone Soup	1
Park, Linda Sue	Seesaw Girl	1
Polacco, Patricia	Rechenka's Eggs	2
Polacco, Patricia	Chicken Sunday	1
Polacco, Patricia	Mr. Lincoln's Way	3
Taylor, Mildred D.	The Well	1
Tompert, Ann	Grandfather Tang's Story	1
Walter, Mildred Pitts	Justin and the Best Biscuits	1

between cultural groups or by authors writing about a cultural group other than their own," or "literature written by members of a parallel culture that represents their unique experiences as a member of that culture" (Huck, Kiefer, Hepler, & Hickman, 2004, p. 22). Even with such a broad definition, only 6 percent (27) of the 452 different titles chosen as read-alouds can be classified as multicultural. Table 3 shows all of the multicultural titles selected by primary-grade survey respondents. Table 4 outlines the same information for intermediate-grade survey respondents.

Table 10.4. Multicultural Books Selected for Read-Alouds by Intermediate-Grade Survey Respondents

Author	Title	Number of Times Listed
Coerr, Eleanor	Sadako and the Thousand Paper Cranes	1
Coles, Robert	The Story of Ruby Bridges	1
Conduto, Michael, and Bruchac, Joseph	Keepers of the Earth	1
Curtis, Christopher Paul	The Watsons Go to Birmingham—1963	2
Curtis, Christopher Paul	Bud, Not Buddy	1
Dingle, Derek	First in the Field: Baseball Hero Jackie Robinson	1
Hamilton, Virginia	House of Dies Drear	1
Mazer, Anne	America Street	1
Park, Linda Sue	The Kite Fighters	2
Robinet, Hariette	Forty Acres and Maybe a Mule	1
Robinet, Hariette	Walking to the Bus Rider Blues	1
Taylor, Mildred D.	Mississippi Bridge	1
Taylor, Theodore	The Cay	2

Table 10.5.   The Number of Multicultural Books and Books Written by and about African Americans Selected for Read-Alouds in Rural Ohio Public School Classrooms

Grade Level	Number of Different Titles Selected for Read-Alouds	Number of Multicultural Titles	Number of Titles by and about African Americans
K–3	274	14 (5%)	5 (2%)
4–6	178	13 (7%)	7 (4%)
Overall	452	27 (6%)	12 (3%)

When this set of books is narrowed further to include only those written by and about African Americans, just 3 percent of the total number of titles selected by survey respondents remains. See table 5.

While some titles written by white authors appeared on multiple questionnaires, the only book written by an African American listed more than once was *The Watsons Go to Birmingham—1963* (Curtis, 1995), a 1996 Newbery Honor Book and Coretta Scott King Honor Book. It was listed as a read-aloud by two intermediate-grade respondents. Only three African American authors, Christopher Paul Curtis, Harriette Robinet, and Mildred D. Taylor, had more than one title listed on returned questionnaires. Table 6 lists the authors, titles, and number of times specific books written by African American authors appeared on returned questionnaires.

Table 10.6.   Books Written by and about African Americans Selected for Use as Read-Alouds by Survey Respondents and the Number of Times Each Book Was Listed on a Questionnaire

Author	Title	Number of Times Listed by Survey Respondents
Allen, Debbie	*Brothers of the Knight*	1
Curtis, Christopher Paul	*The Watsons Go to Birmingham—1963*	2
Curtis, Christopher Paul	*Bud, Not Buddy*	1
Dingle, Derek	*First in the Field: Baseball Hero Jackie Robinson*	1
Hamilton, Virginia	*The House of Dies Drear*	1
Jordan, Delores	*Salt in His Shoes*	1
McKissack, Patricia C.	*George Washington Carver*	1
Robinet, Hariette	*Forty Acres and Maybe a Mule*	1
Robinet, Hariette	*Walking to the Bus Rider Blues*	1
Taylor, Mildred D.	*Mississippi Bridge*	1
Taylor, Mildred D.	*The Well*	1
Walter, Mildred Pitts	*Justin and the Best Biscuits*	1

Table 10.7.   Multicultural Books Selected for Use by Teachers in the Second Phase of the Study

Author	Title
Arkhurst, Joyce Cooper	The Adventures of Spider
Armstrong, William H.	Sounder
Demi	One Grain of Rice
Fox, Mem	Whoever You Are
George, Jean Craighead	Julie of the Wolves
Katz, Karen	The Colors of Us
Park, Linda Sue	A Single Shard
Park, Linda Sue	The Firekeeper's Son
Taylor, Theodore	The Cay

Teachers in the second phase of the study reported the selection of 191 different titles for classroom use during the four weeks of data collection. Of these books, 5 percent (9) can be classified as multicultural using the broad definition. See table 7. When narrowed further, only one title, *The Adventures of Spider: West African Folktales* (Arkhurst, 1964), was written by an African American.

The teachers' commitment to using books that match or support curricular standards, are personal favorites, are favorites of current students, or are favorites of students in years past was mentioned in each of the 12 culminating interviews. However, during their interviews, some of the teachers expressed strong feelings when it came to the importance of presenting multicultural perspectives through children's literature. Of these, three felt especially compelled to use multicultural literature with their rural elementary students, and two others personally believed that multicultural literature was important, but not appropriate for their particular grade level. Interestingly, the lack of racial diversity within their rural communities was one of the reasons given to support both opinions.

Mrs. Anderson (all teachers' names are pseudonyms), who noted the importance of multicultural children's literature to her second-graders, stated, "We are from such a small town with not a lot of diversity." She saw multicultural children's literature as "one way you can get kids used to that and present it to them." Comments made by Mrs. Duncan, a fifth-grade teacher, also specified the importance of multicultural literature in her classroom. She noted that racial diversity is "just one thing that being in a rural area we lack. Kids are not exposed to a lot of multicultural experiences, so that is just something I look for or try to, you know, at least incorporate in some way." None of the titles listed by either of these teachers, however, could be considered multicultural according to the study's definition. In these two particular classrooms, multicultural literature may be set aside for use dur-

ing particular topics or studied in conjunction with certain holidays. This issue was not specifically discussed.

Mrs. Peters, another fifth-grade teacher, recorded two multicultural titles
during the course of the study and emphasized how important the use of
this literature was to her students' futures, especially books containing
African American characters. After more than twenty years of teaching, she
has found that her students often don't know how to react to people of
other races when they leave their rural community and travel or move to a
more diverse area. "Most of the parents of my students don't even understand why we get the Martin Luther King holiday off from school. African
Americans are still referred to as niggers in some of their homes." Mrs. Anderson, Mrs. Duncan, and Mrs. Peters all expressed a similar belief: reading
and discussing multicultural children's literature in the classroom is essential in order to provide students with a framework of understanding, respect, and appreciation for other cultures. Rural students, like those in suburban and urban areas, must learn about the world around them so that
they might better understand their own lives.

Mrs. Freeman, a kindergarten teacher, and Mr. Michaels, a fourth-grade
teacher, believed the opposite was true. Both of these teachers commented
that a lack of cultural diversity and student maturity make multicultural literature inappropriate for read-alouds and discussion in their classrooms. Of
her kindergarten students, Mrs. Freeman believes they are not ready to discuss the different perspectives that multicultural literature provides. "I guess
personally, it's not a big issue to me with kindergartners. We're still into the
'me, me, me' kind of thing, and it's hard for them to even comprehend
those kinds of things."

Mr. Michaels was concerned about the ability of his fourth-grade students
to understand the social issues that arise in some multicultural books and
discuss them appropriately. "I've found that with this age group, 9 and 10
years old, they're really not aware, or they really don't understand a multicultural perspective the way I would like it to be understood. I don't think
they are mature enough to handle that." Mr. Michaels considered them
"just too young at this point," and noted, "I think that this multicultural
perspective lends itself to a more advanced way of thinking that these children don't have at this point."

These comments were made in regard to the class's study of *Maniac
Magee* (Spinelli, 1990), a Newbery winner that discusses discrimination
and the prejudice that exists between some of the black and white residents of a fictitious town. According to Mr. Michaels, these topics "went
over their heads." When asked if the racial composition of the community
in which his students live has anything to do with the "lack of thinking"
he describes, he said, "It probably does. They're not exposed to a lot of
multicultural perspectives."

Overall, the study reveals that most of the books selected as read-alouds by rural elementary teachers are written by authors of European descent and present the views and beliefs of mainstream North American cultures. Additionally, books do not appear to be selected in a haphazard fashion. Teachers report purposely reading aloud books that match curricular topics and support academic standards. However, it appears that personal bias is highly influential to the selection process. Teachers often elect to read their favorite titles and pay little attention to recommendations from professional journals, colleagues, and children's book award recipients. Books with multicultural perspectives, and specifically those written by and about African Americans, are chosen only by teachers who appreciate and value cultural diversity and personally deem its use appropriate for their students.

The literature on classroom book selection reveals similar trends. Studies, mostly surveys, demonstrate that the majority of books selected for classroom use are written by authors of European descent (Applebee, 1993; Luke, Cooke, & Luke, 1986) and contain main characters whose thoughts and beliefs more frequently reflect those of mainstream culture (Applebee, 1993; Jipson & Paley, 1991; McKinney, Fry, & Pruitt, 1997). Julie Wollman-Bonilla (1998) found that some of the practicing and pre-service teachers in her university courses purposely omitted the use of children's books that present nonmainstream perspectives, sociocultural differences, and discrimination. These teachers personally appreciated books such as *Roll of Thunder, Hear My Cry* (Taylor, 1976) and *Tar Beach* (Ringgold, 1991) but rejected their use in the classroom because they believed that the social issues addressed in the books are foreign to the children in their classrooms or that children are not capable of discussing such "difficult" topics. Wollman-Bonilla found that these teachers recognized their biases, but they felt that they were doing what was best for children by not selecting multicultural literature for classroom use.

In a study conducted with pre-service teachers, Colby and Lyon (2004) received different reactions. Students in their teacher education courses were asked to read and respond to an article that outlined the importance of multicultural literature in the classroom. As a result, further discussions ensued. Those who had not initially realized the value of multicultural literature came to understand its potential ability to increase understanding and respect for people from a variety of cultures. One student commented, "Perceptions will not only change for the minority students, but also their majority classmates, and all of them will learn from the experience" (p. 26). As these pre-service teachers explored their own beliefs about the impact of classroom interactions, students came to recognize the power of literature to confront the status quo and prompt discussions that cause students to question social injustice.

DISCUSSION

The importance of classroom book selection is increased by the fact that students' independent reading habits are influenced by the books they listen to and interact with in the classroom (Huck, Kiefer, Hepler, & Hickman, 2004). "Nothing in the entire school has a greater impact on convincing children that books are worthwhile than teachers' reading habits" (Perez as cited in Jacobs & Tunnell, 2004, p. 262). Undeniably, teachers are role models, and the stories they choose to highlight in the classroom become a source of student conversation. These books have the ability to suggest to students that certain topics and themes deserve more attention than others and possess greater value.

Additionally, within the last twenty years, children's literature has begun to play a more prominent role in the classroom. Prior to the 1980s, children's literature was largely ignored by reading methods textbooks and considered an option only when other work was completed. Such is no longer the case. In 1987, Cullinan surveyed state reading and language arts directors across the United States and found that of the 80 percent who responded, all indicated that "a lot of literature is central to a successful program" (p. 29). In 1994, Lehman, Freeman, and Allen found that the majority of teachers they surveyed agreed or strongly agreed that children's literature should "be the primary component of the reading/language arts program" (p. 9). A recent national survey of pre-kindergarten through fifth-grade teachers found that children's trade books were the only texts used for reading instruction by 16 percent of the respondents. Trade books were used to support reading textbooks by 56 percent of the respondents and basals were used to supplement trade books by 27 percent of the population (Martinez & McGee, 2000). Children's literature is also being used to effectively supplement and enrich textbooks during science and social studies lessons (Morrow, Pressley, Smith, & Smith, 1997; Smith, Monson, & Dobson, 1992).

Overall, elementary teachers appear to be selecting a larger number of children's books for more classroom purposes than in the past. If studies demonstrate that personal bias influences what is selected for classroom read-alouds, then it is possible that these same preferences have an impact on what teachers are selecting for use during reading instruction, science, social studies, and other content areas. As Smith, Greenlaw, and Scott (1987) summarize, if the 254 elementary teachers in just their study read aloud an average of 20 minutes per day to their students for 36 weeks, the students would be listening to a combined total of 15,240 hours worth of text dominated by Anglo-European perspectives. Imagine what the figures might be if all of the time students spend with teacher-selected texts were taken into consideration. The thought is staggering.

IMPLICATIONS IN RURAL AREAS

While the number of students attending rural schools may seem insignificant when compared to the population of suburban and urban districts, the impact of rural schools has the potential to be considerable. At present almost one-fourth of the nation's population resides in a rural area (Ayalon, 1995), and while many of those areas are predominantly white, the demographics of the United States are changing. By the year 2020, nearly half of the nation's school-age population will be children of color (Banks, 1993). Because of their importance to the rural community and the fact that they employ a number of local citizens, rural schools have the possibility to influence the thinking of a large number of people. Rural teachers who select, read aloud, and talk about multicultural children's literature with the students provide an impetus for future discussions. After interacting with the books at school, students may take the thoughts and ideas gleaned from class readings and discussions into the community and further pursue these topics with their friends, parents, and other adults.

Rural schools must be able to prepare students to successfully participate in a society that is very different from that known by rural Americans of the past. Advances in technology have made our world a smaller place, and the likelihood that rural students will be living and working with people from a variety of cultures is to be expected. Rural students must be given the opportunity to participate in the world around them through the use of multicultural literature. As Lowery (2002) observes, "Stories help us to overcome obstacles, accept different perspectives, and develop personal goals. Stories allow us to see and recreate ourselves." Through stories, Lowery says, "we learn to make meaning of the life experiences around us and begin to connect with others" (p. 27). Multicultural children's books can help provide a window on the world beyond the social and physical confines of life in a rural area.

Additionally, children of color who attend rural schools need to be able to see their own lives within the books they encounter. Sims (1983) states, "All-white books do not permit black children to develop a strong sense of their own humanity, to affirm their sense of self-worth, or to discover their own identity within a group" (p. 650). In order to validate their importance to society, it is essential for all children to see positive images of themselves reflected within the pages of the books they hear and read at school (Hefflin & Barksdale-Ladd, 2001).

Newbery-winning children's author Katherine Paterson (2000) reminds us that children "live on what they feed upon" (p. 5). When it comes to the selection of read-alouds and other books for classroom use, teachers must ask themselves what they are feeding their students. The effort must be taken to select books that will "truly nourish them, that will enlarge their minds, that will prepare them to make wise decisions when they're grown" (p. 5). Literature is a powerful medium that possesses the ability to perpetuate or dissolve stereotypes. Only when teachers take the time to truly consider the impact of the books they choose to share with students, and the influence personal biases have on book selection, can equity begin to become a reality.

REFERENCES

Altieri, J. L. (1997). The role of children's literature in one rural town's elementary school: A case study. *Reading Horizons, 37* (3), 195-202.

Applebee, A. N. (1993). *Literature in the secondary school: Studies of curriculum and instruction in the United States.* Urbana, IL: National Council of Teachers of English.

Arkhurst, J. C. (1964). *The adventures of spider: West African folktales.* Boston: Little, Brown.

Ayalon, A. (1995). Does multicultural education belong in rural white America? *Rural Educator, 16* (3), 1-6.

Banks, J. A. (1993). Multicultural education: Development, dimensions, and challenges. *Phi Delta Kappan, 75,* 22-28.

Bishop, R. S. (1990). Mirrors, windows, and sliding glass doors. *Perspectives, 6,* ix-xi.

Bogdan, R. C., & Biklen, S. K. (1992). *Qualitative research for education: An introduction to theory and methods.* Boston: Allyn & Bacon.

Chiu, I., & Brennan, M. (1990). The effectiveness of some techniques for improving mail survey response rates: A meta-analysis. *Marketing Bulletin, 1,* 13-19.

Colby, S. A., & Lyon, A. F. (2004). Heightening awareness about the importance of using multicultural literature. *Multicultural Education, 11* (3), 24-28.

Crews, D. (1991). *Bigmama's.* New York: Greenwillow.

Cullinan, B. E. (1987). Latching on to literature: Reading initiatives take hold. *School Library Journal, 35,* 27-31.

Curtis, C. P. (1995). *The Watsons go to Birmingham—1963.* New York: Delacorte.

Dinsmore, J. A., & Hess, R. S. (1999). Preparing teachers for diversity in rural America. *Rural Educator, 20* (3), 19-24.

Fraenkel, J. R., & Wallen, N. E. (2000). *How to design and evaluate research in education* (4th ed.). Boston: McGraw-Hill.

Hefflin, B. R., & Barksdale-Ladd, M. A. (2001). African American children's literature that helps students find themselves: Selection guidelines for grades K-3. *Reading Teacher, 54* (8), 810-819.

Huck, C. S., Kiefer, B. Z., Hepler, S., & Hickman, J. (2004). *Children's literature in the elementary school* (8th ed.). Boston: McGraw-Hill.

Jacobs, J. S., & Tunnell, M. O. (2004). *Children's literature, briefly* (3rd ed.). Upper Saddle River, NJ: Pearson.

Jipson, J., & Paley, N. (1991). The selective tradition in teachers' choice of children's literature: Does it exist in the elementary classroom? *English Education, 23* (3), 148-159.

Kruse, M. (2001). Escaping ethnic encapsulation: The role of multicultural children's literature. *Delta Kappa Gamma Bulletin, 67* (2), 26-32.

Lehman, B. A., Freeman, E. B., & Allen, V. G. (1994). Children's literature and literacy instruction: "Literature-based" elementary teachers' belief and practices. *Reading Horizons*, 35 (1), 3–23.

Lowery, R. M. (2002). Grappling with issues of gender equity: Preservice teachers' reflections on children's books. *Journal of Children's Literature*, 28 (2), 25–31.

Lowery, R. M., & Pace, B. G. (2001). Preparing suburban preservice teachers for rural schools. *Rural Educator*, 23 (2), 32–36.

Luke, A., Cooke, J., & Luke, C. (1986). The selective tradition in action: Gender bias in student teachers' selections of children's literature. *English Education*, 18, 209–218.

Martinez, M. G., & McGee, L. M. (2000). Children's literature and reading instruction: Past, present, and future. *Reading Research Quarterly*, 35 (1), 154–169.

McKinney, L. J., Fry, P. G., & Pruitt, N. E. (1997). The road not taken: Assessing rural teachers' knowledge of multicultural children's literature. *Rural Educator*, 18 (3), 7–11.

Morrow, L. M., Pressley, M., Smith, J. K., & Smith, M. (1997). The effect of a literature-based program integrated into literacy and science instruction with children from diverse backgrounds. *Reading Research Quarterly*, 32 (1), 54–76.

Ohio Department of Education. (n.d.). Typology of Ohio school districts, revised 1996. Office of Policy Research and Analysis. www.ode.state.oh.us.

Paterson, K. (2000). Asking the question. *New Advocate*, 12 (1), 1–15.

Paulsen, G. (1987). *Hatchet*. New York: Simon & Schuster.

Ringgold, F. (1991). *Tar beach*. New York: Crown.

Sims, R. (1983). What has happened to the 'all-white' world of children's books? *Phi Delta Kappan*, 64 (9), 650–653.

Smith, J. A., Monson, J. A., & Dobson, D. (1992). A case study on integrating history and reading instruction through literature. *Social Education*, 35, 370–375.

Smith, N. J., Greenlaw, M. J., & Scott, C. J. (1987). Making the literate environment equitable. *Reading Teacher*, 40 (4), 400–407.

Spinelli, J. (1990). *Maniac Magee*. Boston: Little Brown.

Taylor, M. D. (1990). *Mississippi bridge*. New York: Puffin Books.

———. (1976). *Roll of thunder, hear my cry*. New York: Scholastic.

White, E. B. (1952). *Charlotte's web*. New York: Harper Collins.

Wollman-Bonilla, J. (1998). Outrageous viewpoints: Teachers' criteria for rejecting works of children's literature. *Language Arts*, 75 (4), 287–295.

11

Where Life and Children's Literature Meet: African American Males in the Elementary Grades

Doris Walker-Dalhouse

In early childhood, boys and girls appear to be equally matched on language and literacy ability and early achievement measures. As they develop, during their early years of schooling, an increasing disparity in educational achievement is noted between girls and boys, and this is true especially for African American males (Davis, 2005). These differences are linked to several factors, including differences in gender socialization (Porche, Ross, & Snow, 2004), attitudes toward reading and reading practices that favor girls (Gilbert & Gilbert, 1998; Maynard, 2002; Kunjufu, 2002), and a school culture that lacks caring and nurturing adults (Polite, 1999).

Although the 2004 National Assessment of Educational Progress (NAEP) long-term trends assessment of reading between 1971 and 1973 indicated that many of the differences between black or Hispanic students and their white counterparts have narrowed, racial and gender differences remain (Perie, Moran, & Lutkus, 2005). African American children from two-parent households have been found to have better scores in reading and math (Teachman, Day, Paasch, Carver, & Call, 1998); however, middle-class African American males lag behind their Caucasian student counterparts in grade point average and standardized test scores (Jencks & Phillips, 1998). The 2003 NAEP results indicate that black students in grades four and eight scored lower than white and Asian/Pacific Islanders, and girls of all races scored higher than boys (Donahue, Daane, & Grigg, 2003).

The need to foster reading in all boys is essential. However, the persistent gap in reading achievement between African American boys and their peers must be recognized and understood by educators (Varlas, 2005; Holzman, 2004). Thus, the need for educators to address the reading achievement disparity between African American males and their peers is paramount.

Cai (2002) and Cai and Sims Bishop (1994) suggest that one way to address the disparity in reading achievement in African American males is to use multicultural literature; that is, literature about people who are racially, culturally, linguistically different from the dominant culture. Multicultural literature can improve reading achievement in several ways, as shown by Bauman, Hooten, and White (1999), who conducted a year-long teacher-research project with a group of fifth-grade students (African American, 61 percent; European American, 35 percent) to test a program they developed to teach reading strategies and reading motivation. Multicultural literature and three types of comprehension strategy lessons (elaborated, brief lessons, and impromptu) were presented to students. Students read self-selected multicultural literature and participated in discussion and reading study groups. The results from pre and post informal surveys of the students' reading habits, interests, and their oral and written comments indicate increased reading at home and school, increased valuing of reading, and a greater appreciation of literature and books.

Multicultural literature represents and respects the parallel lives of different groups of people and can promote cultural understanding (Walker-Dalhouse, 1992). Similarly, Tatum (2006) believes that enabling texts or those that focus on sociocultural, spiritual, and economic issues are the best types of texts for African American adolescent males. However, the texts commonly used with African American males in the classroom have been characterized as disabling, because they do not connect emotionally, culturally, or experientially with the lives of these children.

Reading to and engaging children in dialogue about books are essential aspects of later literacy development (Bus, van Ijzendoorn, & Pelligrini. 1995). If teachers are to develop African American boys as readers, they must introduce them to books that tell their stories, address issues in their lives, and validate their experiences. They must also see reflections of themselves, their family, and their friends in the stories and illustrations (Rand & Parker, 2001). Teachers should therefore strive to present these students with books that go beyond traditional male and female roles and that counter feelings of inferiority (Rand & Parker, 2001).

A significant relationship in the lives of African American boys is the relationship with their fathers in terms of their development of male identity and self-worth (Wade, 1994). According to Davis (2005), African American boys begin to conceptualize and form their various identities early. It is thus important for young African American boys to form connections to characters and plots or situations in books that accurately portray the real experiences and perspectives of African Americans and use authentic and realistic language. The characters must be well-developed and their story told in authentic and believable contexts (Heflin & Barksdale-Ladd, 2001).

The literature used must provide a window as well as a mirror that reflects the lives of readers. Sometimes these reflections may be troubling, but they should be authentic and cause the reader to think and to seek productive ways to solve academic and societal issues. This literature can also help students understand and handle social relationships with their family members, peers, and people in their community (McGinley & Kamberelis, 1996). Authentic discussions about the material read should be used to help students analyze and understand reality while learning content covered in the curriculum (Tatum, 2005).

LIFE CONNECTIONS

As a teacher-researcher on a one-year sabbatical, I taught in a magnet school guided by the philosophy of African American educator Marva Collins. According to Collins, "Writing like reading should be part of a total reading program. The most effective reading program becomes most valuable when reading is integrated with all subjects" (1999, p. 37). She recommends character interviews and letters to characters as activities to foster the connection between reading and writing. Collins believes that reading should be a whole-class activity in which reading skills are explicitly taught and in which children are exposed to excellent literature.

My class consisted of thirteen students: 69 percent (9) were female and 31 percent (4) were male; 77 percent (10) were African American; 31 percent (4) were from families classified as having nonlimited income, and 69 percent (9) were from families with limited income and thus were entitled to free or reduced-cost lunch according to federal government guidelines.

Frank

Frank was much larger in stature and bulk than the average fourth-grader, but he was more immature than his classmates. He was very sensitive and frequently cried or pouted over slights or taunts by other students in the class. Although he would engage in rough play such as tag or football, he usually ended up upset over something someone did. When I talked with him immediately after these situations occurred, Frank never really accepted responsibility for his behavior. He felt that his classmates caused his behaviors and that he could not do anything to change things.

Frank's scores on the California Test of Basic Skills at the end of the third grade placed him in the average range in most academic areas. However, his scores in language and language mechanics were below the 25th percentile.

At the start of the fourth grade, the class was administered the Gates MacGinitie Reading Test, Form K. Frank scored 2.2 at the beginning of the school year. Informal tests based on graded word lists and discussions of literature also indicated low performance in reading.

Frank was always eager to come to school. He arrived at 7:30 a.m. and was sound asleep at his desk by 8:00 a.m. His snoring focused attention on him and prompted laughter from his classmates. In an attempt to find out how to help him, I contacted his grandmother, who was listed officially as his guardian, even though Frank was living with his parents. His grandmother thought his sleeping was due to fatigue because of the early school start. I told her that other students had reported that he slept on the bus both to and from school, which did not seem natural. She noted that he also took a nap each afternoon after school. His grandmother promised to take him to the doctor. Later testing revealed that he had narcolepsy, a sleeping disorder.

Although there was a medical explanation for some of Frank's behavioral problems, I became aware that his home life was also a big part of his reading problems. His father, who thought that Frank was too sensitive and pampered by his grandmother, frequently ridiculed him for his less than fluent reading and explanation about what he read. According to Frank and his grandmother, Frank's father would embarrass him in front of his younger brother whenever he mispronounced words or responded to his father's questions about the story. Frank also became particularly upset in his literature group because he felt that the girls did not listen to his ideas during their discussion of the books that they had read. He especially disliked and objected to the actions of another struggling reader named Kelli, a Caucasian female who was also a low-income student but felt superior to Frank. Kelli would say that Frank's interpretations could not possibly be true and that she could not understand why or how he thought they could be true. He also disliked her because she had said that her grandfather probably owned some of his relatives as slaves. This angered Frank tremendously.

Additionally, he became upset by the fact that the other students were quick to correct his statements or to blurt out the pronunciation of words with which he appeared to be struggling as they presented a Readers Theater script or in any segment that he read to support his views about the story. While Frank struggled with pronouncing words occasionally, he possessed several strategies, such as using contextual analysis, rereading of text, and breaking words into syllables. However, Frank's temper often got the best of him. He would call Kelli "stupid" or "dumb" and tell her that if she knew what was good for her, she would stay out of his business. Tears would then roll down his cheeks as his face took on a menacing look.

On several occasions, I used his perception of me as a mother figure to talk with him about his temper. I told him that if I did not care about the person that he was and hoped to someday become, I would not take the time to remind him that he was "too intelligent" to let anyone interfere with the mission that he had set for himself (Collins, 1999). Initially, he chose not to respond but sat with his head bowed and tears streaming down his cheeks.

It was during one of these conversations that I learned that Frank's dad often called him a big baby and laughed at him for being a poor reader. One of Frank's routines with his father was for the father to have Frank read aloud to him. As Frank nervously read, he often stumbled over words. Frank's father, who did not have a high school education, would tell him that he was too big to be reading like a baby. This led to Frank getting more nervous, making more mistakes, and crying. Unknowingly, Frank's classmates were exacerbating his negative, nightly experiences at home by correcting his pronunciation of words. Frank's grandmother provided additional reasons for why Frank was falling asleep as frequently as described earlier. She shared her concerns that his father often had him folding clothes or doing housework until 10:00 p.m. or later, and if the dog needed to go outside at night, it was Frank's responsibility to awaken and take care of him.

Frank was also often caught in the middle of heated arguments between his parents, thus his grandmother was the main source of stability in his life. My one and only opportunity to meet either of Frank's parents was a day after Frank had a physical altercation with one of two Caucasian girls from our class. The incident occurred in the cafeteria, and he was reported to me by the cafeteria staff and my students. He was sent to the principal's office, where he was disciplined. I called Frank's grandmother about the incident and the consequences of his actions.

The next morning, Frank's father appeared with Frank at the classroom door. He told me that he was tired of his son "acting like a fool." When I invited him to come into the classroom to talk, Frank's father did not move. He then yelled at Frank from the classroom doorway and told Frank that he had better not do anything to make him have to leave work to come to school again. Frank's father shook his finger at him and told him to give me his cell phone number to call him the next time he got in trouble. As quickly as Frank's father appeared, he left, leaving his teary-eyed son angry with his classmates for having witnessed his embarrassment. The rest of the morning Frank pouted and complained that others were either looking at or laughing at him. Frank never spoke about the incident or his father, neither did he misbehave at school again.

Kevin

Kevin was a serious-looking student who always appeared to be lost in deep thought. He contributed to class discussions with thoughtful responses or shared questions that required deep thought or reflection. He was very polite and would often throw his arms around me in a tight embrace. He had a passion for video games and karate. Kevin liked the company of the other boys in the class; however, he was argumentative with the girls as he felt he had to defend himself against ridicule. He often repeated answers that his classmates just gave to questions and often repeated questions that were just asked, and the girls would tell him that the question was just answered or asked. Comments made to redirect his attention to class discussions by the art and science teachers, when these behaviors occurred, were often a source of anger for Kevin because the girls repeated them on the way back to their homeroom from the classes. On occasion, Kevin was put out of those classrooms and told not to say anything silly in class again or he would be kept in after school. The art teacher, science teacher, and I thought that Kevin's inattentiveness and forgetfulness were possible signs of attention deficit disorder (ADD). After discussing the behaviors with the school counselor, I realized that Kevin's actions were attention seeking and did not satisfy the criteria designated for the classification of ADD.

Kevin's California Achievement Test scores from the previous year indicated that he was above the 75th percentile in language mechanics. His math computation and total mathematics scores were below the 50th percentile. Kevin's score on the Gates MacGinitie test given at the beginning of the year was 2.8.

Kevin lived in an apartment with his single mother and a baby sister. Conferences with his mother revealed that she worked outside the home to care for her family. Kevin's physical hygiene and the fashionable clothing he wore indicated that his basic needs were being met. His mother tried to meet his emotional needs, but she often found herself overwhelmed with the enormity of being a single mother with none of her family living in close proximity to assist her. Apparently, she moved to the area to try to work out a relationship with Kevin's father. The relationship never resulted in marriage and caused a tremendous amount of stress and acrimony between the two. Although the mother wanted the father to establish a relationship with his son, that did not seem to be what Kevin or his father wanted. Kevin felt that his father favored children that he had from another relationship and disciplined him more harshly than the other children whenever they were together. Their infrequent contacts were characterized by broken promises and negative exchanges between Kevin and his father.

As Kevin became more and more estranged from his father, as evidenced by his refusal to visit him or talk to him on the telephone, he became more distracted at home and school. Kevin told me that his mother screamed at him frequently and called him dirty (profane) names. During one of the conferences that I had with Kevin's mother, she acknowledged that she often became frustrated with Kevin because, whenever she asked him to do anything, she had to repeat her request several times before he did it and he frequently talked back to her. This behavior really frustrated and angered her and led her to call him profane names. Kevin's mother said that she was so frustrated by Kevin's behavior that she often thought that he would be better off living with her aunt and uncle in another city, or in a foster home where maybe he would have a male figure to make him behave.

LITERACY ENGAGEMENT

Both Frank and Kevin were lower-achieving African American male readers. A primary goal for me throughout the school year was to establish opportunities to address content associated with their lives and culture within their literacy experiences. Although we did not have access to books that dealt directly with the relationships between African American boys and their fathers, we were able to address racial and interpersonal relationships. Thus the threads connecting the literary choices used were the themes of racial pride, struggle, and uplift. When presented with the poems "I, Too" by Langston Hughes (1959) and "On the Pulse of Morning" by Maya Angelou (1994), both boys understood the underlying message of embarking on new beginnings in Angelou's poem and of preparing oneself for a future characterized by equity between African Americans and Caucasians. They talked openly about racial equality, saying that although African Americans had not been treated well in the past, a new day was going to come where things were going to be better for black people. As further evidence of their embodiment of racial pride, Frank and Kevin memorized both poems and recited them expressively during class performances and school presentations.

A *Pocketful of Goobers: A Story about George Washington Carver* (Mitchell, 1986) was used in conjunction with social studies, and reading themes on survival and life in America were embedded. Both Frank and Kevin willingly participated in class discussions about the book and highlighted the fact that Carver was an intelligent black man who had to struggle during his life. Students read and discussed the books in literature groups and shared segments from the stories in a Readers Theater. Students were guided in their reading groups by a list of prepared questions about characterization. These included information about the way in which authors use dialogue from other characters, description of the character's thinking, and description of the character's action. They were asked to respond to books in writing as well.

After reading the poems by Langston Hughes and Maya Angelou and Mitchell's A *Pocketful of Goobers*, and because the class was a racially mixed class, we read *Bridge to Terabithia* (Paterson, 1977), which deals with relationships. In responding to *Bridge to Terabithia*, Frank wrote in his response journal that he thought the main characters, Leslie and Jesse, had true feelings for each other. He ended his response entry by saying, "I like this story because it has death, hard times, and friendships." Frank and Kevin's responses to *Bridge to Terabithia* were influenced by their experiences living in low-income areas where life-threatening violence, hard times, and the cultural and ethnic connections between friends are realities. Although *Bridge to Terabithia* is a book outside their cultural experencies, both boys could relate to it on emotional and psychological levels. In his journal entry, Kevin expressed sadness about the death of Leslie and connected swinging on a rope over a swollen river with the consequence of her death.

Another insight about life was revealed in Kevin's journal entry which contained a written interpretation of a proverb. In response to the proverb "You have freedom of choice but never freedom from consequence" (Alston & Thaxton, 2003, p. 118), Kevin wrote: "The proverb means that if you're about to kill someone, your consequence will be death to or from someone else." Clearly both Frank and Kevin understood real life issues and were able to communicate their thoughts orally and in writing.

At the beginning of the year, Frank's reading score on the Gates MacGinitie was 2.2 and Kevin's score was 2.8. During the year, they were exposed to basal literature from the Open Court Collection for Young Scholars' series, which was organized according to the following themes: Risks and Consequences, Business, Medicine, Survival, Technology, and Colonial Life. Students also participated in literature response groups organized around the themes in the series. Creative responses requiring students to write, speak, draw, and act were encouraged. By the end of the year and after introduction to the multicultural reading materials (nonfiction, fiction, and poetry) and practices described above, Frank's reading score increased to 4.3 and Kevin's increased to 4.8. Frank and Kevin appeared to have benefited from the opportunity to be engaged in authentic literature connected with life and with content learning. African American males like Frank and Kevin also need books that help them to develop personal insights about their relationships with others.

LITERARY CONNECTIONS

After my year teaching fourth grade, I returned to my university. A book that was not available at the time, but one that might have been ideal to use with Frank and Kevin, given their relationships with their fathers, is *Just like Martin* by Ossie Davis (1992). *Just like Martin* focuses on the issue of racial equality. It provides a forum for examining the relationship between an African American father and his son, Isaac, who wants to emulate the life and philosophy of nonviolence espoused by the great civil rights leader

Martin Luther King Jr. Isaac's views stand in marked contrast to his father's belief in violence in response to racism. Affected by an incident in which he killed a young mother and her child during military service in the Korean War, Ike Stone, Isaac's father, is a troubled man. After returning from the war, Ike was given a job in the local foundry. One day he responds violently to a racist remark made by a co-worker and beats him with an ax, thus sending him to the hospital. Although acquitted of his actions, Ike lives in a state of anger and sadness and feels that nonviolence is the same as cowardice (Davis, 1992). Isaac fears that his father's beliefs and feelings might lead him to violent confrontation with the racist people in the community, and he hides his father's gun.

Ike is angry when he discovers that his son stole his gun from his truck to prevent him from using it if needed during a rally organized by Isaac and his friends. The situation is compounded when a confrontation takes place during the rally and several men beat Ike as he tries to protect Isaac during the melee. Ike's intense anger causes him to say to Isaac, "The worst thing that ever happened to me in my life was having you for a son."(p. 172). Despite his harsh words, however, it is clear that he loves his son, and that his son loves him.

Ike's love for Isaac, also known as Stone, is demonstrated by his decision to share his painful war experiences with him when the burden of it becomes too great. Another example of his love for Isaac is his decision to stay in town, after being beaten and jailed, so that he can be a part of the civil rights movement in Alabama and protect his son from what he sees as racist acts. Ike's ongoing concern and commitment to supporting Isaac academically, emotionally, and socially is demonstrated when he says, "You're a good boy, Stone. I love you, even if I don't always show it . . . you're smart, get good marks, and I'm saving up every month to send you to college" (p. 40).

Isaac's love for his father is demonstrated after his father denies him the opportunity to attend the famous March on Washington, D.C., where Martin Luther King Jr. delivers his famous "I Have a Dream Speech." Isaac Stone does not judge his father or attempt to disobey him, and he seems to understand and forgive his father for not allowing him to go to Washington. He expresses his feelings by saying, "I love my daddy most when he is mean and ugly, with danger in his eyes, and won't say a word to nobody, 'cause that's when Mama Lucy [Isaac's dead mother] said he needed it the most" (p. 11).

Ike Stone's behavior is driven by a need to protect his son from racism in his Alabama community. Research by Thornton (1997) and Peters (1985) supports the belief that African American parents of all socioeconomic levels feel that it is their primary job to protect and insulate their children from racism and discrimination. They believe that they have to racially socialize their children because the process of racial socialization is the means by which racial identity and preparation for life in America is achieved. As a proud African American male, Ike felt that it was his responsibility to protect and racially socialize his son, even if it meant dying to do so. It is the reality of racism and how to respond to it that is important to consider in interpreting the behaviors of this and other African American families (Peters, 1985).

The role of fathers in the lives of African American sons and the impact of fathers on the academic, emotional, and social development of African American boys are worth exploring through life and literature. The relationship between Isaac Stone and his father resonated with me as a teacher educator and former elementary teacher concerned about the low reading achievement of some African American males. *Just like Martin* and a variety of genres, including poetry, realistic fiction, contemporary fiction, and nonfiction, can make strong connections to the lives of African American males, creating and fostering responses to text that will enable these young men as readers.

LIFE CONNECTIONS

For Frank and Kevin, the father–son relationship was strained, and the nature of this relationship impacted their emotional, social, and academic performance. Clearly, their fathers are not like Isaac Stone's father.

Both boys' fathers exhibited authoritative behavior toward their sons. Research shows that fathers who feel that they have limited economic power and authority in society may exhibit either negative and excessively authoritative behavior in the home or a lack of a sense of authority at home (Wade, 1994). Having to ask for time off from work to come to school because of his son's misbehavior was clearly upsetting to Frank's father. His frustration was evident in his behavior in the classroom and in his expressed frustration at his son's less than fluent oral reading. On the other hand, Kevin's father had children with a woman other than Kevin's mother and had made a home with them. Kevin felt that his father disciplined him more harshly than his other siblings whenever he visited his father. The behavior of his father and his absence from the home resulted in a dysfunctional relationship between them.

A father's love is important to the psychological well-being, health, and behavior of children (Rohner & Veneziano, 2001). Ike Stone expressed his love openly and through some of his actions. His son was psychologically and emotionally healthy and well-behaved. Neither Frank nor Kevin's father openly acknowledged their love for their sons, leaving them vulnerable emotionally, socially, and academically. Yet Frank wanted on some level to be like his dad. In responding to a question on an interest inventory given at the beginning of the school year, Frank wrote, "I want to be a blacksmith just like my father when I grow up."

On the other hand, Kevin refused to take his father's calls and wanted nothing to do with him. Because of his hostility, Kevin's father backed farther and farther away and made no effort to come to see him. Books have the power to transform lives. Examining the issue of father's love through *Just like Martin*, and other stories like it, might lead to insights and understanding of the relationship of fathers and sons and the importance of fathers in the lives of African American boys.

CONCLUSION

Authentic multicultural literature can support literacy development, support home–school connections, develop positive images, and provide a historical context for understanding diverse cultures (McClellan & Fields, 2004). Teachers must be willing to use literature that requires critical reflection about cultural issues (Rabinowitz & Smith, 1998) in an effort to understand these issues and their impact on the lives of the children that they teach.

Researchers and teachers must engage in self-reflection about multicultural literature and about the diverse students they teach (Spears-Bunton, 1999). Multicultural books that depict the unique characteristics of African Americans should be used. These books address a variety of themes; reflect aspects of language, behaviors, traditions, and views; and are intended to promote an understanding of African American history and culture (Sims, 1982). African American students have expressed a preference for multicultural literature (Thornton, 1997). McClellan and Fields (2004) believe that the literacy development of African American children can be supported by the use of authentic African American literature that makes connections between the students' home and school lives, and provides a historical context for cultural understanding.

Hence, teachers who want to create culturally relevant classrooms must broaden their concept of literacy to incorporate literature and orature that encourage students to question and search for answers in what they read (Ladson-Billings, 1992). Meaningful and responsive literacy instruction can nurture the resiliency of African American males by teaching them to value written words (Tatum, 2005), achieve in reading (Conchas & Noguera, 2004), and understand and interact positively with their fathers and other members of their families and communities (Gadsden & Bowman, 1999). Interspersing issues of fathering into class discussions about literature, health, and social studies can prepare African American males to be nurturing fathers (Gadsden & Bowman, 1999). Engaging African American males in reading through critical dialogue in response to text has the potential to help reduce the gap in reading achievement between African American males and their age mates.

REFERENCES

Alston, J., and Thaxton, L. (2003). *Stuff happens (and then you fix it!)*. New York: John Wiley & Sons.

Angelou, M. (1994). *The complete collected poems of Maya Angelou.* New York: Random House.

Bauman, J., Hooten, H., & White, P. (1999). Teaching comprehension through literature: A teacher research project to develop fifth graders' reading strategies and motivation. *Reading Teacher, 53* (1), 38–51.

Bus, A. G., van Ijzendoorn, M. H., & Pelligrini, A. D. (1995). Joint book reading makes for success in learning to read: A meta-analysis on intergenerational transmission of literacy. *Review of Educational Research, 65,* 1–21.

Cai, M. (2002). *Multicultural literature for children and young adults: Reflections on critical issues.* Westport, CT: Greenwood Press.

Cai, M., & Sims Bishop, R. (1994). Multicultural literature for children: Towards a clarification of the concept. In A. H. Dyson & C. Genishi (Eds.), *The need for story: Cultural diversity in classroom and community* (pp. 57–71). Urbana, IL: National Council of Teachers of English.

Collins, M. (1999). *Marva Collins Teacher Power Seminar 2000 Workbook.* Chicago: Marva Collins.

Conchas, G. Q., & Noguera, P. A. (2004). Understanding the exceptions: How small schools support the achievement of academically successful black boys. In N. Way & J. Y. Chu (Eds.), *Adolescent boys: Exploring diverse cultures of boyhood* (pp. 317–337). New York: New York University Press.

Davis, J. E. (2005). Early schooling and academic achievement of African American males. In F. Olatokunbo (Ed.), *Educating African American males: Voices from the field* (pp. 129–150). Thousand Oaks, CA: Corwin.

Davis, O. (1992). *Just like Martin.* New York: Simon & Schuster.

Donahue, P. L., Daane, M. C., and Grigg, W. S. (2003). *The nation's report card: Reading highlights 2003* (NCES 2004-452). U.S. Department of Education, Institute of Education Sciences, National Center for Education Statistics. Washington, DC: U.S. Government Printing Office.

Gadsden, V., & Bowman, P. J. (1999). African American males and the struggle toward responsible fatherhood. In V. C. Polite and J. E. Davis (Eds.), *African American males in school and society* (pp. 166–183). New York: Teachers College Press.

Gilbert, R., & Gilbert, P. (1998). *Masculinity goes to school.* New York: Routledge.

Heflin, B., & Barksdale-Ladd, M. A. (2001). African American children's literature that helps students find themselves: Selection guidelines for Grades K–3. *Reading Teacher, 54* (8), 810–819.

Holzman, M. (2004). *Public education and black male students: A state report card.* Schott Educational Equity Index. Cambridge, MA: Schott Foundation for Public Education.

Hughes, L. (1959). *Selected poems of Langston Hughes.* New York: Knopf.

Jencks, C., & Phillips, M. (1998). *The black–white test scores gap.* Washington, DC: Brookings Institute.

Kunjufu, J. (2002). *Black students—middle class teachers.* Chicago: African American Images.

Ladson-Billings, G. (1992). Liberatory consequences of literacy: A case of culturally relevant instruction for African American students. *Journal of Negro Education, 61* (3), 378–391.

Maynard, T. (2002). *Boys and literacy: Exploring the issues.* New York: Routledge.

McClellan, S., & Fields, M. (2004). Using African American children's literature to support literacy development. *Young Children, 59* (3), 50–54.

McGinley, W., & Kamberelis, G. (1996). Maniac Magee and Ragtime Tumpie: Children negotiating self and world through reading and writing. *Research in the Teaching of English, 30,* 75–113.

Mitchell, B. (1986). *A pocketful of goobers: A story about George Washington Carver.* Minneapolis: Carolrhoda Books.

Paterson, K. (1977). *Bridge to Terabithia.* New York: Avon.

Perie, M., Moran, R., and Lutkus, A. D. (2005). *NAEP 2004 trends in academic progress: Three decades of student performance in reading and mathematics* (NCES 2005-464). U.S. Department of Education, Institute of Education Sciences, National Center for Education Statistics. Washington, DC: Government Printing Office.

Peters, M. (1985). Racial socialization of young black children. In H. McAddoo & J. McAdoo (Eds.), *Black children* (pp. 159–173). Beverly Hills, CA: Sage.

Polite, V. C. (1999). Combating educational neglect in suburbia: African American males and mathematics. In V. C. Polite and J. E. Davis (Eds.), *African American males in school and society* (pp. 97–107). New York: Teachers College Press.

Porche, M. V., Ross, S. J., & Snow, C. (2004). From preschool to middle school: The role of masculinity in low-income urban adolescent boys' literacy skills and academic achievement. In N. Way & J. Y. Chu (Eds.), *Adolescent boys: Exploring diverse cultures of boyhood* (pp. 338–357). New York: New York University Press.

Rabinowitz, P., & Smith, M. (1998). *Authorizing readers: Resistance and respect in the teaching of literature.* New York: Teachers College Press.

Rand, D., & Parker, T. (2001). *Black books galore! Guide to great African American children's books about boys.* New York: John Wiley & Sons.

Rohner, R., & Veneziano, R. (2001). The importance of father love: History and contemporary evidence. *Review of General Psychology, 5* (4), 382–405.

Sims, R. (1982). *Shadow and substance: Afro-American experience in contemporary children's fiction.* Urbana, IL: National Council of Teachers of English.

Spears-Bunton, L. (1999). Calypso, jazz, reggae, and salsa: Literature, response, and the African diaspora. In N. Karolides (Ed.), *Reader-response in secondary and college classrooms* (2nd. ed., pp. 311–326). Mahwah, NJ: Lawrence Erlbaum.

Tatum, A. W. (2005). *Teaching reading to black adolescent males: Closing the achievement gap.* Portland, ME: Stenhouse Publishers.

———. (2006). Engaging African American males in reading. *Educational Leadership*, 63 (5), 44–49.

Teachman, J., Day, R., Paasch, K., Carver, K., & Call, V. (1998). Sibling resemblance in behavioral and cognitive outcomes: The role of father presence. *Journal of Marriage and the Family*, 60, 835–848.

Thornton, M. C. (1997). Strategies of racial socialization among black parents: Mainstream, minority and cultural messages. In R. J. Taylor, J. Jackson, & L. M. Chatters (Eds.), *Family life in black America* (pp. 201–215). Thousand Oaks, CA: Sage.

Varlas, L. (2005). Bridging the widest gap: Raising the achievement of black boys. *Association for Supervision and Curriculum Development Education Update*, 47 (8), 1–3.

Wade, J. C. (1994). African American fathers and sons: Social, historical, and psychological considerations. *Families in Society*, 75, 561–570.

Walker-Dalhouse, D. (1992). Using African-American literature to increase ethnic understanding. *Reading Teacher*, 45 (6), 416–422.

12

Fences, Physical and Proverbial: Pre-service Teachers' Engagement with *The Other Side* by Jacqueline Woodson

Peggy S. Rice

> The rest of my life is committed to changing the way the world thinks, one reader at a time.
>
> —Jacqueline Woodson

Scholars such as Rudine Sims Bishop (2000) have noted that although quality African American children's literature is published, its inclusion in school curriculums is limited, as teachers tend to avoid using these books to engage their students in critical conversations. When I have attempted to engage my students, who are pre-service teachers, in critical conversations about African American children's literature, they tend to resist. The European American pre-service teachers are especially resistant and tend to silence other voices, an aspect Beach (1997) addresses as he identifies various stances of resistance in high school students' responses to multi-cultural literature. For instance, he identifies "individual prejudice" stances, such as "denial of racial difference" and "reluctance to adopt alternative cultural perspectives."

This resistance is reflected in the following discussion that occurred after I read aloud a section of *Leon's Story* (Tillage, 1997) to a class of pre-service teachers. In the selected passage, Leon's mother is seriously injured and his father killed. Leon, an African American growing up in the 1950s, observes a car full of European American boys knock down his father and then come back and run over him. "The car came back and pulled over to where my father was and the driver ran completely over him, as though he was running over a dog or something. And my father got caught underneath the car and they drug him almost back up to the house where we were living" (p. 67).

Professor: What is your response to this story?

European American Student 1: I think the violence is too graphic to share with elementary children.

European American Student 2: I do, too. People don't behave like that anymore. The civil rights movement made a huge difference.

African American Student 1: You don't know what you are talking about.

African American Student 2: Yeah, stuff like that happens. I'd share this book with elementary children. It is important for them to hear these stories, especially students who are not black.

(Tense quiet fills the air.)

Professor: What other thoughts do you have about this story? How do you think your cultural identity has shaped your response to the story?

(No one responds. Tense quiet continues.)

Overcoming this resistance is not a simple task. Fostering respect for literary characters in African American children's literature requires readers to "try on" the perspectives of these characters and to consider the possible implications of those perspectives in the reader's life, a goal that is difficult to achieve (Smith & Strickland, 2001). Beach (1997) and Smith and Strickland (2001) recommend involving readers in activities designed to help them enter into the world of the story, such as writing from the perspective of a character, or engaging in dramatic activities. This chapter presents research I conducted with a group of pre-service teachers enrolled in my senior seminar class for elementary education majors whose concentration area is elementary English language arts. I incorporated recommendations by Smith and Strickland (2001) and Beach (1997) as I investigated the influence of imagination and the arts as response activities on pre-service teachers' engagement with *The Other Side*, by Jacqueline Woodson (2001).

The Other Side is a first-person narrative from the perspective of Clover, an African American child. In the story, a fence separates the white neighborhood from the black neighborhood. Clover's mother has told her not to climb over the fence as it isn't safe. At the beginning of the summer, Clover observes a white child, Annie, climbing up on the fence and staring over at Clover's side. Sometimes Clover stares back at her. One day when Clover is jumping rope with her African American friends on her side of the fence, Annie asks if she can join them. Sandra, one of Clover's friends, refuses to let her. In addition, although Clover and her Mama see Annie with her Mama when they go into town, they don't talk to each other. It rains a lot that summer and Clover notices Annie playing outside in the rain by herself, but Clover's Mama won't let her go outside. In the middle of the summer, the rain stops, and Clover is happy to go outside. She goes close to the fence, and the two girls introduce themselves, smiling at each other. They sit together on the fence, as they don't want to disobey their parents about going onto the other side of the fence. Clover and Annie continue to sit together on the fence throughout the rest of the summer. Clover's mother notices but doesn't say anything. After a while, Clover asks her African American friends if Annie can join them jumping rope. The girls all jump rope together until they are too tired. The book ends with Annie commenting, "Someday somebody's going to come along and knock this old fence down." Clover responds, "Yeah. Someday (p. 32)."

THE PROJECT

My specific research questions are as follows:

- Were critically thoughtful responses apparent in the pre-service teachers' responses to African American children's literature when imagination and the arts are used, as after reading activities? If so, what is the nature of the critically thoughtful response?
- Are differences apparent between the African American and European American races? If so, what is the nature of any differences that occurred?

Setting

This study was conducted at a midwestern university with a group of pre-service teachers enrolled in a senior seminar class for elementary education majors whose concentration area is elementary English language arts. The class focuses on the trends and issues in the teaching of elementary English language arts, in which the pre-service teachers read and discuss articles from journals, such as *Language Arts* and the *Journal of Literacy Research*. Two topics of focus prior to implementation of the project were critical literacy and visual response/oral presentation of literature. The classes tend to be comprised of European American students, so this class was unique in that approximately 25 percent of the students were African American.

Throughout the semester, I noticed that the African American pre-service teachers and the European American pre-service teachers often responded differently in discussions regarding multicultural topics, specifically those involving African American children's literature. For example, when we discussed *Leon's Story* (Tillage, 1997) as a text for social justice, the European

American students expressed views that racism was "back then" and "things are different now," views with which the African American students disagreed. There is an element of truth in each perspective, in that life for African Americans has changed in some respects following the civil rights movement; however, overt acts of racism still exist. The discussions and engagement with the African American children's literature were limited in scope, as neither perspective was open to discussion and tension emerged with the opposing views.

Participants

Fourteen pre-service teachers participated in the study. Four of the participants were black females and ten of the participants were white females. One of the African American participants was twenty-three years old; three of the European American participants were twenty-two years old; the remaining ten participants were twenty-one years old. All of the participants were unmarried; however, one of the twenty-one-year-old African American participants had a three-year-old daughter. Three of the African American participants were raised in the inner city of a midwestern city in which the population was at least 75 percent African American; one of the African American participants grew up in largely European American areas of cities in three different regions of the United States. Seven of the European American participants were raised in midwestern communities in which the percentage of European Americans was at least 94 percent. The population of these communities ranged from 2,000 to 17,000. Three of the European American participants were raised in predominately European American suburbs of midwestern cities in which the European American population was at least 90 percent. With the exception of the African American participant who had lived in three different cities and one European American participant, all of the participants had friendship circles that consisted primarily of members of their own race.

NARRATIVE INTERPRETATION

Sociocultural theorists recognize the influence of readers' "inner texts," such as ideas, experiences, and meanings (Witte, 1992) on their interpretations of narrative. These theorists acknowledge that readers are active participants in the construction of meaning, and that meanings are socially constructed with multiple interpretations, depending largely or partially on one's discourse community. One's "identity kit" (Gee, 1996) or "cultural identity" (Ferdman, 1991) based on one's social and cultural experiences forms a base for interpretation of words, meanings, and ideas. Hall, Critcher, Jefferson, Clarke, and Roberts (1978) have argued that interpretations are based on our "cultural maps" that provide a framework for constructing the meaning of new events. Thus, our "cultural maps," which are created by our sociocultural frame, provide the backbone of our "inner texts" and result in situated meanings (Gee, 2000) that shape our responses to books we read.

Situated meanings were evident in the pre-service teachers' responses to *Leon's Story*. The European American pre-service teachers had not experienced the type of racial prejudice experienced by Leon in the 1950s, nor were they aware of the contemporary lives of African Americans, so their cultural identity provided constraints in terms of their response to the story as events that happened "back then." They firmly believed that "things are different now." At the same time, the cultural identity of the African American pre-service teachers enabled them to respond to the racial acts of violence depicted in the story as events that still happen to members of the African American community. Although the African American pre-service teachers had not personally experienced the type of racism depicted in *Leon's Story*, they were aware of similar experiences within the African American community, and they shared these stories after the activities with *The Other Side* (Woodson, 2001).

Social constructivists such as Vygotsky (1978, 1987) foreground the importance of social interaction in learning and the need for social interactions that enable us to build on and extend previous understandings. Bakhtin (1981, 1986) emphasizes that our social interactions do not necessarily generate new understandings, an aspect I noticed in our discussions of *Leon's Story*. For Bakhtin, new links of meaning are invented only when we engage in dialogue in which two perspectives intermingle to generate new points of view, new positions, and new understandings. When the pre-service teachers shared their responses to *Leon's Story*, resistance to each other's perspective emerged rather than dialogue, and they were unable to move beyond the resulting tension that surfaced.

TRANSFORMING RESPONSES TO AFRICAN AMERICAN TEXTS

In order for new links of meaning to be formed, critical thinking must occur. The conflict and tense quiet that surfaced when the pre-service teachers shared their responses to *Leon's Story* prevented critical thinking from occurring. According to Bailin (1998), critical thinking involves three dimensions: (1) critical challenges, in which students assume various roles related to a particular controversial issue; (2) intellectual resources, in which background knowledge is essential as well as attitudes such as a willingness to listen to and consider the views of others; and (3) critically thoughtful responses in which an understanding and appreciation of various points of view is evident. All three of these dimensions can be promoted by educational drama and other types of imaginative responses, such as interior monologues (Bigelow & Christensen, 1994).

CRITICAL CHALLENGE

In light of the lack of engagement and critical thinking I observed in the class discussion of *Leon's Story*, I selected Woodson's *The Other Side* as a focus for the project, as the plot addresses the influence of racial segregation on children, includes the voice of an African American protagonist along with a European American character, and includes limited dialogue. The limited dialogue in *The Other Side* lends itself to drama conversations.

Drama conversations occur at the "edges of the text," and the story becomes a "narrative prop" (Heath, Branscombe, & Thomas, 1986) for teacher and students to create a world that intersects and interacts with both the story world and the actual world of the students. To accomplish this, small groups engage in improvisation among various characters in the story (Wolf, Edmiston, & Enciso, 1997). For example, in *The Other Side*, the primary voices that are heard are Clover's and her Mama's; however, as readers, we know that other characters' voices exist in the story world, such as the voices of Sandra and Clover's other friends, or the voices of Annie and her mama in conversation. What were these conversations? Drama conversations provide opportunities for children to explore alternate ways of thinking as they enter into the world of the story (e.g., Edmiston & Wilhelm 1998), and "*believe* in the possibility of their character" (Wolf, Edmiston, & Enciso, 1997, p. 497), thereby engaging in critical thinking. For example, the participants in a study by Edmiston and Wilhelm (1998) were able to "walk in the shoes" of the characters and demonstrated a deeper understanding of the social injustice of slavery.

INTELLECTUAL RESOURCES

In order to deal with the critical challenge, students need to draw on many intellectual resources; background knowledge related to the issue is essential (Bailin, 1998). With this in mind, we first engaged in activities with *The Story of Ruby Bridges* (Coles, 1995) in order to develop an understanding of racial relations between African Americans and European Americans during the late 1950s and early 1960s. I also decided to sequence response activities with *The Other Side*, so we began with responses aimed at the center of the text, to draw participants into the story world before moving to the edges of the text. Attitudes such as "open-mindedness, fair-mindedness, and the willingness to consider a variety of points of view" are essential for critical thinking (Bailin, 1998, p. 13). As empathy and affective understanding are related to these attitudes, I selected the following response activities aimed at developing these aspects and to build belief and commitment: quickdraw, classroom theater, drama conversations, and interior monologue.

Quickdraw

Before reading the story aloud to the participants, I told the participants to close their eyes, picturing the characters and action in the story and imagining themselves in the story while I read the story to them. In addition, I told them they would sketch an image "symbolic of their response to a character or scene in the story and then share that image with a partner" when I had finished reading the story to them. Researchers, such as Wolf, Edmiston, and Enciso (1997) have used this strategy to "set the stage" for dramatizing at the edges of the text.

Classroom Theater

After the students shared their sketches with a partner, I distributed two scripts of *The Other Side*. One script presented the story as told by Jacqueline Woodson; the second script was adapted to convey Clover and Annie in contemporary times, reflecting back on that summer. I told the participants they would participate in classroom theater with one of the scripts. Classroom theater blends creative drama with readers' theater, so that participants have opportunities to dramatize at the center of the text without memorizing a script (Wolf, Edmiston, & Enciso, 1997). The participants selected their roles and practiced "bringing the text to life." I videotaped the performances, so the participants would be able to view them later and reflect on their performance.

Drama Conversations

After presenting the story as depicted in the 1950s, the research participants selected roles and engaged in the following drama conversations: (a) Clover and her Mama, (b) Annie and her Mama, (c) Sandra and Clover's other friends, (d) the black side of town, and (e) the white side of town. After each drama conversation, participants not engaged in the drama conversation acted as reporters. I was their editor, telling them that I had heard about the story and wanted them to investigate the attitudes and experiences of the people in the town. Once the drama conversations depicting the characters during the 1950s were completed, participants engaged in drama conversations depicting the characters during contemporary times after Clover and Annie are grown up, as follows: (a) Clover and Annie, (b) Clover and Sandra, (c) Annie's Mama and Clover's Mama, (d) Clover and her Mama, (e) Annie and her Mama, (f) Sandra and Clover's other friends, (g) the black side of town, and (h) the white side of town. Again, participants not engaged in the drama conversation acted as reporters. Each pre-service teacher participated in four drama conversations.

Interior Monologue

Empathy for others can be developed through imaginative response activities such as interior monologues, which are "the imagined thoughts of a character in history, literature, or life at a specific point in time" (Bigelow & Christensen, 1994, p. 110). This strategy provides structure for critical thinking about the perspectives of others, but it also enables student choice. For example, in a unit on the Vietnam War, the participants in Bigelow and Christensen (1994) could write from the point of view of an American pilot, a North Vietnamese man, a Native American marine, or a Buddhist monk. Upon completing the drama conversations, participants wrote an interior monologue (imagined thoughts) from the point of view of a character of choice in either the historical past or contemporary times. Participants shared their interior monologues, followed by comments from the audience.

CRITICALLY THOUGHTFUL RESPONSE

According to Bailin (1998), critically thoughtful responses reflect an appreciation of the various points of view, as well as an appreciation for the complexity of the issue being addressed. They also reflect an understanding of the various aspects of the context, including open-minded and fair-minded consideration of the various positions and arguments, that leads to sound reasoning about an issue. Critically thoughtful responses would take the form of the role drama but could also include drawing, writing, and discussion. Were critically thoughtful responses apparent in the pre-service teachers' responses to African American children's literature when imagination and the arts were used, as after reading activities?

DATA SOURCES

In order to evaluate the participants' engagement with the text and determine the extent to which their interpretations were critical, data were collected from several sources: field notes from observations; transcripts of the interactions that occurred during the various activities; ratings the participants gave for their level of comfort after they participated in each activity, along with their written explanations; ratings and explanations for the extent to which each participant thought that each activity enabled her to "walk in the shoes of the characters"; and written responses to the questions, focusing on their response to the activities as a whole, such as: What types of insights have you gained from participating in these activities? What types of insights have you gained from participating in these activities with African American literature? What types of insights have you gained by participating in these activities with members of a race different from yours?

ANALYSIS AND RESULTS

Ratings were tabulated and percentages calculated for the level of comfort and the extent to which each participant thought that each activity enabled her to "walk in the shoes of the characters." Separate percentages were calculated for the African American participants and the European American participants. I used a clustering technique (Beach, 1983) to identify the nature of the written responses. I used the constant comparative method (Bogdan & Biklen, 1992) to determine patterns among the written responses, as well as to determine emerging themes and revealing comments from my field notes and transcripts of the interactions that occurred during the various activities. In order to establish trustworthiness (Lincoln & Guba, 1985), theoretical perspectives, data sources (field notes, transcripts, and written documents), and methods were triangulated.

Fostering Respect for Literary Characters

In an attempt to reduce the tension others have experienced in discussions of multicultural literature (Beach, 1997; Smith & Strickland, 2001) and to increase engagement so that the participants were able to "try on" the perspectives of the characters and to consider the possible implications of those perspectives in their lives, the study incorporated a broad range of response activities designed to enable the participants to enter the story world. Overall, the African American pre-service teachers were more comfortable than the European American pre-service teachers participating in these activities (see table 12.1). With each of the activities, 75–100 percent of the African Americans indicated that they were extremely comfortable responding to the book in this manner. The primary reason expressed by the African American pre-service teachers for feeling extremely comfortable was having an opportunity to share their ideas and feelings. At the same time,

Table 12.1. Pre-service Teachers' Comfort Rating for Participating in Each Activity

	Percentage of Responses					
	African American			Euro-American		
Activity	Extremely Uncomfortable	Comfortable	Extremely Comfortable	Extremely Uncomfortable	Comfortable	Extremely Comfortable
	1	3	5	1	3	5
Sketching an image that showed your response to the story	0	25%	75%	0	20%	80%
Sharing the image that showed your response to the story	0	25%	75%	0	10%	90%
Making decisions about your first classroom theater performance with group members	0	25%	75%	0	10%	90%
Presenting your first classroom theater performance	0	25%	75%	0	25%	75%
Making decisions about your second classroom theater performance with group members	0	25%	75%	0	20%	80%
Presenting your second classroom theater performance	0	0	100%	0	30%	70%
Making decisions about first drama conversation with a group	0	0	100%	0	50%	50%
Presenting first drama conversation	0	0	100%	0	70%	30%

Responding to others' first drama conversation	0	100%	20%	60%	20%
Making decisions about second drama conversation with a group	0	100%	10%	60%	30%
Presenting second drama conversation	0	100%	10%	80%	10%
Responding to others' second drama conversation	0	100%	40%	60%	0
Making decisions about third drama conversation with a group	0	100%	0	80%	20%
Presenting third drama conversation	0	100%	20%	60%	20%
Responding to others' third drama conversation	25%	75%	30%	60%	10%
Making decisions about fourth drama conversation with a group	0	100%	30%	50%	20%
Presenting fourth drama conversation	0	100%	20%	80%	0
Responding to others' fourth drama conversation	0	100%	20%	70%	10%
Writing an interior monologue	0	100%	10%	30%	60%
Sharing your interior monologue	25%	75%	10%	50%	40%
Responding to others' interior monologues	25%	75%	10%	20%	70%

Table 12.2. Pre-service Teachers' Rating for the Extent to Which Active Participation Enabled Them to Walk in the Shoes of Characters

	Percentage of Responses					
	African American			Euro-American		
	Lowest		Highest	Lowest		Highest
Activity	1	3	5	1	3	5
Quickdraw	50%	0	50%	60%	20%	20%
Classroom Theater	0	0	100%	10%	60%	30%
Drama Conversations	0	0	100%	0	20%	80%
Interior Monologue	0	0	100%	10%	30%	60%

the comfort level of the European Americans varied a great deal depending on the activity. For example, up to 40 percent of the European American participants were extremely uncomfortable with the drama conversations. The primary reason expressed by the European Americans for feeling extremely uncomfortable was a fear of offending the African American pre-service teachers. The drama conversations were the activity in which the highest percentage of European Americans (80 percent) felt they were most able to walk in the shoes of the characters (see table 12.2). Thus, even though the European American participants were not as comfortable as the African American participants, the dramatic activities created spaces for them to enter the story world and try on the perspectives of the characters.

Consider the following scene in which four of the European American pre-service teachers and three of the African American pre-service teachers were in-role as adults in Clover's African American neighborhood during the 1950s:

Af. Am. 1: We're neighbors of Clover's family on the black side of the fence. Now ladies, I think this interaction is a very bad thing. You, you know what can happen when they come there?

Eur. Am. 1: What should we do?

Af. Am. 2: We can keep our children away from theirs. There's some time before something happens like in Rosewood. They'll be here soon to burn down our houses and chase our men off.

Others: Yeah.

Eur. Am. 2: I think if they come over to our side, we should just keep our kids inside.

Eur. Am. 3: Yes, mine will definitely be inside or kept a close eye on.

Af. Am. 1: I think we need to go over and talk to Clover's mom, you know, she doesn't seem to worry about her daughter playing with that, that . . . What's her name?

Others: Annie.

Af. Am. 3: I know my little girl came home talking about Annie. I was like, Annie, who's Annie? And it happens to be this little girl across the fence and you know this is really alarming to me. I cannot allow this. This is dangerous for our whole community, now.

Af. Am. 2: Yes, it is.

Af. Am. 1: We need to set up a meeting.

Eur. Am. 4: If one comes in, all will come in. We just can't lose the little bit that we have.

Af. Am. 3: Yeah.

Eur. Am. 1: If their kids come over, their parents will get mad about it.

Af. Am. 4: I cannot afford to lose this house. We'll be out on the street and I cannot afford to do that.

Af. Am. 3: We've worked too hard to get here.

Af. Am. 1: Let's see. We'll meet at Clover's house at 7:00 Thursday to talk to her mom.

Others: Right.

[Conversation ends.]

In the preceding conversation, the cultural identities of the pre-service teachers influenced their contributions. Even though the European American students "tried on" the perspectives of the African American characters, their initial contributions tended to lack urgency in comparison to those by the African American pre-service teachers. In particular, the contributions by the African American pre-service teachers consistently reflected an understanding of extreme consequences and an urgent need to address the situation before it could escalate due to the lack of power of the African American community in regards to the European American community. Thus, although the European American pre-service teachers exhibited a willingness to listen to and consider the views of others, their background knowledge provided initial constraints. In the following interactions, as the reporters question Clover's neighbors, the European American actors are able to develop background knowledge through the contributions of the African American actors, as evidenced in their critically thoughtful responses.

[Reporters enter.]

Reporter 1: Why are you interrogating Clover's mom? That's not very fair.

Af. Am. 1: (laughs) We're not interrogating Clover's mother.

Reporter 1: Why are you telling her what she has to do with her daughter? That's not your business. She is an adult.

Eur. Am. 2: We're just going to ask her what she is doing.

Af. Am. 2: We're thinking about the good of the community as a whole, not just Clover.

Eur. Am. 4: Yeah, we all need to stick together or they might take over.

Af. Am. 1: Did you hear what happened to Mr. John down the street? He was just down there trimming his yard and Mr. Farmer came and shot at him. He said he was too close to the fence. Now, if they're going to shoot at him even if he doesn't cross the fence, if we cross the fence, we'll all be lynched.

Reporter1: If they are shooting at black people who are too close to the fence, why are they letting the kids sit on the fence?

Af. Am. 3: They don't know that the kids are doing that.

Eur. Am. 1: The white girl initiated it. She sat there staring.

Reporter 1: Well, I noticed the little black girl sitting on the fence, too.

Af. Am. 3: It's that Clover girl sitting on the fence with Annie; my child hasn't been sitting on the fence.

Af. Am. 1: That's why we're having conversations with all of our children. They're not allowed to sit on the fence, and they are not going over the stupid fence because I don't want this community to burn down. I don't want harm to come down to my family.

Reporter 2: You said that you've had conversations with your children about how to react to this whole thing, so does that mean you're telling your kids what to do? Why not let the kids think for themselves?

Eur.Am. 1: We just let them know what could happen.

Eur. Am. 2: Right.

Af. Am. 1: We're telling them the realities of life. They're gonna grow up and be adults in this world and they're going to be the ones that face white criticism from white people. Therefore, they might as well learn from now when they're five and learn how to deal with it rather than get beat down by the police in the street when they're twenty-five. So, I'd rather tell my child now, than let them grow up and end up getting in the street somewhere. Now, I'm not telling my child what to think. I'm telling them what's real.

Reporter 2: Well, by keeping this segregation, I mean, how can that solve any problems? You know, if you keep white from black, how can that solve problems?

Eur. Am. 1: It's gonna keep our children safe.

Af. Am. 2: It's not that we like to be separate. We have no choice. We're limited in our actions.

Eur. Am. 2: We're going to keep our children inside because of this whole situation. We have to keep them safe.

Reporter 2: Okay. You said you're trying to inform your children. You're trying to educate them on the reality and you're trying to help them deal with it, but you're not letting them deal with whites by keeping them in the house.

Af. Am. 2: Oh, no. My child can go outside to play, but she can't go across the fence.

Reporter 2: That is how you let her deal with reality?

Af. Am. 3: This is our reality, our community.

Af. Am. 1: Do you know what happened the last time someone black crossed the fence? This was in another segregated community. That whole community was burnt down and people were shot dead in the street and kids left with no parents, all because someone crossed the fences. So you know, I don't want that to happen to this community. If that means I have to pull my children into my house, so they don't play with these kids, that is what I have to do, because I'm not going to lose my family, my house, my property for some stupid reason like that.

Eur. Am. 3: My family has worked too hard. My husband and I just don't want to lose my house. We just don't. We just don't.

Reporter 3: I know you all have said that you have worked hard. Don't you think that the white people have to work hard, too?

Af. Am. 1: We have to work three times harder. Do you know how hard it is for me to buy a car, because I am black? Do you know how hard it is for me to shop in town?

Eur. Am. 4: I have three jobs right now.

Reporter 3: Do you think that no white person has three jobs?

Af. Am. 2: Oh, my goodness, I make minimum wage. My bosses are all white men. My husband makes minimum wage and all of his bosses are white men.

Eur. Am. 4: I am the lowest in the company. Everyone's white above me. I can't go any higher, so why would they be making as much as me or less than me? I don't even have a seat on the bus when I come home from work.

Eur. Am. 1: They live on the other side of the fence, and they don't want us to get up high.

Af. Am. 3: It is like an ocean.

Reporter 2: How can one fence divide like the sea?

Af. Am. 2: They wanna keep us low. They don't want us to be superior.

Af. Am. 1: There is a physical fence and there is a proverbial fence. There is a fence in society that won't allow us to go further.

Eur. Am. 2: White people come in and take the better jobs. I just never get a break.

Eur. Am. 1: They don't have to work as hard as us, either.

Eur. Am. 3: Yeah, because they've got the white color.

Eur. Am. 1: They get to sit in the front of the bus, you know, we have to sit in the back or stand.

Af. Am. 1: Lots of times, there is no seat. We have to walk three miles, four miles, five miles a day in the dead of winter after being at work for twelve hours, working three times harder. We come home and still take care of our family. This is not a discussion about a fence, this is a discussion about survival. This is what it takes for my family to survive.

Af. Am. 3: And their kids get to ride a bus to school and our children have to walk.

Reporter 2: I think this is a case of ignorance, where neither side knows enough about each other to have a credible statement to make.

Eur. Am. 1: I don't think it is coming from our neighborhood. It is definitely coming from their neighborhood.

Reporter 2: Have you made the effort to go over there and find out?

Eur. Am. 1: They are the ones who make the rules. They are the ones who say we have to sit in the back of the bus. We are not making those rules. They are the ones that are ignorant. They are segregating us. If we don't follow, we're gonna get hurt.

Reporter 1: Maybe we need to talk to them.

This lengthy drama conversation illustrates the manner in which the drama conversations created spaces for the European American pre-service teachers to "try on" the perspectives of the characters of a different race. In the initial part of the discussion, the African American pre-service teachers' contributions reflected the lack of power of the blacks much more so than the contributions by the European Americans. Following the lead of the African American pre-service teachers, as the reporters continued to ask questions, the European American pre-service teachers contributed critically thoughtful responses that demonstrated an understanding of the inequity of power that enabled whites to segregate blacks at this time in history.

In our final meeting, the pre-service teachers wrote their interior monologues, imagined thoughts of the characters, and shared them orally. After each interior monologue was shared, others would respond with their comments. All of the pre-service teachers selected a character from their race. Among the African Americans, the selections were as follows: Clover in the 1950s (1); Clover in contemporary times (2); Clover's Mom in the 1950s (1); Sandra in contemporary times (1). Among the European Americans, the selections were as follows: Annie in the 1950s (7); Annie in contemporary times (1); Annie's Mom in contemporary times (1); a white neighbor child in contemporary times (1). Each of the pre-service teachers said they selected these characters because they felt that they could relate to her.

Following is an interior monologue of Clover in the 1950s:

Today was a strange day. I was outside playing with my friends and I saw that girl sitting there [on the fence]. I wish I knew her name. I wonder if she likes to jump rope like me and my friends. I wonder why I never see her with friends and why she looks so sad all the time. I could not imagine being alone, like her with no friends to jump rope with and sing the Cinderella rhyme, which is my favorite. I wish I could go over that fence and jump rope with her. I always ask Mama why I can't go over, but she always says the same thing over and over (It just isn't safe!).

Following is an interior monologue of Annie in the 1950s:

Those girls on the other side of the fence sure look like they're having fun. I know Mom said not to go over the fence because they are "colored folks" and "different from us." Still those girls don't look mean or anything. They're just jumping rope. Maybe I could teach them some new rhymes! Hmmm, you know, if I just sit up on the fence, I'm not going over it. Maybe I can just talk to those girls from there. I really would like to make some friends, even if I could only talk to them.

The interior monologues reflect critically thoughtful responses. The pre-service teachers were able to consider the perspective of the character in that context and empathize with the characters. Thus, respect for the literary characters is evident; however, the pre-service teachers did not "try on" the perspective of the characters of a different race.

PRIVATE EXPERIENCE TO PUBLIC DOMAIN

As literary theorists (e.g., Rosenblatt, 1991) note, the reader's imaginative creation of the story world forms the base for further discussion. Entering the story world and adopting the perspectives of the characters enabled the participants to bridge the two worlds and engage in dialogue (Bakhtin, 1981, 1986) that included critically thoughtful responses, as evidenced in the interchange in the preceding section. An additional important aspect of this dialogue is that it enabled the participants to move their private experiences regarding racism into the public domain. Prior to our engagement with *The Other Side*, participants were not comfortable voicing their experiences with racism. The sharing of the following experiences generated discussion about racial relations in contemporary times.

Af. Am. 1: I think back then racism was just more out in the open. Now, I think people are still very racist, but, you know, more covered up. I mean, I have experienced a lot of things. People try to be nice in a different way, to divert from racism basically.

Professor: Would you share an example so we can understand?

Af. Am. 1: Oh, my gosh! I was in Burger King. I went over to grab some fries while my car was getting fixed next door. As I was sitting down, one white lady, she came right over and sat next to me. She asked me how old I was and I told her. And she said, "You know, you color folks just don't age right. You guys just age so nicely." I was just like, "Colored folks?!" It is stuff like that.

Af. Am. 2: I was gonna give another example of racism. When we first moved into my neighborhood, it had three black families in it. My mom said, it is not that she is teaching me to be prejudiced, but she said, "Watch. It's called white flight. As soon as more black families start moving in, watch the white people start moving out." And that's exactly what happened. This lady that lived two doors from us, her kids started to grow up with us, 'cause we are all around the same age. They would come to our house to play on the swing set and monkey bars. Before long, her mom, their parents, built a house in a predominantly white neighborhood. They didn't even wait to sell the house. They just built the house and moved. I guess she felt she could tell my mom. She said, "We're moving, because the neighborhood is just not what it used to be." It's not like the neighborhood had gangs and loud music. It was just black families moving in.

Eur. Am. 3: Well, my Dad is extremely racist. At times, he can be a goodie and hide it. But I think a lot of the problem is that some parents teach their children to stay with the attitudes of the fifties. I mean, like, I've had black people yelling at me and say, "Your family had black people as your slave." And I know for a fact that they didn't because I was new in this country. My ancestors were not even here at that time. But just because I'm white they think that I have had slaves, and I've had that comment made to me many times. Plus, like, what did I do? I'm not racist.

CONCLUSION

The results of this study demonstrate how using imagination and the arts as response activities to African American children's literature increases engagement and critical interpretation for pre-service teachers. These types of activities create spaces in which readers are able to move beyond the situated meanings (Gee, 2000) that are created by their sociocultural frame. Readers are able to overcome resistance and foster respect for literary characters, an aspect that has been difficult to achieve with African American children's literature (Beach, 1997; Smith & Strickland, 2001).

More specifically, the inclusion of dramatic activities, such as drama conversations at the edges of the text, provides opportunities for readers to "try on" the perspectives of the characters. As Heathcote notes, "Drama is not stories retold in action. Drama is human beings confronted by situations which change them because of what they must face in dealing with those challenges" (1984, p. 48). In drama you "put yourself into other people's shoes and by using personal experience to help you to understand their point of view you may discover more than you knew when you started" (p. 44).

This power of drama was evident in the responses the pre-service teachers provided in terms of the insights they gained from participating in these activities. Following are thoughts from some of the European American pre-service teachers:

> "I have thought about things that I may not have thought about unless another student said it."
> "I learned a lot about myself and how I really feel on the issues discussed."
> "I have realized that racism and segregation are still in our society."
> "I have never been racist, but I do have new feelings. I really didn't realize how strongly African Americans still feel about these issues."
> "This discussion has made me realize that we still have a long way to go before we can all look at each other without labeling people a color."

Following are thoughts from some of the African American pre-service teachers:

> "I have gained another point of view. I am able to see how someone of another race may take the same story, scene, or action and portray it in a different manner."
> "Most of all, I've gained a sense of understanding of people, not just black/white people. I feel like I can work on race relations because I know where white people are coming from."
> "Racism is still as prevalent today as it was in history. It is just hidden more. As an African American, it has allowed me to show or tell the white students a black person's point of view of racism and how we are treated. It gives white people an opportunity to see what it means to be black. It has given me the incentive to be more open with issues."

The inclusion of other imaginative activities, such as the quickdraw, classroom theater, and interior monologues helped create the space necessary for dialogue (Bakhtin, 1981, 1986) to occur. These activities were more comfortable for the pre-service teachers to engage in and helped develop trust within the community. For example, there was a visible difference among the interactions of the races as the pre-service teachers participated in these activities. The first time we met, the African American pre-service teachers sat together on one side of the room while the European American pre-service teachers sat together on the other side of room. Members of the races talked quietly among themselves or were sitting quietly. At our final

meeting, the races were integrated and the atmosphere was much more re-
laxed. Everyone was chatting.

Educational Importance of the Study

Scholars such as Rudine Sims Bishop (2000) recognize the limited inclusion of multicultural children's literature in elementary classrooms. In order for this to change, educators must overcome their resistance to critical
engagement with African American literature, as well as to acknowledge and
transcend the threat that exists in a critical literacy classroom—difficult
tasks to accomplish. This study provides some insights into the power of
imagination and the arts for engaging pre-service teachers in African American multicultural children's literature and transcending the threat that exists in critical literacy classrooms. With noted African American authors
such as Jacqueline Woodson writing stories "to change the way the world
thinks, one reader at a time," (1995, p. 711), these are indeed important aspects to consider as we move toward creating a more equitable society.

REFERENCES

Bailin, S. (1998). Critical thinking and drama education. *Research in Drama Education, 3* (2), 145–154.

Bakhtin, M. M. (1981). Discourse in the novel. In C. Emerson & M. Holquist (Eds.),
The dialogic imagination: Four essays by M. Bakhtin (pp. 259–422). Austin: University of Texas Press.

———. (1986). *Speech genres and other late essays.* (Vern W. McGee, Trans.). Austin:
University of Texas Press. (Original work published 1979.)

Beach, R. (1983). Attitudes, social conventions, and response to literature. *Research
and Development in Education, 16,* 47–54.

———. (1997). *A teacher's introduction to reader-response theories.* Urbana, IL: National
Council of Teachers of English.

Bigelow, B., & Christensen, L. (1994). Promoting social imagination through interior monologues. In B. Bigelow (Ed.), *Rethinking our classrooms: Teaching for equity
and justice* (pp. 110–111). Milwaukee: Rethinking Schools.

Bishop, R. S. (2000, December). *Cross-disciplinary perspectives on children's and young
adult literature.* Paper presented at the National Reading Conference, Scottsdale, AZ.

Bogdan, R., & Biklen, S. (1992). *Qualitative research for education: An introduction to
theory and methods.* Needham Heights, MA: Allyn & Bacon.

Coles, R. (1995). *The story of Ruby Bridges.* New York: Scholastic.

Edmiston, B., & Wilhelm, J. (1998). Repositioning views/reviewing positions
through drama: Forming complex understandings in dialogue. In B. J. Wagner
(Ed.), *Educational drama and language arts: What research shows* (pp. 116–153).
Portsmouth, NH: Heinemann.

Ferdman, B. M. (1991). Literacy and cultural entity. In M. Minami & B. P. Kennedy (Eds.), *Language issues in literacy and bilingual/multicultural education* (pp. 347–390). Cambridge, MA: Harvard Educational Review.

Gee, J. P. (1996). *Social linguistics and literacies: Ideology in discourses.* London: Taylor and Francis.

———. (2000). Discourse and sociocultural studies in reading. In M. L. Kamil, P. B. Mosenthal, P. D. Pearson, & R. Bar (Eds.), *Handbook on reading research: Vol. 3* (pp. 195–207). Mahwah, NJ: Lawrence Erlbaum.

Hall, S., Critcher, C., Jefferson, T., Clarke, J., & Roberts, B. (1978). *Policing the crisis: Mugging, the state, and law and order.* New York: Holmes & Meier.

Heath, S. B., Branscombe, A., & Thomas, C. (1986). The book as narrative prop. In B. B. Schieffelin & P. Gilmore (Eds.), *The acquisition of literacy: Ethnographic perspectives* (pp. 16–34). Norwood, NJ: Ablex.

Heathcote, D. (1984). *Dorothy Heathcote: Collected writings on drama and education* (L. Johnson & C. O'Neill, Eds.). London: Hutchinson.

Lincoln, Y. S., & Guba, E. G. (1985). *Naturalistic inquiry.* Newbury Park, CA: Sage.

Rosenblatt, L. (1991). Literary theory. In J. Flood, J. M. Jensen, D. Lapp, & J. R. Squire (Eds.), *Handbook of research in teaching the English language arts* (pp. 57–62). New York: Macmillan.

Smith, M. W., & Strickland, D. S. (2001). Complements or conflicts: Conceptions of discussion and multicultural literature in a teachers-as-readers discussion group. *Journal of Literacy Research, 33* (1), 137–167.

Tillage, L. (1997). *Leon's story.* New York: Farrar, Straus & Giroux.

Vygotsky, L. S. (1978). *Mind in society: The development of higher psychological processes.* New York: Plenum Press.

———. (1987). *Collected works: Problems of general psychology: Vol. 1.* New York: Plenum Press.

Witte, S. P. (1992). Context, text, intertext. *Written Communication, 9* (2), 297–308.

Wolf, S., Edmiston, B. & Enciso, P. (1997). Drama worlds: Places of the heart, head, voice, and hand in dramatic interpretation. In J. Flood, S. B. Heath, & D. Lapp (Eds.), *Handbook of research on teaching literacy through the communicative and visual arts* (pp. 492–505). New York: Macmillan.

Wolf, S., & Enciso, P. (1994). Multiple selves in literary interpretation: Engagement and the language of drama. In C. K. Kinzer & D. J. Leu (Eds.), *Multidimensional aspects of literacy research, theory, and practice* (Forty-third Yearbook of National Reading Conference) (pp. 351–360). Chicago: National Reading Conference.

Woodson, J. (1995, November/December). A sign of having been there. *Horn Book,* 711.

———. (2001). *The other side.* New York: G. P. Putnam's Sons.

Index

Abbott, Robert, 35

activism, 43

The Adventures of Spider: West African Folktales (Arkhurst), 196

aesthetic stance, 139

African American authors, chosen for read-alouds in rural schools, 195

African American children: African American literature as a source of pride for, 97; concerns about education of, 4; educational achievement and, 3–4; embracing the linguistic knowledge of, 146–47; nontraditional literary response types, 144–45. *See also* African American males

African American children's literature: activism and, 43; addressing social justice and, 21; countering racism and, 21; cultural consciousness and, 98; importance of, 3. *See also* multicultural literature

African American English. *See* African American Vernacular English

African-American Inventors (McKissack), 18

African American literature: cultural consciousness and, 97–98; dominant themes in, 98; educational value of "speakerly" texts, 145; as a source of pride for African American children, 97

African American males: development of male identity and, 204–5, 213–14; example lives, 205–9; out-of-school literacy, 111; reading achievement and, 203–4; significance of multicultural literature to, 204–5, 213–14; summer reading program study, 111–25. *See also* father–son relationship

African American mothers: enforcement of racial boundaries and, 83. *See also* African American women

African American Vernacular English (AAVE): embracing children's knowledge of, 146–47; literature analysis and, 141–44; overview of, 128; performance during literature discussion, 140–41; reading

About the Contributors

Patricia E. Bandré is an assistant professor of reading education at the University of Arkansas at Little Rock. She holds a doctoral degree in children's literature and reading education from Ohio State University. Her research interests focus on the acquisition and use of read-alouds in the classroom and student response to read-alouds. Prior to completing her doctoral studies, she taught intermediate-grade students in rural Kansas.

*Wanda M. Brooks is an assistant professor in the College of Education at Temple University. She teaches graduate and undergraduate courses related to literacy acquisition and instruction. Her current research interests include examining the reading processes of African American students as well as young adolescent literature and reader responses. She has published in *Reading Research Quarterly, New Advocate, Journal of Children's Literature, English Journal,* and *Journal of Negro Education.*

Susan Browne is an assistant professor in the department of reading at Rowan University in Glassboro, New Jersey, where she also serves as a university liaison to a Camden county professional development school. Her research interests include reader response theory, critical literacy, culturally responsive pedagogy, and children's literacy practices in nonschool settings. Formerly a school district of Philadelphia classroom teacher, she continues to serve as a teacher consultant for the Philadelphia Writing Project.

Gregory J. Hampton is an assistant professor of African American literature in the Department of English at Howard University. He has published articles in the *English Journal, College Language Association Journal, Children's Literature in Education, Obsidian III,* and *Callaloo.* His fields of interest are nineteenth- and twentieth-century American, African, and African American literature; contemporary world literature; African American studies; women's studies; literary theory and criticism; science fiction; children's literature; and jazz studies.

KaaVonia Hinton is an assistant professor in educational curriculum and instruction at Old Dominion University. Her scholarship focuses on literacy materials created specifically for blacks; literature for adults, children, and young adults, especially works labeled multicultural; critical biographies of black writers; and literary criticism. She is the author of *Angela Johnson: Poetic Prose* (2006).

Elizabeth Marshall is an assistant professor at Simon Fraser University where she teaches courses in children's and young adult literature. Her work on representations of gender and sexuality in texts for young readers has appeared in *Reading Research Quarterly, Children's Literature Association Quarterly, College English, Alan Review,* and *The Lion and the Unicorn.*

Michelle H. Martin is an associate professor of English at Clemson University, specializing in children's and young adult literature. She is the author of *Brown Gold: Milestones of African American Children's Picture Books, 1845–2002* (Routledge 2004) and co-editor (with Claudia Nelson) of *Sexual Pedagogies: Sex Education in Britain, Australia, and America, 1879–2000* (Palgrave 2003). She has published in *The Lion and the Unicorn, Children's Literature Association Quarterly,* and *Obsidian III.* The work in this volume is a part of a book project on the children's literature of Arna Bontemps and Langston Hughes.

*Jonda C. McNair is an assistant professor in the Eugene T. Moore School of Education at Clemson University. Her work has appeared in *Children's Literature in Education, Language Arts, Journal of Children's Literature,* and *New Advocate.* She is a past recipient of the Grant-in-Aid Award sponsored by the Research Foundation of the National Council of Teachers of English. The title of the grant proposal was "I Never Knew There Were So Many Books about Us: Parents and Children Reading African American Children's Literature Together." Her research interests include children's literature, with a special emphasis on books written by and about African Americans; early literacy development; and multicultural education.

Karla J. Möller is an assistant professor of language and literacy at the University of Illinois at Urbana–Champaign. Her research focuses on children's literature and literacy education, specifically on the availability and use of multiethnic and multicultural literature and on literature discussion pedagogy in elementary classrooms. Her most recent work is on conceptualizations of struggling and capability with regard to literacy events, and on engagement and dialogue of children and teachers related to reading culturally diverse literature. She is a past recipient of a Spencer Dissertation Fellowship and is currently working on multiple projects in a racially and linguistically diverse public elementary school, where she has been an active researcher and volunteer since 2004.

Nina L. Nilsson is an assistant professor in the Department of Curriculum and Instruction at the University of Kentucky, where she teaches undergraduate and graduate courses, including the clinical practica in reading diagnosis and intervention for the Literacy Clinic. Formerly an elementary teacher and reading specialist, she works with schools and districts to conduct literacy instruction workshops. Her research interests include literacy issues relevant to diverse learners, multicultural children's literature, and strategies designed to facilitate reading comprehension.

Kimberly N. Parker is a doctoral candidate in the Department of Curriculum and Instruction at the University of Illinois at Urbana–Champaign. Her research interests include African American young men and their reading engagement, as well as African American young adult literature.

Peggy S. Rice is an associate professor of English education in the English Department at Ball State University, where she teaches courses in children's literature and elementary English language arts methods. She conducts research examining pre-service teachers' and children's responses (written, verbal, dramatic; individual, and group) to various types of children's literature. She is interested in discovering ways in which children's literature can be used as a vehicle to develop understanding of marginalized groups.

Doris Walker-Dalhouse, a former elementary teacher, is a professor at Minnesota State University, Moorhead. Her research and writings address sociocultural aspects of literacy. Her work appears in periodicals including *Childhood Education, Young Children, NRC Yearbook, Reading Teacher*, and *Journal of Adolescent and Adult Literacy* and in the books *Literacy Development of Students in Urban Schools: Research and Policy* and *Reading for All in Africa*. She has served on the board of directors for the International Reading Association and the National Reading Conference.

*The editors' names appear in alphabetical order as both shared equally in editing this book.